AF192369

D. C. KATSONGA

Reluctantly Surrounded By Politics

GROWING UP IN A DICTATORSHIP

novum ◢ pro

This book is also available as e-book.

© 2024 novum publishing

ISBN 978-3-99146-492-1
Editing: Charlotte Middleton
Cover photo, internal illustrations & author's photo: D. C. Katsonga
Cover design, layout & typesetting: novum publishing

The images provided by the author have been printed in the highest possible quality.

www.novum-publishing.co.uk

Print product with financial
climate contribution
ClimatePartner.com/16547-2311-1001

CONTENTS

Acknowledgements

To my wife, Jayne, and our two sons, Luso and Phiri.
You inspire me.

To Mr Ken Andrew Nicholson for saving my life.

Personal rights must be respected in biographical texts. Therefore, don't mention someone's name unless you have their permission to do so (preferably in writing). It should also not be possible to draw direct conclusions about the person (e.g. by describing family relationships or giving their address). If you do not have such permission, it is in your own interest to change the names and, if necessary, the circumstances so that, in the worst case, no legal action can be taken against you as the author.

The short stories in this book are based on my real-life experiences and are recounted as accurately as I remember them. I have addressed the concerns you mentioned. However, I have changed the names of some individuals, including those who have passed away, to respect their privacy and for the reasons you highlighted.

WE ARE MADE TO BE

The journey through life is always perilous, and there is generally no expertise on how to move forward from one day to the next, from one year to the next.

To those who last the distance, don't boast. You have made it this far and achieved this because your life path was pre-determined by a power greater than anything you have encountered in your life.

How often have certain *accident moments* missed you? How often have you missed a flight that crashed later? How often have you not married a partner who later turns out to be a killer? Survived a shipwreck and you did not even know how to swim? The only survivor of a horrific road accident? How often have I avoided snake bites while digging for mice in Mwanza?

We are here because we were meant to be here, doing something which was also pre-determined.

An illiterate sports personality makes millions and owns an aircraft, yachts, etcetera, while somewhere a university graduate is languishing in poverty! Fate! Pre-destiny!

How often have you met a former classmate who is now a brain surgeon or a NASA scientist and yet, in class, you and others thought their life would come to nought? Individuals who were stars in class have underachieved in their later lives. What is life all about, I ask. Does the answer matter? Perhaps not.

Where I hail from, it is taught right from birth that the way to success in adult life is through a good education. While in the developed world the situation is varied and as they say, nature is abstract, to find meaning in it one needs to accept that in nature, there is no chaos. This is why it is believed that everything in life is linked to everything else.

'Believe that we are, not because we have chosen to be, but because we were meant to be.'

Chapter 1

JOURNEY TO MUTARE

As the tropical summer mid-afternoon sun did its worst, I decided to stop and cool myself with a soft drink at a roadside cafe. I had just passed a road sign which read 'WELCOME TO MARONDERA' and, apart from feeling a little dehydrated, my six-foot fourteen-stone frame needed stretching.

The driver's seat in the brown twelve-year-old Peugeot 504 was in an advanced state of dilapidation. Due to wear and tear, the leather upholstery covering the seats was light brown and black, and there were more traces of the original shade of brown on the passenger's seats than on the driver's. Likewise, the springs on the left side of the driver's seat had completely relinquished their responsibilities, and the owner, a close friend of mine, had advised me that to have a comfortable drive, I would need to sit on one buttock, the right one. He was the kind of chap who could be relied upon for helpful suggestions like that! As to the general state of the car, well, let me say I was quietly confident that I would be able to complete the three-hour drive from Harare to my destination, the small border town of Mutare, a town on the north-eastern border with Mozambique and back to Harare, a well over five-hundred-kilometre round-trip.

As I parked the car under a huge mango tree, which danced with the odd rhythm of a drunken Ngoma dancer at a 'welcome' party, a gentle fruity breeze, the most agreeable present from the spirits, one might say, wafted by.

Marondera seemed to be a popular country oasis for drivers in transit. There were several cars and a few trucks parked at the far end of the row of shop fronts. Standing or squatting next to the mango tree were vendors, mostly young women, selling, among other things, all manner of vegetables, wood carvings, and traditional clay pots.

My heart skipped a beat at the sight of a woman near a café door carrying a bamboo basket full of mushrooms of many varieties. She immediately reminded me of my mother, Mai naMlauzi. She knew all the edible mushrooms which grew in the bushes around our farm in Thondwe, and she used to tell us, 'Davie, sight isn't everything when it comes to mushrooms; they can be any colour. What you must look for is the *ant test*. Look at the mushrooms, and if ants are attacking them, they are not poisonous to human beings.' We lived safely by this rule, and I now wondered if this woman had also used the ant test when she picked her mushrooms.

At the café, I bought myself a can of ice-cold Coca-Cola and a piece of soft smoke-cured wild-game meat. I was told it was buffalo and very tasty it was too. Inside and even on the veranda, all the seats were occupied, so I walked out into the car park and ate my snack leaning against my brown chariot. The temperature was considerably lower under the tree, and the ice-cold drink helped to cool me down by making me sweat a little before cooling me down. Naturally!

On the other side of the street, the little market was busy. Cars stopped by the roadside, their occupants picking what they wanted from the variety of goods on offer, quickly paying, and speeding away. I could imagine that prices were cheaper here than in the bigger towns, where most of the customers would be living. For a few minutes, I watched some children play hopscotch noisily at the far end of the car park, shouting and calling each other names for cheating. I saw myself in them and thought, how time flies.

Suddenly, my interest was distracted by an old, gaunt-looking man carrying two charcoal-grey medium-sized pots traditionally decorated with dark-brown triangles around the rim. They looked beautiful. He addressed me in the local language, Shona, which I was not very good at, which he soon grasped, judging by how I responded and quickly changed to English.

'Pots, Bwana, clay pots, very cheap. Only three dollars each,' he exhorted as he proudly handed me one for a closer appreciation and hopefully a sale!

His bushy white beard had a light-brown nicotine stain, which, I am sure, had been left by years of smoking, just above and below his mouth, and I noticed that when he smiled, his teeth, the ones he still had, were also tobacco-stained dark tan.

I can truthfully say that I did not want to buy pots. I did not need pots, and I was just about to return the pot I was holding when he began to cough violently. His fragile body looked as if it were going to fall apart under the intensity of the coughing fit. Still, after about a minute it relented, and he swallowed hard and seemed temporarily to have recovered. I do not know what he saw in the direction where the children were playing, but at that moment he started to laugh, slowly at first and then hysterically. Tears poured from his sallow, dark eyes and like narrow, flowing streams, disappeared into his bushy beard. Turning back to me, still smiling broadly, he continued with his sales pitch. 'Are you taking both, then? They are locally made – our cottage industry, as they say, in Harare. The wife will certainly be good to you tonight. *Women just love pots.*' He did not know all my defences were already down the moment I saw him cough; this was overkill.

I quickly paid him the asking price of six Zimbabwe dollars, plus two extra dollars for the effort, anxious to escape before the salespersons launched another attack on me. 'Thank you, Bwana,' he said, pocketing the money gleefully. 'These are the last ones I am selling today. The money doesn't last, though. I'm like a productive mango tree. As soon as there is a ripe one, someone plucks it. It's the wife, you know. She never lets me near her if I fail to sell at least two pots a day. Sometimes she even refuses to cook for me. She is Manyika, from Honde Valley in Mutare. Difficult women, if you ask me, but then, if I had not married her, I would probably have married someone exactly like her. It's fate, I suppose,' he concluded philosophically. I could only smile compassionately.

As I pulled away, I noticed the old man had lit another cigarette and gone into another coughing fit. I wondered whether I should have used the extra two dollars to buy him a cough mixture, but then again, perhaps the Manyika wife had everything under control.

I had also expected a road sign showing which direction Marondera Prison was located. My father and other nationalists, fighting against the imposed Federation of Rhodesia and NyasAaron d in 1960, had spent some months there. Perhaps I may have to make a special trip to visit this eerie structure and connect with the macabre stories of torture Father had narrated to us after his release. I am not sure the other seventy-two detainees incarcerated at various detention centres fared any better.

Between Marondera and the next town of Rusape, there were many tobacco and maize farms along the road, with the occasional barn silhouetted against the vast canvas of a cloudless sky. Now and again, I could see herds of cattle grazing lazily, fertilising the land with their waste as they did so. It was a sight which reminded me of the late Frankie Howard, a British comedian, who once said, 'Don't look a gift horse in the mouth, for it's the other end that feeds the rhubarb.'

I did not stop at Rusape, but judging from the buildings I saw from the car, the town seemed larger than Marondera. Before long I reached the lower slopes of the eastern highlands on which Mutare is situated, and from then on the journey would be uphill.

When I had been driving for less than an hour, I needed to rest my right buttock and relieve the pressure on my bladder. Pulling into a deserted lay-by where the only signs of human life were empty cigarette packets and Coca-Cola and beer bottle tops, there was also a little hut with a large window, on top of which were the words 'KUMBIRAI NO.1 TEA ROOM. OPEN 24 HRS A DAY'. It was closed! As I took a few steps into the bush, the sun was still up but far off and weak, as though being forced out of the sky at the end of the day against its will. Standing in front of a huge Masuku tree, I took in my surroundings. A rainbow carpet of wildflowers spread itself towards the nearby hills to my right. Red-chested mpheta, the yellow-winged pumbwa, maphingo, African starlings, and other birds sang above and around me. Wild fowls raised a cry in the bushes to my left as they flew and disappeared over the ridge. I felt a great sense of tranquillity. I was at peace with myself, at one with nature, and lost in my world.

I was brought back to earth by the sound of a huge over-loaded lorry which made such a commotion as it struggled uphill, leaving behind a trail of dark diesel clouds, that one would have been excused for thinking that an old steam locomotive was approaching. Awakened from my reverie as the birds contemptuously took flight, I jumped back into the Peugeot 504, into my favourite position in response to the state of wear of the driver's seat. It was time to continue my way.

The going was slower now. The road had become very winding and steep, and the car could not be encouraged to go any faster. Now sulking as it slipped out of sight behind the many layers of hills and mountains, the sun had turned the blank sky to a pale, murky, and sombre blue extending to a pale yellow and finally, a bright orange as it was approaching the western horizon in the distance. The fact that there would be stars any minute now, millions of them, taking their places in the night sky, did seem to make quite a difference to the way the sun slowly moved out of sight.

I had been driving for over an hour when I finally saw a road sign which readCHRISTMAS PASS 5MLS. MUTARE 8MLS'.

On reaching the top of Christmas Pass, arguably the highest point in Mutare, the road veered suddenly to the left, making a bow shape, and still rising. The town, now visible below, appeared as a collection of tiny lights, nestling in the natural bowl in which it sat at the foot of the surrounding hills.

The descent into the town itself was very hazardous and slow, due to the many bends which needed to be negotiated with care. Barely visible to the northeast, in the dying sky, were mountain ranges that seemed to go on forever. Somewhere there lay my homeland, my country, Malawi. A five-hour drive would put me among my people, those to whom I would not have to explain who I was. They knew me. They had known me since birth. They were people who would offer me food, water to drink, and a place to sleep without question. They were people who knew the source and meaning of my name in the land of my ancestors, Land of the Lake, where laughter comes easily, and the welcome is as golden as the rising sun.

Bringing the Peugeot to a halt in front of the Mutare Sun Hotel, which was situated on the left side of the road, I thankfully stretched my legs and reflected on the story which had first brought me to this place and had been told to me by my maternal uncle, whom I had met only once during my school holidays, some twenty years or so earlier.

Uncle Davison Filipo had spent around eight years working in a South African asbestos mine. Each time, he was contracted to work for three years. In the end, he would pack all that he had amassed and book a train ticket, destined for Blantyre, Malawi. The train always passed through Botswana and overnighted at a place called Francis Town, which he pronounced Forest Town. This town, he said, had the most beautiful women one could ever wish to see. As he waited for his connection, which was on the following day, he was drawn into conversation by one of these women. He may have used the phrase 'picked up', and he may even have given the impression that it was he who did the picking up, but now I know a thing or two about Botswana women, I somehow don't doubt who did the picking up – this woman, whom he described as being so beautiful that she had a 'beauty spot all over her body!'

The following morning, she lifted him and carried him on her back to the bathroom, which was about ten metres from the house, bathed him all over – she was thorough too! – and carried him back into the house the same way. After breakfast – a calabash of fresh milk, which was still warm from the cow's udder, and a huge piece of roast beef – he decided to marry the woman. Who would not? *Marriage-deserving women don't come any better than this.* After a few months, he had used all his money and most of his hard-earned goods, some of which were intended for his parents, brothers, and other members of the extended family in Malawi. Everything was gone. Now there was only one thing for him to do: go back to Johannesburg, back to the mines.

Three years passed, at the end of which he got as far as his beloved Feresi Town and met yet another woman with a beauty spot all over her body. So, he had apparently described her to his buddies. This time she was better behaved than the first, or so he thought, but he was wrong, and after a year, it was back to the mines yet again. Another three years passed and this time, on his way home, he knew he had to be strong. When the train stopped overnight in Francis Town, my previously weak uncle decided to sleep standing up at the station. Offers did come, but he resisted them all.

The following day, everything moved smoothly, and my uncle was in Harare by late evening. After a few hours of rest, the train continued its journey, arriving in Mutare just before midnight. One of his workmates was getting off there and since the train was overnighting in Mutare, the friend offered my uncle accommodation at his home, which wasn't far from Central Mutare station.

As the family was celebrating the return of their son, my uncle's eyes caught sight of someone, a young woman, who just happened to be his friend's sister. Her eyes were also arrested by him. Yes, you have guessed it, he missed the train to Blantyre the following morning and set up home with his Mutare lass, encouraged by his friend. Once again, all his money was 'lost' there.

There were gold mines in Mutare, where my uncle could have sought work, but the pay was more attractive in Johannesburg, so he made yet another trip to South Africa. This time he worked for only one year before his employers, the same ones he had worked for previously, discovered he had cancer of the lungs. Rather than tell him the truth about his condition, they told him that one of his parents had died and that he had to go back home. At the same time, a letter was secretly sent to the recruitment office in Malawi, alerting them of the true state of my uncle's health. He was sent by air directly to Malawi, and somehow his wife, my auntie, was not told of this turn of events. By then she had borne him a son, and he believed she loved him. Shortly before he died, he mentioned her name to my maternal grandmother, Mai aNakhoni, and that of her village in Mutare. As far as I knew, no one had made any attempt to contact the widow in Zimbabwe. This could have been because of the disappointment caused by my uncle marrying a foreigner, and worse still, a Zimbabwean. The belief was that Zimbabwean and South African women married for money and were lazy. To quote my grandmother, aNakhoni, 'They spend all their time painting their nails and looking into a mirror to see if their faces have changed.'

I had first come to Mutare to meet my auntie and give her the news about her husband's death and reassure her that he had not voluntarily deserted her. The sad truth is that my mission had not been a success. The whole village had been wiped out by the Smith government during the liberation struggle, and those who lived there now were all new inhabitants.

Never mind, I had thought, they are now reunited, and he would have told her everything himself and probably a lot more.

Leaving Mutare, I paused in the same hotel car park, resting my weary buttocks, and I asked an old man about the mountain ranges I could see in the distance. In answer to my questions, he could only say, 'Yes, Malawi is beyond those mountains. It is very far from here; it takes us the whole day on a bus ride to get there.' He could not have known that with those few words, he transformed the nature of my journey from a one-off search for a disowned lady to one of a regular pilgrimage. Somewhere behind those mountains, my parents, brothers, sister, and friends were going about their everyday chores, unaware of my whereabouts, my hopes, my dreams, and sometimes my despair. If only I were a bird. All that freedom of movement, no passport, and no fear of shadowy figures in the night, but for now, only my eyes could take me, a political outcast, to where I could not go myself – to Malawi, my home country, still under the tyrannical rule of the president for life, Dr Kamuzu Banda.

Chapter 2

FATHER AND MOTHER

My father was a no-nonsense character. An ex-politician and a very prominent businessman, anywhere he went, people either loved him, loathed him, or even feared him. As a man who had almost become a priest, Father commanded respect within the Roman Catholic Church from both blacks and whites. On most Sundays, he played the pipe organ at St Montfort Catholic Institute in Blantyre during Mass.

Although his job meant he knocked off very late at night, he never missed his early morning Sunday Mass, and all of us got used to going to church every Sunday.

I remember one day we arrived in church about two minutes after the Mass had started and found that the two chairs which Father had brought to the cathedral for his and Mother's personal use were occupied by a white couple. There were, I must add, other chairs vacant, but my father chose not to take them. Instead, he insisted to the deacon that the couple be moved to the other seats. As the entire discussion with the deacon was carried out in Latin, the other party looked on somewhat bemused, but eventually the couple complied and my parents took to their pews, and we all peacefully paid attention to the prayers thereafter. This incident happened in around 1961, when such behaviour from the 'natives' was unheard of!

Father later told us, as he drove us home, that he knew the white couple personally. They worked at the African Lakes Corporation (Mandala), and they were very cruel to their workers. He told us that he was sure they were racist and that they had deliberately sat on those seats just to spite him and Mother. 'That's why I couldn't take it! We are all created in God's image, and we are also created equal. Boys, as you grow older and into the world, you should not allow anyone to treat you differently because of reasons known to themselves, whatever these reasons might be. Never allow that!' he said assertively.

My father had dropped out of training for the priesthood at the age of thirty-two or thereabouts, by which time he was fluent in English, French, and Latin, . The reason he gave for failing to complete his training was 'poor health', but as I never saw my father ill in all my life, I found it hard to accept that poor health had been the reason for his change of heart. I prefer to think that he had probably found different ways of serving the Lord.

He also picked up Portuguese and Yawo later in his working life, in Mozambique and Eastern Malawi respectively, along the shores of Lake Malawi in Mangochi.

My father came to Mwanza from his home village of Ligowe, Traditional Authority Mlauli, with his parents, as a baby in around 1912.

His father had married an Ambo (part of the current Chewa) tribe woman with a Chibwe clan name. The history of the Ambo people is that they had trekked southwards from the Katanga area of the modern-day Democratic Republic of Congo and Northern Zambia area to the Zambezi valley in search of less congested and better agricultural land and pastureland for their animals. Their settling in this area coincided with the arrival of the warlike Mputa's Ngoni people, who were running away from Chaka Zulu's reach after the latter had defeated them on the battlefield fought on the veld of the Durban-Natal area of South Africa.

It didn't take long for the Ambo people to capitulate to these warriors, and they were soon assimilated into the Ngoni culture after several skirmishes, and quite a good number of them started to identify themselves as Ngonis. By the time Grandfather betrothed her, a generation or so later, Miss Chibwe was a complete Ngoni lass, otherwise his parents wouldn't have sanctioned the marriage in those days.

Grandfather became a senior member of the church when the Roman Catholic Church opened its first mission in N'nenu.

After a few years, as the church continued to expand with its missionary work, th Mission is N'nenu decided to open a new mission at Mwanza Boma, and they chose my grandfather to escort them on this trip. The journey was on foot and about thirty-five kilometres. Their first stop was Kanduku Village, where they were welcomed by Chief Chithundu, now Kanduku, in the early evening. After introducing themselves and what their intentions were, they were given food and water and a place to sleep until the following morning.

At sunrise, as they were getting ready to depart, Chief Chithundu offered them two men to accompany them on their search for a suitable place to set up their new mission. These two men were Mr Chitsotso and his young brother, Mr Mando. The former later became my maternal grandad.

A church was constructed in no time at all, and alongside it a primary school was also built. Grandfather Katsonga became a church elder and a primary school teacher at Saint Paul's. Mr Chitsotso was his deputy in church activities.

Having appreciated the sunny, mild climate in Mwanza, the Italian missionaries decided to introduce citrus fruits from Italy. They brought in tangerines, oranges, and lemons. These seedlings were being shared between the N'nenu and Mwanza missions, and it was my grandad who was physically being sent to N'nenu to bring the Mwanza supplies.

In the almanac of Saint Paul's church in Mwanza, this information is available, and it makes me proud and thankful to my grandfather that he played a major role in the economy and nutrition of the Mwanza district, because the area is now the biggest producer of these fruits in the whole country.

It was not surprising when, after he had written and passed his Standard Six examinations, my father decided to go to a seminary, Nankhunda Seminary in Zomba, to be exact. This decision, commendable as it was, was not welcomed by my grandfather, who felt that Standard Six was the highest level of education a NyasAaron d boy could attain before going into the job market. He refused to fund my father's decision at Nankhunda. Since my father was so determined to go ahead, he approached his father's cousin in Lisungwi, Mr Lembani. It was he who funded my father's education at Nankhunda Seminary. My father used to reminisce about how tough life was then, spending three days on the road walking from Mwanza to Nankhunda, crossing terrain awash with wild man-eating animals and snakes and crossing crocodile-infested rivers on his way to and from school at the opening and closing dates of semesters.

Just to buttress the annoyance Father still had against Grandfather, whenever there was a tiff between them, Father always reminded his father, 'It's Uncle Lembani who helped me achieve a better and improved education when you completely refused ...' I do not recall Grandfather ever defending himself against this accusation.

After four or five years at Nankhunda Seminary, Father was sent to Kachebele Seminary to complete his studies and be ordained as a priest. Two months before ordination he decided to quit, as I have already said, due to poor health.

He later got a job as a French teacher at a seminary in Dodoma, Tanzania. He was there for two years, and he returned home to map his way forward.

I recall him giving me French tutorials at home during my vacations when I was in Form Two in secondary school. I didn't know Father was fluent in French until this time. After going through my school report, he called me and said that he would be giving me extra lessons in French, because a sixty-five percent score wasn't good enough. On day one, he came out to the veranda carrying an old, tattered French textbook, which he later informed me he had used in Tanganyika in his early years. It was hard following his approach, because a lot of improvements had been made to the teaching of French since his time. The textbook which was in use at the time, entitled *Pierre et Seydou* was like the equivalent of the modern-day French Made Simple. Although I found the exercise helpful and very interesting, the time my father chose to do it was, in my view, most inappropriate. My mates and I used to play football on a nearby field from four p.m. almost every day if it was not raining. Sadly, my father used to get up from his siesta at around the same time, have his cup of tea or coffee before returning to the night club for the late shift, and he lovingly chose those playtimes minutes for the French tutorials. Alas!

By now, Grandfather Katsonga and his deputy, Mr Chitsotso, had become close as workmates but also as family friends. It was this working together which cemented their friendship to a level where they agreed to encourage their children to enter into marriage. This is how my father met Mai Namlauzi, my mother. So, my father did not have to go through all those time-consuming and sometimes expensive rituals of courting. To some extent, he might have been happier to do the same for us when we were old enough to join the adults' league, but by then he knew and accepted that time had moved on.

Soon after my parents married, Father sought work. He was undecided about what to do, as there were very few good jobs open to black Malawians at that time. He would have continued with teaching, but local salaries were worse than in Tanzania. His decision to start work as an office clerk in Mozambique was largely because the Portuguese colonialists paid better than their British counterparts in Malawi.

Father, with his new bride, was off to Mozambique. Their first destination was a place they called 'Dona ana', where Father found a job as an office clerk. The Portuguese found him unusually interesting because of the language skills he had, and the fact that he was a Roman Catholic, like most Portuguese people in this area, was an added advantage.

The employer was a very prosperous vegetable farmer, who also ran two restaurants in the area. From time to time, when Father found himself in the restaurant kitchen, he would watch the cooks work and ask questions, and when he got home, he would attempt to reproduce the dishes the cooks were creating in the restaurant kitchen.

Slowly, his cooking skills began to pick up and in no time at all he could, and did, stand in for one absent cook. He was a natural, one could say! By the time he moved to what he described as a 'better job' in Tete, where my sister, Naphiri, was born, his Portuguese was fluent. He later worked in hotels in Quelimane and Beira, also in Mozambique.

With all the catering experience he had gained in Mozambique, Father decided to start his own hospitality business. Research, of a sort, had convinced him that the best place to open a pub and restaurant was on the lakefront, something he might have picked in Beira. His chosen location was to be Mpondasi in Fort Johnston (Mangochi). One might say he chose well, as Mangochi is now the number one tourist resort in the country.

It must have been after a long day of swimming and basking on the golden sands at Mpondas' beaches that my parents' thoughts began to wander and, on one such day, I was conceived. Maybe they had fish for supper, for I enjoy seafood so much!

Growing up, I noticed from my brother and sister that, when Father called them, they responded, 'Papa!' and, when it was Mother calling, one responded, 'We Mayi!' I later discovered that 'Papa' meant 'Father' in Portuguese, another relic from his tour of duty in Portuguese East Africa, now Mozambique. Why he didn't wish us to respond to him in NyasAaron d's official language, English, or in our own Ngoni language, I will never know. Perhaps this is proof that Portugal's policy of) was effective! Assimilado - the term given by Portugal to their African subjects in Angola, Mozambique, Guinea Bissau, and probably elsewhere like Macau and Goa, from the 1910s to the 1960s, who had reached a level of 'civilization', according to Portuguese legal standards, which theoretically qualified them for full rights as Portuguese citizens. In practice, the system was not implemented in a way which would produce the intended result, that of 'close union of races of different degrees of civilization that help and support each other loyally'. However, this notion of 'close union' was never fully attained. And as to, 'We Mayi', this was a term from adulterated Zulu word, 'Umama', meaning, 'Of Mother', a response which endearingly gave one's mother complete ownership of the child she was calling.

There were several household rules we had to religiously follow. Every morning, as soon as father was up and at the breakfast table, we had to go and greet him in English. 'Good morning, Father,' we would say, kneeling on one knee, or if we found him standing up, we took a bow before greeting him. That was a true Ngoni (Zulu) value. In the evening, just before retiring to bed, the routine was the same – 'Goodnight, Father.'

We were instructed never to eat and walk at the same time. That meant that coming from school, no matter how hungry we felt, if we were offered a snack by a friend, we could accept and keep it until we got home. Another rule was, 'Do not accept food at anybody's house.' I recall Cousin Jessy was caught breaking this rule at the Njobvuyalemas, one of our neighbours, when we lived in Ndirande, Blantyre. When Father was informed of this disobedience that evening, he looked sternly at Cousin Jessy and asked, 'So, we do not provide you with enough food to eat in this house?' Cousin Jessy did not respond. She simply looked to the floor.

'NaMlauzi, Chisozibele!' We, at least I, did not understand that order and how it related to Cousin Jessy's transgression. However, the situation became clearer at dinner-time when, apart from the everyday family meal, there was a basin full of nsima and two deep dishes, one of vegetables and the other of beef stew. 'Jessy, that's for you, and I want you to finish it, because you have demonstrated we are failing you on the food front!'

'I am sorry, Uncle, I will not do it again,' she promised before her sobs and sniffles began. Chisozibele was a name given to one of the big saucepans father had bought in Harare, then Salisbury – Sozibele! – the prefix 'chi' in Chichewa signifying large size. From Cousin Jessy's experience, we all lived in fear of Chisozibele and made sure we simply did not accept food at anyone's home, no matter how hungry one was or how appetising the food was – rules are rules!

My Mother, Mrs. Dalia Katsonga (Nee Dalia Filipo Chitsotso) from Kanduku Village, Senior Traditional Authority Kanduku, Mwanza District, Malawi.1962.

My father's active involvement in politics was influenced by whenthe Federation was imposed on Rhodesia and NyasAaron d, and his racialist experiences in Portugal's colonised Mozambique.

He became a leading member of the NyasAaron d African Congress, and late in 1955, to facilitate his political ambitions, the family moved to the largest town in the country, Blantyre. There my father opened a pub for imported drinks such as whisky, brandy, gin, etcetera. These were drinks which could only be sold by those with a special licence, a document which was normally only granted to whites. My father was the first black Malawian to be allowed to sell such drinks by the colonial government.

Politically speaking, this had worked against him, because his opponents countered that he was favoured by the federal government, and it was partly the root of the 'stooge' label which stuck on him. It was simply not so. They ignored, or failed to understand, his Roman Catholic background and learning, where hatred and the carrying of grudges are seriously discouraged. There were times when he would stop the car and give someone a dressing down in the middle of the street for calling him a stooge as we drove by. He was simply trying to explain his position politically, which he thought the Malawi Congress Party was misrepresenting. This is how I slowly became aware, from the age of five, that my father was chastised by some sections of the population, although at that tender age I was unable to understand or appreciate the full facts behind their opposition to him.

On 6th July 1958, the Ngwazi returned home after about forty years of self-imposed exile. After addressing the tens of thousands of those who had come to welcome him, he was driven into Blantyre town by my father, John Chester Katsonga, in his black-and-white-roofed left-hand-drive Chevrolet, registration number BT6325, driven from Chileka to Blantyre for a closed meeting with his new political team. He was, from that day, to be our house guest in Chirimba for well over a month. I hope I will be forgiven for boasting that I was arguably the first toddler in Malawi to wet the Ngwazi's pants a few times during this period! Bless him!

It is documented that Dr Kamuzu Banda was a member of the Labour Party whilst in Britain, a left-of-centre party. On the other hand, my father was a conservative, right of centre!

In 1959, a state of emergency was declared, and leading political figures, including my father, were arrested. Awakened in the early hours of the morning by loud banging and shouting at the door and the flash of torch lights by the police, Chalela and I had watched, horror-struck, from our bedroom door as our father was dragged out of the house only half-dressed. His request to change from his pyjamas into something more decent was ignored and, shocked, we were ordered back to bed by our mother. It was soon after its internment that Dr Kamuzu Banda failed to interest my father in joining the Malawi Congress Party, and he thereafter formed his political party, which he named the Christian Liberal Party, with encouragement, among others, from Archbishop Theunissenen. Malawi had become a one-party state. I remember playing Hide-and-Seek in what remained of the Kwacha taxi when we moved to 'Four Miles' in Zomba in 1964. It was parked on one of the plots, rusting away and having some parts of it cannibalised by Mr. Silombera, who had his garage only a stone's throw away across the road, a forgotten symbol of the country's political dawn and history. Father had parked it about ten metres away from his bedroom.

My late Father, John Stanislas Chester Katsonga 1958. A businessman, politician, and a linguist [apart from two local languages, he spoke English, Portuguese, French and Latin]. He came from Ligowe Village, Traditional Authority Mlauli, N'nenu District, Malawi.

It was the first thing he saw either from his ain bedroom window or when he opened the door to go out. I wonder what went on in his mind at the sight of what was a relic of the country's recent political history.

One afternoon, my brother, Chalela, and I came back from school to find the old car was no longer there. Mother told us it had been bought for spares by Mr Silombera across the road.

House rules were very traditional. As a Ngoni (or Nguni) parent, there were three things Father felt he had to instil in us: hard work, obedience, and loyalty to family and friends. As far back as I can remember, we were supposed to be up early enough to greet him before he left for work, even on those days when we wanted to have a lie-in. It was a must. We all had to develop alarm clocks in our heads to be up when he was up. Evenings were the same – we had to bid him goodnight. All this was second nature to us, indeed to any proud Ngoni family. It was expected that 'children should be seen and not heard'. We only sat together with my father when there was no one visiting him. Otherwise, by tradition, we were only supposed to 'chat' with him when we were alone as a family and there were issues to be discussed or one of us had broken one or two of the house rules we lived by.

Naturally, there was punishment for breaking any of these rules, and often I was the culprit. I recall one Saturday in 1962 – it must have been Saturday, for we were neither going to school nor were we going to church – when Chalela woke Father with a report that I had beaten and bitten him on the forehead, which was sadly true. As he was delivering the report, I dressed up quickly and ran out of the house without anyone seeing me. Father came into the bedroom, cane in hand, and must have been disappointed not to find me, but when a search around the house proved fruitless, I am sure his anger slowly turned into parental concern. Sending the servants half a mile up the road to check at the home of a family friend proved no more successful and, as there was still no sign of me when they returned, they were asked to check in the nearby bushes. It was Chalela who found me, now helping with the search. I could see an element of concern and sorrow when our eyes locked onto each other's. He pretended to continue with the search. He did not want to hand me over to Dad for the punishment I deserved. The time now was just before seven o'clock in the morning and, as Father was leaving for work, I could overhear him saying, 'Tell this boy I am coming home for lunch. He will never learn!' he concluded as he banged his car door shut. I listened to the fading sound of the car with great relief as it sped off towards Rangely Stadium. His last comment referred to an incident the day before when I had cut one of the new dining-chair cushions with a razor blade, which had resulted in a caning.

A few minutes after Father's departure for work, Chalela called out, 'Davie, you can come out now; he's gone. Let's play.' Until this day, I did not know that despite our daily squabbles, my brother, Chalela, loved and cared about me as his kid brother. I must have been eight years of age. Our frequent squabbles reduced immensely from this day onwards.

What I found hard to understand about my father was that he did not think twice about caning us for small matters but if, on the other hand, the offence was serious, he did not even shout at us; he just spoke to us. Take, for example, the year I was supposed to be in Grade Three at the Catholic Institute in Blantyre but found myself back in Grade Two. For the entire previous school year, I had left home on time, but other than going to class, I had chosen to spend my time playing on the swings in Jubilee Park. My ever-loving brother kept my secret from Dad. This was at the time when Father was at a crossroads in his political career, so he never had time to check our school progress or homework.

The headmaster, Mr Chiphala, knew about my truancy, but for reasons known to himself, he did not tell my father. Perhaps he did not want me to face the wrath of Father's well-known temper, or indeed his silence was to save his own skin. One Sunday, during that year of Sundays, after attending church service, I saw the headmaster approaching us as we walked into the car park. My little heart was almost in my mouth. I am sure the headmaster knew I was petrified, because he bent down and whispered to me that he was not going to report me.

He and my father had a short chat, mostly about the weather and how the school was performing. And I remember him saying as he left, 'See you in school tomorrow, you two,'

Chalela and I both responded in unison, 'Yes, Sir.'

I still did not go to school until the following school year, by which time things were cooling down politically as far as Father was concerned. I suspect he was not spending a lot of time on the political circuit at that time. Consequently, this availed him more of family issues than was the case earlier. Naturally, he wanted to know how we were getting on in school. Chalela was all right. He was intelligent. I was the problem. 'No brains and lazy,' he used to call me. As for Sister Naphiri, certainly there were no issues there – she was Father's favourite and doing exceptionally well at Saint Mary's Girls' Catholic Boarding School in Zomba.

'You're in Standard Three, Davie. How is it going?' Dad asked one Saturday evening after supper.

'I'm in Standard Two, actually,' I replied. I am certain my face went all white as I said this, not that anyone would have noticed.

'Why?'

'Well,' I continued, 'when we went to school, the headmaster showed me a queue I should join. I joined it and it led to Standard Two,' I confidently explained.

'And you didn't ask why you were still in Standard Two? I'm going to school with you boys tomorrow. I don't understand. You should be in Standard Three,' said Father, angrily shaking his head.

On the following Monday, he quietly drove us to the Catholic Institute Primary School where, on arrival, we all got out of the car and Father led us to the headmaster's office. I do not know how many deaths I died from the car park to that office. It was like death by a thousand cuts – simply unbearable and unable to extricate me from the problem I had foolishly created.

Without the usual niceties of a greeting, Father went straight to the main issue. 'I would like to know why my son, Davie, is in Standard Two and not Standard Three, where he should be this school year.'

'Ah! Sir, Davie missed all his examination papers, and he was never in class most of the time.'

'Why didn't you tell me? I even recall the other day when we met in the church car park, and I asked you how the school was doing. Even then, it never occurred to you to give me this very important information, Mr Chiphala. Look, as far as I am concerned, my son is Standard Three! That is all there is to it! I'm sure you'll make sure this is so,' my father concluded firmly as he ushered us out of the office.

As Father left the schoolyard, Chalela and I proceeded to our respective classrooms. Within minutes, the headmaster walked in, whispered to the teacher, called my name and asked me to follow him. He was taking me to my new class, Standard Three. I was almost two weeks behind my new fellow pupils at this point.

The subject being taught as I took my seat was arithmetic. Standard Two consisted of H.T.U. (Hundreds, Tens, Units) and I was not good at it then as I sat down, looked at the blackboard and noticed to my horror that this time those letters had an extra 'T'. It was now T.H.T.U. This was simply too much for me I have never liked the subject since. I did, however, pass my final exams that year, and I even remember the headmaster congratulating me for my hard work. *What hard work?* I wondered. This was in 1963. Chalela and I were then ferried to Zomba Catholic Boys' Primary School. It seemed Father wanted to have a change of scene from politics, from the tinderbox of Blantyre. Although Zomba was the capital city of Malawi at the time, it was Blantyre where the real action was! Besides, the fact that his father and sisters were already in that town must have made his decision to move his business closer to them a little easier.

Of the three children, I stayed at home the longest, which gave me an unplanned opportunity to observe how my parents related to each other. Before this, I was quite aware of the love which existed between them. As a wife, my mother did as she was told, and her husband brought home the beef. The arrangement was something no one in my culture could fault. It was, in our cultural sense, simply perfect.

My mother's contribution to the restaurant side of the family business was cooking and baking. I remember days when she was so tired but still felt she must continue her preparations. It was on days like these that I never went out to play. Although we had many servants, Father preferred my mother, his dear, hard-working wife, to prepare certain dishes. Often, I was there too, mincing, whipping eggs, cutting onions and tomatoes, etcetera. One afternoon, busy in the kitchen, my face crudely and accidentally dusted with flour, for it was on a windy day – I must have looked like a traditional Nyau dancer – from the corner of my eye I caught my mother standing still, her eyes looking at me with a degree of sadness, perhaps disappointment. 'My son, how I wish you were a girl,' she said ruefully as she continued with her work. Unsure of how to respond to these words, for I did not know exactly what she meant, I carried on working, thinking that perhaps I should involve myself in more 'manly' chores than cooking, but despite the confusion in my young mind I still enjoyed helping Mother in the kitchen.

At first, Father was happy with my input in the kitchen for the family business, until he noticed changes in my behaviour every time he had a tiff with my mother. At times, I did not think he was acting fairly and, being thirteen years old at the time, I did not know how to hide my facial expressions, which inadvertently graphically reflected my feelings. I was very protective and supportive of my mother. There was nothing wrong with their marriage per se, just little things that, in my view, were less than just to Mother.

Just to buttress the above point, on one trip to Mwanza to visit my maternal grandmother, my mother and father decided to be a little less conventional than usual and have a picnic on the way. Mother prepared two grilled Piri-piri chickens and some other items to tempt the palette, which were packed and loaded into the car ready for the journey. It was a very relaxed drive on what was a bumpy gravel road from Chileka to our destination and, soon after crossing the Shire River, my father spotted in the nearby bush to the left a big outcrop of a rock with a flattish top about twenty metres from the road. 'That's a nice spot for a picnic, wouldn't you say, Nam?' he asked confidently, bringing the car to a halt. I am sure I speak for everyone, including my parents and my brother, as well as myself, when I say we were all looking forward to demolishing those two chickens.

A big mat was laid on the rock, all the food was set out and hands washed, and Father had already blessed the food when he, turning to Mother, inquired, 'Where's my Piri-piri powder?' He never ate his food without Piri-piri.

'I think I forgot to pack it,' replied my mother resignedly. 'But there's already enough of it on the chicken. Look, the chicken is looking red because of it!' Mother tried to explain.

'Over twenty years of marriage, and you still don't know what your husband likes,' fumed my father. 'Come on, pack everything. We will eat at your mother's.' This was the end of the beginning of our picnic.

After Malawi had been given self-government in 1963, Father had to reflect on events which preceded this momentous event. In 1962, his deputy in the Christian Liberal Party, Ponde-ponde, was murdered by supporters of the Malawi Congress Party. This was the first reported political murder in Malawi, and from then on, Father had to have bodyguards wherever he went. Life had become increasingly dangerous for the whole family, and he felt he had no other choice but to leave politics altogether rather than do the unthinkable and join the Malawi Congress Party, a move he had always vowed he would never make. Being involved in politics for my father was a duty he felt he owed his people, quite apart from his other interests in his professional life, but from then on he concentrated his energy on his business, and when life in Blantyre became unbearable for him, even after quitting politics, he sold everything and settled in Zomba in 1963, as I have already said earlier.

Father was a very active man. He successfully ran a nightclub in Zomba between 1964 and 1968 before moving to Lilongwe, where he built another nightclub at the new (now old) airport, which became the best and busiest nightclub in the city and the entire central region in Malawi at the time – not my words but results from tourism inspectors!

Father left the Zomba joint to my elder brother, Chalela, and concentrated on the new investment in Lilongwe. After a few years there, he won a tender to run the Airport Caterer's Cafeteria, which was shortly followed by another victory, another tender to build a motel, which was part of the Capital City Development Corporation. Our capital city was being moved from Zomba to Lilongwe, and the main sponsors, Canada and South Africa, wanted a Malawian to run this establishment, which opened in 1977 and was called Chester's City Motel (now the Lingadzi Inn).

Looking back now, the transition from politician and businessman to just a businessman was a very hard road for my father. He had gradually become calmer and a lot more relaxed. Despite his quitting politics, at mass rallies, President Dr. Ngwazi Hastings Kamuzu Banda did not stop taking a dig at him every so often. There were those people the president did not seem to like much, and many of them ended up in mysterious 'accidents' or detention but, for some reason, Dr Kamuzu Banda spared my father from such extreme extra-judicial punishments. Maybe he decided he would get more satisfaction from slowly and continuously tormenting him at his political rallies, thus inflicting death by a thousand cuts, or perhaps he was still thankful for my mother's home cooking during the early months of his return from exile! I am sure Dr Kamuzu Banda's intelligence (loosely speaking) people advised him that they had no evidence my father was scheming against him, yet the uncalled-for oral attacks continued unabated.

One incident, which happened in broad daylight in 1969, served as a reminder to my father that his political enemies had not forgotten him. Driving from Lilongwe to Zomba, my mother by his side, he was halfway up a very steep hill, then called Kasupe, when he came upon two Caterpillar Gladers apparently engaged in some road repair work. They signalled him to pass, but as he did so they both set off in motion, forcing his car towards the edge of the escarpment and the approximately one-hundred-and-fifty-metre drop below. It took all of Father's driving skills and an element of luck to avoid escaping this attempt on his life. Reaching the local town at the top of the mountain within two minutes, Father insisted on walking back and confronting the Caterpillar Gladers' operators, but Mother stood firm and suggested he report the matter to the police station only a few metres away. He relented, and a statement was made at the police station, after which two police officers wanted to be taken to the spot where the incident was reported to have taken place.

Once there they did see the tyre marks of the Caterpillar Gladers, which were visible and fresh and so were the tyre marks of my father's car, but there was no sign of the Gladers themselves nor of anyone working on that stretch of the road, as my father had reported. The police promised to investigate the matter, and that was the last he heard from Kasupe Police.

Up to the final days of his business life, Father had a loyal bodyguard called Peter, who came from Domasi in the Zomba District. Among other things, my father liked Peter because of his loyalty and physical presence. He also had a good sense of humour, which at times could be dark. I recall one afternoon when we were in Lilongwe, when Father remembered that one of his old friends was in the hospital at Likuni. Flowers, a card, and foodstuffs were purchased, and we were soon on our way to Likuni General Hospital. When we arrived, there was a doctor and a nurse at the man's bedside, so we were asked to wait along the corridor just outside the ward. It was very busy, with people walking up and down, and a few doors along the corridor Peter saw an old man in a wheelchair, looking rather helpless, his head hanging sideways over his right shoulder and his arms dangling weakly by his sides. He was also completely bald. We then noticed there was a tube which, although we could not see where it came from on his body, appeared to be entering an orifice in the man's neck.

'What's that?' Peter asked my father, pointing at the tube.

'It's a feeding tube,' Father explained in a low voice, 'for food in liquid form, like tea,' he concluded.

'How about sugar?' queried Peter, a wry smile on his face. 'Er ... er ... er ... how does he know if they've put enough sugar in it?'

'I don't think in his condition that is an issue he is bothered about, Peter!' retorted Father.

I always wondered why Peter had no wife for all the time he was with us. Then one day, after washing Dad's car, he excused himself to go off for a few minutes to have his breakfast while Father was having his.

'So, you will have to prepare it yourself, Mister? Perhaps you should get yourself a wife! Why don't you have a wife?'

'I did until one year ago, but she passed away. We had two daughters together, both of whom are now married.'

'Do you see them? I mean, do you visit them sometimes?'

'I could, if only I knew where they were,' he responded with a somewhat dejected tone.

My father died on the 12th of March 1986 in Zomba, a time when one mysterious heavenly body was visiting planet earth. It was a comet, which even Aristotle conceded ignorance about in *Meteorologica*. Aristotle thought the comet was a body with clefts which held some inflammable gases which keep on igniting as they escaped, hence the brightness of the comet. He later admitted he did not know much about this heavenly body and yielded to what science was finding out at that time.

In 1066, Halley's Comet appeared, and it was blamed for bringing bad luck to the Normans, who were vanquished at the battle of Hastings during the comet's appearance. Many Christians have their interpretation of Halley's Comet. I had overheard my dad's fellow Roman Catholic friend telling my dad that he could see Mother Mary holding a rosary in the Ikeya Seki comet in late 1965, when this very bright heavenly body was visible in the night sky with different interpretations. He told us the end was, thus, nigh. I was only in Standard Four – why should I continue to work hard if my education were soon to be curtailed, I thought to myself. I was ten at the time.

There is a connection between us as human beings and other things in the known and yet unknown universe. That's my belief. Religious? Probably, or just an acknowledgement that a God is controlling all of us and the entire Universe!

Halley's Comet was very visible in the night sky. This comet visits Earth once every seventy-six years, and it's only in recent years that science has come to understand this legendary heavenly object. To me, it felt like this time, it had come to tell my father that his number was up! It was like it had come to take him into the afterlife. He was born two years after the last appearance of the comet and died during its next visitation. Whatever science says today, there are a lot of mystical explanations about this comet. Bengalese people see Halley's Comet as burning torches thrown into the sky by forest spirits. In Australia, Aboriginals see Halley's Comet as flaming sticks ridden by great Shamans.

Parliament, which had not yet moved to Lilongwe, was sitting at the time. Only one parliamentarian attended the funeral. She was my father's niece and at the time a serving Member of Parliament for Mwanza Central Constituency. It was then rumoured that there was an order flying around Parliament warning Members of Parliament not to attend the funeral. The niece had to plead that as she was a family member, she was allowed to appear at the funeral. To the embarrassment of the ruling Malawi Congress Party, the funeral attracted thousands of people from as far away as Mozambique, Zimbabwe, Zambia, South Africa, the northern and central regions of Malawi, to most of the districts in the southern region of the country.

Regretfully, I was not among the mourners present. I was thousands of miles away in England, unable to make the journey to pay my beloved father my last respects, because I was a persona non grata in Malawi at the time.

The day he died, about noon my brother Mark called me almost immediately, bless him, to deliver the sad news.

On the previous night, Owen Mbilizi and another Zimbabwean friend of ours were having a drink just before supper, and I heard someone calling my name at the door and I answered it. There was no one there. Coming back, my two friends asked me what I was responding to. I explained, and none of them had heard anyone calling me. We continued chatting, and I heard the same voice calling me by my name, and again I went to answer the door where, yet again, there was no one! Was I sober? Yes! I was drinking juices that evening, because my girlfriend, who later became my lovely wife, Jayne, did not approve of me taking alcohol. She was the one preparing supper in the kitchen. She too, like my two friends, had not heard the calling.

The next day, for the first time in my university life, I simply decided not to go for lectures I woke up and was feeling a little stressed and unhappy, without anything to blame for my low mood, and that's when Mark called!

Science has not yet researched the spiritual world to explain the phenomena I have just narrated! I believed then, just as I do now, that the persistent voice calling me the previous night was my father's spirit informing me that he was about to leave this world. The weakness I felt and the mood I was in the following morning was probably also spirit induced. They did not wish me to hear the bad news while in a public place.

As we leave home and become independent of our parents, I feel that something within us stops to remind us exactly what our parents represent in our mature lives. I did not know what my father represented in my life at this point. I was thirty-one years old at the time, happy that both my parents were alive and well, praying that one day I would see them again. That was all! But on hearing of my father's passing, I felt unprotected, vulnerable, and exposed to a world I did not trust. So, even when my father was old and passive in most things, he was still my protector. His passing revealed this to me, and I had to start rebuilding my self-confidence as myself and not Chester Katsonga's son!

Chapter 3

MUSICAL MAGGIE AND THE LOOSE CHANGE REFUND – THIS IS TO JONI THE MAN! MALAWI POLITICS IS IN FLUX

My brother and I had been to two primary schools by the time we moved to Zomba Catholic Boys' Primary School. First, we were sent to Chakana Junior Primary School in Ndirande. My brother had been at this school a year earlier. My parents were forced to send me to school a year earlier than had been planned because, they later told me, I had started to use obscene language which I had picked up from the playground.

I was the youngest in class. This was a time when Class One had learners who were in their teens! I found everything difficult, starting with classwork and physical education. The teacher, Mr Ngoleka, must have thought I was simply weak in the head. I did look a little older for my age because of my height. One day, during physical education, he whipped me in the face, bursting the area below my right eye open. This did not enhance my love for going to school.

A year later we were transferred to St Montfort Primary School; some called it the Catholic Institute. For the entire first year, I never attended classes. Each morning my brother and I could leave home, and while my brother went to class, I escaped to play truant at the Coronation Park nearby.

We lived around the Chichiri area on Lali Lubani Road, if one is coming from the stadium end. The houses, until 2020, was the last building on the right. It is just possible there are now new buildings after it towards the Polytechnic Hostels.

From our house to Rangely Stadium, there was no house at all, just open prairie. I remember during March and April we used to catch mphala-bungu or imphe. These were butterfly caterpillars. They make a very good snack when fried and sun-dried. I used to like them, and when I find some in one of the markets in Blantyre, certainly in Mwanza, I buy them. You will never have a better-tasting savoury and wholesome snack!

Across the road were several houses. Most of them were government houses. Adjacent were the Chiozas. They had a home-help they, and we, used to call Atati. We had a very short cook, and we used to call him Ashoti, meaning 'a short person'. He seemed not to mind. Occasionally, Atati could be seen crossing the grassland on his way to or from the nearest shop in that area. It was towards the Water Board staff residence area. Ashoti, being a practical joker, would call out to Atati, 'Oi! Atati! Could you give us some tobacco, please?' Atati would stop as Ashoti would walk quickly, hurrying towards him. Once there, he would engage Atati in a conversation while gently massaging his bald head. Atati didn't seem to mind at all. Strangely, bald people did not, and they still do not, like people massaging their bald heads. Come to think of it, most people simply do not like having their heads massaged, certainly not by just anybody!

Life at Zomba Catholic Primary Boys' School started rather badly for my brother and me.

The Malawi Congress Party had just won the general election, and those who did not support the party were now seen as traitors. Father, as ex-chairman of the Christian Liberation Party, was one such person, and by association so were we, his family. The fact that he had left politics altogether a few months earlier made little difference to most people, including Dr Kamuzu Banda himself, who continued to castigate my father any time he felt like it, which was often. We faced a great deal of bullying from other pupils at school, but I remember that some sympathised.

Harry, a short, square-faced, and particularly rough boy, who enjoyed a fight at least twice a week or until he ran out of opponents, made friends with me and threatened to beat anyone who tried to bully me or Chalela. Most pupils were scared of him, and his protection worked quite well, for the attempts quickly died down as the news about our link to Harry spread through the school playground. He had the reputation of being a mean fighter, whose elder brothers were even meaner and could be relied upon to add extra muscle, should the need arise.

For the protection Harry was providing us I paid him one penny, which was a third of my pocket money, each school day. For some reason, I do not think nor do I know if my brother ever contributed to this service, and I also do not recall if he demanded it or if it was just a token of my gratitude, but in no time at all, we became very close friends and we began playing truant together, more often than not going fishing for the entire day for as many school days a week as we wished. Our studies suffered. Mind you, having played a similar silly game in Blantyre two years earlier, it was not hard to go along with Harry when he proposed we should skip classes and go fishing along the Likangala River less than half a kilometre from our school. I enjoyed fishing. This was the first time we were being taught and were required to use 'dip pens', and I wasn't enjoying the experience, always going home with dirty, inky fingers and clothes.

Our teacher told us that the use of dip pens evoked a beautiful feeling and could be a relaxing, rewarding process. Unlike a fountain pen, a dip pen handle did not have an internal reservoir; the ink was held in the metal nib, which used its capillary channels to regulate the ink flow. We were told how these dip pens would improve our handwriting beyond recognition. Every desk was designed to sit two learners, and they had two orifices on both ends in which a small ink receptacle would be inserted for the pen dipping. The government supplied the ink.

Understandably, something Mother did not appreciate was the washing off of these ink marks. Most of them would not entirely disappear through a normal wash. She was happier when I started returning from school with clean uniforms without ink marks; she must have thought I had now mastered the art of using a dip pen. Luckily for me, she did not get the whiff of fish on my clothes, or if she did, she might have linked the smell to the fish from nearby Lake Chilwa, which we frequently had for our meals at home. They were more affordable than meat and were readily available. Still, I was almost caught when she found a sachet of salt and Piri-piri powder in my short-trousers pocket.

'Why do you have these in your school uniform pocket?' she asked while handing me the offending sachet. She continued, 'Have you been having meals in people's houses?' My mind quickly moved to the Chisozibele punishment.

'Er ... er ... my friend, Harry, and I use salt and Piri-piri on our cassava and sweet potatoes.' I blushed, head bowed, lying to Mother.

'Weird! I have never heard of anyone using Piri-piri and salt on sweet potatoes and cassava,' she commented without showing any sign of pleasure either in the tone of her voice or in her facial expression. My friend, Harry, and I used to use these on our catch from the Likangala River. At the end of each expedition, we would light a small fire on a rock by the riverbank and roast out salt-and-Piri-piri-marinated little fishes, which we used to pierce with a wooden skewer. The fishes were almost always less than six inches long. We always ate all the catch since there was no safe and authentic way of bringing the fish home.

During the few days we stayed at school, I noticed a beautiful girl who always offered to carry my books as we walked home after classes – what a treasure she would have been to the World Women's Emancipation League! Her skin was light mahogany, and she was of medium build, although her sharp mushrooming breasts placed her evenly between the two worlds of big and little girls. God must have spent the entire day designing her pearly-white teeth, for when she smiled, even the roosters noticed, stretching their wings one wing at a time! She was just over thirteen years of age, and her name was Margaret. With her dazzling, toothy smile on display, the more she offered to carry my books, the closer and fonder I got of her. I was slowly but surely becoming infatuated with her. I was almost ten.

The 6th July came and went and NyasAaron d became Malawi. The country was now an independent state, and the leader, the Messiah, Ngwazi Dr Hastings, 'the destroyer of the stupid Federation', (Transition by Farai Sevenzo. No.85 [2000], pp.4-29,

Published by: Indiana University Press) became the prime minister of Independent Malawi with the British monarch as the Head of State at least up to 1966, when Malawi became a republic.

Father told us not to participate in the celebrations, because, he said, it might not be safe, so we all stayed home. Within a month of these national celebrations, Malawi had its first Cabinet crisis when more than eight out of the eleven Cabinet ministers rebelled against the prime minister. Support for each side was based on tribal lines, Zomba, the capital city, itself being Yao-dominated. Henry Chipembere, whose supporters came from an area which ran from the southern tip of Lake Malawi to the southern border, was the most prominent in the rebellion. He was a Yao and came from Mangochi District. Those found loitering and wearing a commemorative badge for our country's independence were made to eat it if caught by Chipembere's supporters.One morning, soon after arriving at school, we were ordered back home because the headmaster, Mr Ngwaru, told us there were 'troubles' in town. He also said that if anyone asked us whom we supported, we should first look to see what colours they were wearing. Dr Kamuzu Banda's supporters wore red; Chipembere's wore black. The town was littered with roadblocks manned by rough-looking and badly behaved characters who wore their colour on their sleeve. We spent two weeks away from school, during which time one of the most colourful party officials in Zomba was almost killed by Chipembere's people. His home was a big red-brick bungalow, which stood along the Blantyre-Zomba Road, roughly three hundred metres from our place. He managed to survive by hiding in one of the big, leafy mango trees across the road, opposite his house. This serious situation was made humorous because of the man's size.

Being seriously overweight, pot-bellied, and short, the mental picture conjured up of him climbing into one of those trees was simply hilarious to the locals. After surviving that attempt on his life, he went into hiding further afield, and I am certain he must have found a very safe house somewhere, for I never saw nor heard about him again.

What we, as children, found surprising was the way our friend George's father was able to organise an army of guerrillas without the authorities noticing. They came in lorries. Father's workers were outside the nightclub, and we were playing around the trees at the back, when we were forcibly called to help pick up stones which were being put into sacks and loaded onto the lorries. By then I had an idea as to what was happening – a sketchy idea but an idea all the same. We were later to hear that George's father and his marauding men had chased traders from the market square and stolen most of their earnings for the day. Shopkeepers in the surrounding central town trading centre suffered a similar fate. The fighting continued but now with the police and army involved. As the government forces were kept busy, those ministers who had crossed the Life President were making their way across the border into neighbouring countries. Out of the eleven senior ministers, about seven were forced to flee the country, including Henry Chipembere. This did not deter George's father, brave Silombera. He fought on.

One early August afternoon, when the sun was high in the sky, we followed army vehicles as they sped up the road towards Silombera's house. People nearby said he was inside. The house, which Silombera had built himself, was the most beautiful in the district. It had two floors, the only one in the area to have two, and it was painted yellow. It was a local landmark. When the soldiers surrounded the house and began shooting, Silombera shot back, surprising, even shocking, the charging army. Somehow 'Great Houdini' Silombera escaped, and as they searched the house, he began shooting at them from the nearby Namilongo hills. In retaliation, the angry captain ordered the house to be demolished. Perhaps he was simply duty-bound! It was all very easy. They drove one of their personnel carriers right through the house, and soon that beautiful landmark was nothing but a heap of rubble and mangled iron sheets.

The fighting developed into a real guerrilla war with Silombera fighting from Mangochi, which was within Chipembere's home area. A few months later, he was captured, 'tried', and executed.

Subsequently, his widow was to become my mother's best friend. On the day he was hanged, the whole district was in a sombre mood. For me, it was more to do with George, whom Chalela and I played with. Silombera had been 'the daddy next door', and I do not think he deserved to die this way but, if that was what the penal code was, what else could one do? Accepting its provisions is, arguably, the biggest component of being a good citizen. Didn't Socrates, the Greek philosopher, perish for a similar belief?

After Silombera was captured, the government, for the sake of reconciliation, had the choice of releasing Silombera or holding him in detention. But no, Dr Kamuzu Banda decided to take his life. In his defence, I suspect Dr Kamuzu Banda would say that he was only following the law, and perhaps he was – and the worst was yet to come!

Those two weeks were probably the slowest days in my tender life. For once, I did not want to be away from school, from Margaret. She lived in a village three miles from my home, but I had never been there, and the school was the only place where we could meet with each other. I suppose, having gone through the painful Silombera saga, one way or the other the seeds of pacifism were deeply sown in my heart that fortnight! At long last, we got the all-clear that the fighting had stopped, and it was safe to go to school.

When I told Harry I was not going fishing with him because I did not want to miss nature study, he was both upset and startled. 'But you don't like nature study, Davie. Just admit it – you want to be with Maggie.' I owned up, and Harry, looking dejected, sneaked out of the schoolyard for the river, alone.

That day, as I attended the nature study lesson, glassy-eyed and with a lingering smile on my face, I was oblivious to whatever the teacher was saying. I was so happy, happy just to sit in the same room as Margaret. Occasionally, she would turn her face in my direction and smile, which lifted my spirits no end. If Harry had bothered to ask me what I had learnt in nature study that day, I do not know what my response would have been. I noticed nothing – apart from Maggie, that is. She continued to carry my books after classes, and she also sang to me. Her repertoire included some old folk songs, in which she substituted some of the words with my name. I suppose that was at the height, the zenith, of our relationship.

One of the songs had lyrics like:

> *My man, Davie,*
> *I will always be your woman.*
> *To the day I die*
> *That's my wish.*
> *Only if you could buy me,*
> *A silk dress,*
> *A dress I can wear 'til my dying day.*

It is difficult to describe my feelings when she sang this song. I felt super-human, a man in control, a man with everything, a man with the keys to her heart and beyond. I wondered why it was that some people took a long time to find their lifetime partner. At the age of ten, I had found mine. To show the woman I loved her, the one-penny-a-day protection money meant for Harry was now going to Margaret, in the form of an advance dowry, I suppose! Since the friendship between Harry and me had now been cemented through our truancy and fishing trips, his protection services were now almost free.

Following a few months of bliss, I was more than a little depressed when one Monday morning Margaret failed to come to school. As I sullenly walked home, carrying my own books, after what had been a very long day for me, worse was yet to come. Two girls from her village stopped me and told me the reason Maggie was not at school was that her mother had beaten her when she found out Maggie was having 'Ugandan talks' with a chap in their village called John. 'Don't tell her we told you this,' they added. Those words were like someone was twisting a dagger in my heart. I could not accept, nor imagine, my Maggie with another.

What had happened to all that 'I'll always be yours 'til the day I die?' I wondered. Perhaps I had delayed too long buying the silk dress, I thought. My dreams were now in ruins. I knew I must end the affair and end it quickly. I did not know how I was going to last out until the following day when I could see her and get rid of the pain, the lump in my throat, and plug the gaping hole in my bleeding heart!

By the time I arrived home, I just could not eat; I simply wasn't hungry. In truth, I had lost the will to live, to face the world, to carry on, and deciding to go on a hunger strike, I faked a headache as an excuse for not eating. I seriously considered ending it all. My caring mother promptly produced two aspirin tablets. I resolved to do without supper too, but weakened by emotion and the wonderful aroma coming from the kitchen, I gave up the hunger strike that night, deciding I had sacrificed enough already. Anyway, I did not fancy the idea of dying before I had had time to tell Maggie we were through because she was a cheat.

I met Harry on my way to school the next morning. He could see I was down-hearted, and we discussed ways in which I could get even with Maggie. He was full of ideas, some of them very original.

'You see, Davie,' he started, thoughtfully, 'I could beat her together with the boyfriend. Or just the boy. On the other hand, you could ask for your money back.'

'What money?' I asked, confused.

'All the pennies you've been giving her – and for what? She must return them, Davie. Show her you're not a fool.'

A fool, I thought. Yeah, I should indeed teach her a lesson. Beating her, or the boyfriend, would be too easy.

When I arrived at school that morning, I cast my sad chestnut-brown eyes like a searchlight around the playground, hoping to spot Margaret, but when the bell sounded for assembly, there was still no sign of her. I sat, unseeing, unhearing, through the first two lessons, local history, followed by arithmetic. Harry, who had decided not to go fishing that day, tried to cheer me up with some jokes but to no avail. I hurried out of the classroom as soon as the bell rang for the first interval at nine forty-five a.m. and found Maggie at the far corner of the playing field, alone and looking rather lost. She was in her well-pressed school attire, a blue knee-length skirt, and a plain white round-necked blouse. The urge to clear my chest was overwhelming as I half-walked half-ran towards her. Reaching her, I tactfully and sensitively spoke my carefully chosen words.

'I want my money back.'

'What money?' she asked, a puzzled frown on her face.

'You know, the pennies I've been giving you – I want them back,' I said assertively. At that moment a gust of wind wafted by, lifting Maggie's skirt embarrassingly high, revealing her pink bloomers underneath – a sight I found most restorative – but I pretended not to notice. As they say, anger and foolishness are very close brothers.

'All right,' she sighed resignedly. 'All right. I'll give them to you tomorrow.'

With these words, I ran to Harry, who was waiting a few metres away.

'Did she give the money to you?' he asked expectantly.

'No ...' I started.

'She hasn't refused to pay, has she?' Harry queried, getting visibly excited.

'Listen, Harry – tomorrow, she'll bring the money tomorrow.' I could not bring myself to say anything more. My emotion-filled voice was beginning to chokingly fail me; it was like I had a huge frog stuck in my throat. Somehow, the twenty-four hours' grace period was too long to allow a girl like Maggie after what she had done, Harry reasoned.

'She'd better not mess up, silly girl,' he concluded as we walked back to the classroom.

First thing in the morning on the following day, Maggie called me just before assembly and from her skirt pocket produced one shilling and sixpence. The amount was comprised of one-penny coins, the ones with a hole in the middle, and there were two Tickies (the NyasAaron d Ticky was worth three pennies). These had the head of King George on one side and three arrows on the flip side. She said that according to her calculations, that was how much I had given her over the few months of our whirl-wind relationship. I had expected to get a feeling of satisfaction with this settlement, but instead I felt a little ashamed and nas-ty. The whole experience did not heal or seal the gaping hole in my heart, as I had hoped it would. I still had strong feelings for Maggie, but I felt there was no way back. I had to nurse myself back to normalcy after all this. Puppy love? Certainly! Still, the intensity is perhaps similar to other love heartbreaks at any age. I have, through the years, realised this fact.

Maggie stopped coming to school within a few months of this incident, and the story was that she had married her new boyfriend, John. He was eighteen. I imagine, like me, he was a music lover, or maybe he had a good line in silk dresses. Either way, Maggie's songs were for him now, not for me. I had to find another musician and hopefully without a John lurking nearby!

Chapter 4

MY UNCLE WILLARD

Cool gusts of wind blew dry mango leaves across the front yard. It had rained a little in the night, and a warm steaming vapour, which rose from the ground, promised yet another hot day. The surrounding mango and thombozi trees were already teeming with various types of birds spotting different types of plumage, as if in competition with each other. They also sang just as competitively, with none of them giving room to listen to the song being sung by the next group. Their way of welcoming a new day. I was eight, a year and a bit younger than Chalela.

From the narrow red-earthed road which led to our house there appeared the figure of a man carrying a suitcase in one hand and a hold-all in the other. He was walking towards our house, and when he was a few metres from the veranda he slowly lowered his luggage, wiping his sweaty face with the open palm of one of his free hands as he did so. Chalela and I were busy in the time-honoured occupation of two small boys, that is, doing nothing, when the man shouted, 'Where's your mother, boys?' Chalela and I hesitated. 'Where's your mother?' asked the stranger for a second time, more firmly and slightly louder this time.

'In the kitchen,' answered Chalela, somewhat surprised at being interrogated so early in the morning.

'Go call her,' the newcomer ordered, and being the younger one I stood up and slowly walked towards the kitchen.

'Hurry up! And while you're at it, bring me some water to drink!'

In response, I quickened my pace, and as I did so I could hear him continue, 'You need knocking into shape, you two.' I did not like the sound of this stranger!

Hearing the conversation outside, Mother came to see who it was. 'Ah! It's your Uncle Willard. Don't you remember him?'

'I don't think they do,' responded the stranger, 'but they will before I leave,' he added with a conspiratorial wink towards Mother, and he wickedly smiled at Chalela and me.

Uncle Willard was a nomad. It was his chosen way of life. He was single and used to appear like a cloud drifting across the sky, here one moment, gone the next, and in between he never told anyone of his next port of call. The family had given up hope of him ever settling down, and according to Mother, it had been roughly four years since his last visit. It was rumoured he had children here and there, although the family never got to meet them, and Uncle Willard never discussed or owned up to the fact that he had illegitimate children. Mother liked Uncle Willard, mostly because he made her laugh. He looked strong and tall, with a round, handsome, clean-shaven, funny face, one which made one smile just looking at it. He was also hard-working and useful to have around the house and on the farm, as we were later to discover.

Following an old Ngoni tradition of sharing and togetherness, five households, which consisted of those of my two aunties, my Grandfather, and my cousin Jessie, used to have supper together every night. Each household would prepare their meal and take it to a particular house which was chosen on a round-robin basis every week. That night it was our turn to act as hosts, and reed mats were spread on the front yard of our house. The night was pregnant with a thousand sounds from God's creatures, each one telling its story in its own unique way but which the next creature dismissed as mere noise. These stories were delivered beneath a sea of flickering stars, a confident giant of a moon coolly outshining them all. Mothers could be heard calling their brood for supper, crying children, laughing adults and then silence as we each took our positions to eat.

Men ate together away from the women, who ate with the younger children. The older children joined the men, and it was from them that they learned table (mat) manners while enjoying the food.

After the main dish, which was nsima with red kidney beans, beef stew, chicken stew, and a variety of vegetables, it was time for dessert, my favourite part of any meal. The summer season had brought us, amongst other things, sweet potatoes, pumpkins, green maize, and fresh groundnuts, and on most nights, each household would bring one or two of these items, boiled and steaming hot. It was after the desserts that both groups, men, and women, merged and storytelling began. There were folk tales, 'true lives', cultural and such like, which used to continue late into the night. When I got up the following day, I would often be unaware of how the stories had finished, or indeed, how I got into bed. I might have lasted through the first story or on occasion the second but rarely beyond that.

Uncle Willard had his unique style of telling a story, and it was so disappointing, particularly to the women, when he was not around at these gatherings. He was the star performer, and his stories would often start something like this.

'It was during the driest summer ever – 1949, it was, long before you children were born. Your sister was only two at the time. Get me some water to drink, Davie, and hurry up or you'll miss the story. Things were bleak, and the chief decided to make some offerings to the ancestorial spirits. Beer was brewed and a bull was slaughtered – did I just hear a hyena laughing? It's far off, anyway.'

'No, it's Chalela,' Mother joked, causing everyone to break into laughter.

'Stop interrupting!' ordered the storyteller. 'The chief was accompanied to the nearby hill with these offerings well prepared, but a week, a month, two months passed and still the skies kept their blue colour and the sun shone. The heat was unbearable – I don't know if it's just me but I am feeling hungry already. Davie, go get me some sweet potatoes from your mother. Why are you limping? That boy never sits down; he's up and down, up and down, the whole day. He never rests! The offerings had to be repeated. We were dealing with greedy spirits here! This time, the skies opened before the chief and his elders arrived back in the village. Don't drink too much water, Davie. I won't escort you to the loo tonight!'

This was followed by another interruption from Mother. 'I thought you said you'd tell them a funny story tonight.'

'I've over-eaten, Sister. I can hardly breathe properly. Tomorrow, I'll tell them. Okay, you lot?'

'No, please tell us some more, Uncle Willard,' we would plead.

'Yes, tell the children a funny story. The one you promised them.'

'All right, all right. Any more pumpkins?' he would ask, a ready, cheeky smile on his lips. 'Well, now ...'

As far as Chalela and I were concerned, Uncle Willard was a workaholic. Each morning our bedroom door would open, and just as the sun came up, Uncle's voice commanded, 'Wake up, boys. We're going to the field. I've got your hoes ready.' We usually ignored him for a minute or so. 'Did you hear me? I'll give you three minutes and no more!' I often wondered how he worked out his minutes, for he never wore a wristwatch. Chalela would get up, and while he was pulling on his khaki shorts with one hand and rubbing his eyes with the other, Uncle Willard would return and pull my blanket off my completely naked body. 'If you don't get up, I'll pour cold water on you!' This was enough resistance from me, and I would cave in, though reluctantly.

We would be working in the field soon after six. Mother usually brought us breakfast at around seven-thirty, and we continued weeding until noon. The first week of working this way was hard, and when we complained to Mother she replied, 'Your father thinks you need discipline, and he gave your uncle a free hand toinstill in you true Ngoni values.'

'Can't we learn about them in stories, Mom?' asked Chalela, hoping to bring about a change in our fortunes. Some hope!

'Leave me alone, now. Work never killed anybody, and you'll soon be going back to school anyway,' Mother would dismissively respond with a little loving smile on her lips.

During the second week I decided this sort of suffering had gone on long enough and one day, just before noon, according to my shadow, I told Uncle Willard I was going home. I reasoned that I had done enough work for one day and was tired.

'You're right, Davie. Now, let's see. Right – just do these four ridges. The same for you, Chalela, just four more ridges, and that is it for the day,' Uncle replied persuasively. I stood erect and looked at those four ridges planted with maize, groundnuts, beans, and sorghum. Uncle Willard expected us to take out the weeds carefully and painstakingly grow in between these crops, as I had done the entire morning. Not me! With my hoe on my shoulder, I headed home, running, with Uncle Willard in hot pursuit. My young, long, and still growing crane-like legs were no match against his long and mature crane-like legs, and when Uncle Willard caught up with me, he gave me a caning, but I still refused to work. Instead, I ran to my mother in the kitchen, who immediately sympathised and gave me a pineapple to peel while we waited for Chalela and Uncle Willard to return to the house. I was beginning to doubt Father's wisdom in giving Uncle Willard free rein. The good thing was that soon after such an incident we would be friends again – until the next time!

After lunch, just as Chalela and I were about to disappear to play with other children, Uncle Willard would at times call us back. 'I think I should cut Davie's hair before you go out to play. Go on, get the tools from your mother.' My heart would sink. I hated getting my hair cut, especially by him. I found the whole experience most depressing and demanding, not to say painful. You were expected to keep still for minutes on end, look this way and that, turn here, turn there, and if that was not enough torture, in the meantime, one could hear the other children playing nearby. I could not bear it.

ehind the house was a small patch of a pineapple garden, roughly half an acre. At the far end was a big flattish granite rock, which Uncle Willard had chosen for the site of his small, rickety barber's chair. He did not even ask me what style I wanted, like a short back and sides or a 'Kojak' or a 'Cadet Cut (now renamed an Ollie Cut since Oliver North came on the scene). He would just start removing the hair wholesale!

'Don't make your neck too rigid,' he would complain. 'Turn this way, no, not so much, back the other way just a little. Do you want me to finish the job or not?' I did not care but dared not say so. When he accidentally nicked me with the pair of scissors behind my neck, I could not say anything the first time, but the second time it happened I could not control myself.

'You've cut me, haven't you, Uncle? I can feel the blood flowing.'

'No, it's only a little nick,' Uncle Willard would flippantly respond.

'Yes, but there's blood, Uncle,' I would moan while squirming in my seat

'Next, you'll be telling me you've eyes behind your neck. Will you please shut up while I finish cutting your hair, big head!' I had no choice. The idea of going around with a half-finished haircut did not seem like an option at all.

Uncle Willard would not allow me to have a mirror nearby as he cut my hair, so the first mirror after my ordeal would be Mother. On this day, she had been plaiting her longish African hair and perhaps contemplating her next chore. She was uncomfortable with idleness. The beauty of her light mahogany skin and the kindness in her nature were so evident in her face as the setting sun's rays reflected on it. When she noticed my presence and then my bare head coming towards her, I could easily see she was trying very hard to stifle a laugh.

'It's not looking good, Mom, is it?' I queried, expecting some reassurance. Her response came between barely controlled bursts of laughter.

'What do you want me to say, Son? It's all right. It's good.'

At this point, I knew the haircut was badly done and that I was looking awful, and I felt uncomfortable and unsure of joining the others to play. They would laugh at me, I feared.

'There's no need to sulk, Son. Your hair will grow back soon,' soothed Mother. With these words, I disappeared into the house, intending to stay there until my hair grew back. The prospect of being seen in that state by the other boys was too risky, but my resolve only lasted a few minutes, and my friends, as expected and dreaded, had a good laugh at my expense although the amusing spectacle did not last long. There were many activities, sometimes moving flipchart-like on the playground, occupying our growing minds.

That night, Uncle Willard made this announcement. 'Boys, this Saturday we're going hunting.'

'But we don't have any weapons!' exclaimed Chalela, his eyes alight with the promise of the hunt just announced.

'Davie, go into my bedroom and bring me the sack from behind the door,' ordered our beloved, funny and industrious uncle.

I ran quickly in anticipation and was back in under a minute.

'I've made your weapons,' Uncle Willard declared. 'I thought of making assegais, but those need a lot of skill and strength to use. Let's see ...' He paused as he took the contents from the sack. 'This one is for you, Chalela, a bow and arrow with a club-diamond-shaped tip designed to hit a target without piercing it. And for you, Davie, here is a sharp-tipped arrow and a smaller bow to match your strength.' We both thanked him. I was so excited with my weapon and so was Chalela with his.

On the following day, there was no dissent at the maize fields. I did as I was told, and we even found time to laugh at Uncle Willard's jokes. He had this ability to impersonate, so easily, anyone he set eyes on. The way a person spoke, walked, or even thought was mimicked by him. The day before, a skinny old man, who lived nearby, had passed by on his way to the market, which was over three miles away. He commented on the quality of the work Uncle Willard was doing and added that he was planning to push himself a little harder before the weeds overtook his maize field. 'Talk about optimism. For all he knows, he may not even make it to the market,' said Uncle Willard as soon as the old man disappeared down the road. 'I would like to push myself harder,' he continued, this time impersonating the way the old man spoke to a tee. Chalela and I found the way he sounded extremely funny. I was beginning to like him.

Saturday, the day I looked forward to, the day Uncle Willard had promised to take us hunting, finally arrived. A beautiful day it was too – clear skies and a gentle breeze limiting the effects of the growing heat from the sun. Our free-range chickens were busy picking insects from the short grass around the house, stopping intermittently to stare at me with one eye and then the other whenever I made a move. There was no human sound, no voices. This tranquillity was broken when two hens began to peck at one another rather violently, sending feathers flying. And there was a voice – Mother calling us for breakfast.

'What time are we leaving, then?' Chalela queried Uncle Willard shortly after we had finished eating our sugared M'gaiwa maize-meal porridge.

'I take it you've never gone hunting before?' replied Uncle Willard, a gentle, mocking smile on his face. 'We'll leave once the sun has gone further west.'

'You won't be going far, will you?' asked Mother, suddenly concerned.

'Don't worry about us. When Ngoni men go on a hunt, all the women should be doing is cleaning the saucepans in anticipation,' stated Uncle Willard, squinting into the bright early-morning sun.

'Just be careful, boys,' called Mother resignedly as she disappeared into the kitchen.

Later, after lunch that day, we set off into the hills, which on one side descended into Thondwe River at a small waterfall called Kumadang'oma.

The hunt was a disaster. The nearest we got to killing anything was when my sharp-tipped arrow lodged itself into a baboon's leg. The baboon quickly disappeared into the thicket, leaving me with a bow I could not use on this hunt.

Frustrated and disappointed, we sat down on a rock overlooking the river, and we could hear the falling sounds of its fast-flowing waters as it reached the mini-falls. The sun had become pale and distant. It was still daylight, and we sat still, each of us lost in his thoughts.

'Never mind, boys. It wasn't a good day for hunting,' said Uncle. 'We should try again next week. Next time we'll be using a different approach. Somewhere upriver.' Chalela and I listened with great interest although we did not verbally respond.

'Come on, cheer up, boys.' Uncle Willard began to laugh gently and slapped me jokingly on the back so hard that I was forced into an impromptu forward jiggle before he got hold of me and sat me next to him.

'All right. I'll now tell you a short story from home, Kwa a Kanduku, Ku Mwanza.

'Once upon a time, there were three young men who went hunting up in the hills. Accompanying them was a younger muscular man, who did not know much about hunting. After hours offruitless searching, they suddenly heard elephants braying down in the swamp – excitement at last. Before setting off on the attack, the immature would-be huntsman saw a juvenile elephant close by, on its own.

"Why don't we go for that young elephant?" he suggested. "I can handle it on my own." He was told by the others that the elephant before them might be three months old or thereabouts and that it could still be dangerous.

"I'll take it single-handedly, with my bare fists. They don't call me Nyanga-ya-Theka (Half a Horn) for nothing, you know!" he boasted. The others, having failed to dissuade him from his plan, simply watched as he walked towards his quarry, which was grazing in the late afternoon sun with an air of confidence about it. Wisely, the other three kept their distance from the upcoming confrontation. The young man took off his shirt, took a deep breath, held it there, and gathering all the energy he could muster, he let fly one massive punch to the elephant's head. The animal did not even wince. Another punch followed, and another, then with one sudden movement, the animal's long trunk coiled around the now frightened and desperate-looking young man. The elephant swung its trunk three hundred and sixty degrees twice then suddenly let go. As a glider, the young would-be hunter took to the sky, landing face down in a swampy puddle a few metres away. The little elephant looked towards the other three as if to say, "How about the rest of you – do you want to have a go too?" The braying of the little elephant had aroused the interest of an older elephant, which could be seen speeding to where the boys were. It was not a time to wait and watch. They all showed clean heels as they ran up the hill towards their home.'

Mother was sitting on the veranda when we got back. The way her motherly smile lit up her face, like a ray of sunlight brightening a darkened landscape, showed her relief at seeing us safely back.

'We'll try again next week. Something wasn't quite right today,' Uncle Willard defensively told her. 'Something to do with the direction of the wind.'

'So, we won't be having supper tonight, then? I didn't prepare anything apart from the pots and some freshly dug onions!' teased Mother.

'I've never enjoyed an onion supper before, as you know, Sister. How about adding something easy to go with the onions?' Uncle Willard asked cheekily.

'What have you got in mind?' retorted Mother.

'Er ... er ... well ... I saw one young rooster limping this morning. To see one of God's creatures suffer like that ...'

'No. I'm not letting you finish off that poor, lovely thing, Brother.'

'You're missing the point, Sister. I don't think you're happy to see the rooster limp around like that. Who knows how long, if ever, it's going to take for the leg to heal.'

'No. You're not eating my rooster. If you want chicken, there are lots of wild fowls in the bush – guinea fowls, wildfowl – but certainly not my rooster!' Mother seemed to conclude, but these negotiations went on for almost an hour. The Bible was even brought into play a couple of times to support Uncle Willard's argument. That is when Mother's resistance waned. For goodwill, he promised to bring not one, not even two, but three birds the next time we went hunting.

Once again, the day to go hunting arrived, another dry, sunny day. The wind was gentler compared to the last time we had gone hunting. Uncle Willard ordered us both to take a bath but not to use soap. He reckoned that any soap or perfume was easily picked by wild animals as a sign of imminent danger.

We had been in the bush for less than thirty minutes when Chalela spotted a bushbuck. He whispered excitedly to Uncle while pointing to where the animal was. We were both ordered to squat as Uncle did likewise. He quickly aimed his arrow from his sturdy bow and let go! The animal shrieked and tried to run as Uncle ran in pursuit. It did not go far. The arrow had lodged between the front leg and the neck; it had perhaps severed some vital organs inside it.

Uncle quickly cut its neck but not completely severing its from its body. This he did to drain the blood from the carcass, which he claimed spoiled the taste of the meat if not done that way. Using some vines, Uncle tied the dead animal to a piece of dry bamboo and handed it to Chalela to carry. He made sure the severed end of the carcass was at a slanting angle. Looking back, it must have been around twenty kilograms or thereabouts.

After an hour or so, Chalela complained about the weight and that he needed a rest. He also complained that because of the carcass he was carrying he was no longer hunting with us. Surprisingly enough, Uncle Willard seemed to understand Chalela's lament, and he decided to hide the dead animal in a big leafy tree nearby. We were hunting on private land, which Father had acquired some years earlier.

The hunt continued, and by now the sun was showing some signs of exhaustion. No longer was it bright nor was it hot. Its colour had now changed to orangey-red, and it looked very distant. Down the hill and towards the river, we could see a variety of animals taking their last drink of water just a short distance from Kumadang'oma Falls before retiring for the night.

Uncle Willard whispered to us to pick one animal to aim at. Chalela picked another bushbuck, I picked a springbok, and Uncle Willard picked a kudu. He said he was going to count to three, and at that point each one of us should let go of their arrow. I missed; Chalela and Uncle Willard both had a hit each!

We had to pursue the kudu for some distance before it got tired. Perhaps at this point it had lost too much blood to continue running, and just before we could get to it, a man carrying an axe appeared and gashed the dying animal on the head with a lot of violence as he shouted, 'Msomoli wangawu!' We were told a moment later by Uncle Willard that those words meant that the man was laying claim on one part of the animal for finishing it off, usually the front leg and the head. Chalela's animal had fallen a few metres from where the hit took place.

We now had simply too much meat to carry. Uncle Willard sent us back home to the village to bring extra help. At this point, he had already gutted one of the carcasses, and wrapped the entrails, liver, lungs, heart, and pancreas in some mpoza leaves tied using Luzi, he said, 'First, stop by at the house and give this to your mother. Tell her she should begin cooking immediately.' I could see what Uncle had in mind. It was easy to get people for the singular chore of carrying the meat now that the harder part had already been accomplished.

Such meat would usually be shared by all involved in the hunt, including those who simply took part in the skinning and gutting of the animals. Certainly, all those who helped with the carrying of the meat also got their pound of flesh, emphasis on the word, 'pound'.

Those who were unable to go hunting because of illness or age and couldn't play any role in this exercise were also given some of the meat, although, as expected, not the choicest of cuts. The rest of the meat would be salted and dried for future use.

Uncle Willard was simply a work dynamo. If it was not working in the field or going hunting, he would always find something for us to do or at least learn. He was very good with the making of mortars and pestles for pounding maize to make flour for the traditional staple food. He made quite a few for Mother, and within a few months, he became the artisan for our village and surrounding villages. He was being paid money or alcohol for his sweat. He was in high demand. At the height of all this, one morning as we were having breakfast, he simply said to Mother, 'Sister, I will be leaving for Ncheu this week.'

I hadn't realised how fond I had become of Uncle Willard until that morning. I just couldn't imagine life without him around on the farm.

'What is in Ncheu?' queried Mother.

'Well, that's where I have settled.'

'Settled?' asked Mother with a stern but kind tone.

'Sister, I am sorry I did not inform you. I have a wife in Ncheu. I came here because I was not getting along with my in-laws, but I now think I can handle the problems we have. I promise to bring her over here one day. She is a very good woman; it's the in-laws who make my life unbearable sometimes.

'You two,' he said, looking at us, 'do not destroy your bows and arrows. We will go hunting again when I return.'

It was now September, a period for bushfires. Our over-grown arable land with its natural forest had already experienced its portion of this annual man-made destruction. Grass, tree-stumps, and a variety of other plants were showing their resilience by growing new shoots of growth – new and fresh leaves were visible all over the ground around the uncultivated areas of the farm.

Mother and her friends and us boys were all around the house when we heard the barking of dogs and the sound of a man shouting, 'My bushbuck! My bushbuck! My bushbuck!' The sound was coming from the right side of the farm, the area where we had gone hunting with Uncle Willard a couple of months earlier. The noise was coming closer and closer, and all of us had our eyes glued in the direction of the shouting and dog-barking. We then saw the bushbuck crossing at great speed the driveway that led to our house. Behind it was the hunter followed by around five dogs. This first time any of us had witnessed a barefoot human being, or even one with shoes on, outrun his dogs in a situation like this!

'Oh, how I wish your uncle was here! I would have asked him to use the short-cut in the direction of the bushbuck and try to gain ground, Msomoli! It's nsima, red kidney beans and khwan-ya (bean leaves) tonight.'

We couldn't have agreed with her more. It was midweek, and Father was not coming until the weekend. He usually brought us groceries including beef and fish. And for families in need of mortars and pestles for the preparation of their maize flour, they simply had to find a new craftsman, and that wasn't going to be easy. Such artisans were not easy to find in the area at the time. My Uncle Willard was going to missed by several people for various reasons. I was not very perturbed by his departure, because my mother would be resuming her role as my barber. She was a better one than Uncle Willard. Working in the fields would also be at a comparatively slower and more tolerable pace.

Chapter 5

A SMALL WORLD OF MAGIC AND WONDER

In 1966, while the political bloodletting was still on the rise, the Ngwazi (all-conquering hero) His Excellency Dr. Kamuzu Banda was full steam ahead with his development plans. The grandest of them all was, at the time, the transfer of Malawi's capital city from Zomba in the southern region to Lilongwe in the central region.

There was a lot of talk from his whispering detractors that he had chosen Lilongwe because it was very close to his home district of Kasungu. Well, what they chose not to mention was that Lilongwe was centrally located. This was intended to make it fairer for people from both ends of the country to access government services at a centrally positioned point, and it was also going to create, directly and indirectly, thousands of new jobs.

I was eleven at the time, and the memory of Margaret was fast becoming a fading emotion struggling to leave one corner of my heart completely. It did not take too long for me to find a new occupant of that space in my bruised but healing heart. In my class, there was a beautiful girl with Nubian facial features and height. Her name was Lucy. Her desk was to my immediate right. Thus, I could look in her direction without swivelling my head too visibly for her, or others, particularly the teacher, to notice. Each time I arrived at school I used to look around the playground just to see if Lucy was there. I attribute my poor academic performance that year to her, not that she was aware of this. Apart from developing a habit of greeting her each morning and saying goodbye at the end of our school day, there was nothing else that Lucy and I discussed. Each time I spoke to her I couldn't tell whether my close attention was being appreciated or not, but still I persisted.

The rains had come. These were the first rains which, at the time, the pre-climate change period, used to fall towards the end of October and certainly before the 15th November.

During the school holidays, which had just ended, our friends, Enock and Ojesi, from the same Kumbengule village, had spent the time in Domasi, towards the shores of Lake Chilwa. Chalela and I were surprised when news began to spread that these two brothers were performing some strange and hard-to-understand magic. We became interested, and on the next morning we confronted the two brothers with this information, and they confirmed the rumour. We were then invited to the next show, which was to take place on the evening of the following Saturday.

We arrived at the place for the show just before sunset, and we found most of our friends were already there. I could see the two brothers running around preparing for the magic show. Eventually, we were all called to a spot they had chosen. The expectant and excited group gravitated toward them as one unit tied together by an invisible elasticated rope. We encircled them. In the middle of the circle was a fire-cured clay pot, in which we could see bits of roots and fresh green leaves soaked in water. There was also a wooden pestle just over a metre long and with a diameter of roughly three inches. This kind of pestle was generally called the 'groundnuts pestle'. Enock and Ojesi washed the pestle using the water in the clay pot. They then called for our attention. 'We are now about to begin our performance called Cham'godo. We will start to sing a song, which you will be asked to join in with. The louder you respond to the song the better will be the magical performance. I will start thus.

'Cham'godo, Cham'godo,
Anthu ache ndi omwewa (Cham'godo, these are the very people)
You respond, Cham'godo,
Akupanga makani (They are hard to convince)
You respond, Cham'godo,
Muwagwetse anthuwa (You should floor them)
You respond, Cham'godo,

Hey, hey, hey, hey, hey, hey, heeee,
You respond, Cham'godo,
Cham'godo taimba mulongo wako ndi Madiwane (Cham'godo, sing,
your sister is Madiwane),
You respond, Cham'godo.

'A very simple song, isn't it?' he asked rhetorically. He then invited three volunteers who would wish to participate in the magic show. Three of our friends did – Fred, Tilekeleni, and Louis.

'Tallest in front, shortest at the back. I will then place the pestle on your shoulder. You are all facing the same direction. Hold onto it with all your strength, yes?' All this was done, and the singing started in earnest. Slowly at first and immediately after we could see the three young people struggling as if a huge and active weight were pushing them down. As the singing reached even higher decibels, the three participants were now destroying some newly germinated maize crops in a nearby garden, and they eventually had to drop to the ground what had become a *living* pestle while it was on their collective shoulders.

Different groups of three presented themselves to Enock and Ojesi to take part in the magic show. My brother, Chalela, Thomas, and I joined in and we, just like the others before us, were floored by Cham'godo. For the next few days, the whole village had chins wagging about this magic show. Boys who were a bit older and most of them in their late teens came to the show, took part, and there was no different result.

Up to this day, I do not know how Cham'godo worked.

A few years ago, in 2015, I returned to Chief Kumbengule's area in Zomba in search of Enock and Ojesi. I found that George's mother, their auntie, and her other children, I do not recall how many, were the only ones still in the village. The rest had either passed on or had left the village. As for Enock and Ojesi, they both had joined the Malawi Defence Force. Enock had died the year before, but his elder brother, Ojesi, had retired and was living in the Naisi area within Zomba District, about fifteen kilometres from Kumbengule Village. I persisted, and using the map I had been given by the auntie, I managed to find Ojesi.

The ravages of a hard life were etched on his face. Although he was only three years older than me, Ojesi could have successfully passed for my father. He looked very old! After reminiscing for a while about the good old days, I mentioned Cham'godo.

'Oh! Yes, I remember,' he said, his sallow eyes brightening up.

'Could you perform it for us these days?' I asked him with very expectant eyes.

'No. You see, people have been asking me about that for some time now. Sadly, out of the six roots and herbs, I can only remember one. I am sorry.' Disillusioned, we still chatted about a lot of other boyhood incidents before I bid him farewell.

I could not desist from cheekily reminding him of the days when we and our chums would go to the wetlands to play where people grew sugarcane and other winter vegetables. We also enjoyed picking a variety of wild fruits which grew around that area. Apart from these fruits, there was also an onion-like plant, a bulb.which Ojesi had told us if one cut it in half, as one would do with an onion, and rubbed the cut end of it around the genital area, in a month's time or so, one would see some little hairs sprouting. The wild bulb was very itchy, and Ojesi had warned us not to scratch if we were to get the desired result. It was no easy feat to follow that instruction but, to those who persevered, and you have guessed it, *it worked*!

It's amazing how, at that age, eight through to eleven, you want to be a teenager with all the benefits in double time. I would have reminded him of the Makunganya gang and loads of other escapades we got involved in but for time! Still, hurriedly, I couldn't leave before reminding him of the day he encouraged me to climb into a mango tree where there was an attractive yellow mango hanging next to a nest of murder hornets, the huge dark brown type called maphang'ombe (which translates as cattle killers), found in Zomba and other districts in Southern Malawi. He assured me that these insects reacted aggressively against quick or sudden movements, so I should approach the mango fruit stealthily. As a reward for taking this challenge, he would start to teach me how Cham'godo worked. I managed to do as instructed, but because the fruit was at the tip of the branch where two wasps were, the branch began to shake up and down in response to every movement I made. Consequently, I was stung by both wasps. One bite was on the lower lip and the other on the left side of the nose. I screamed and was on the ground in record time.

The shaking of the branch had also helped the mango to detach itself from the tree, and Ojesi had it in his hand. 'Oh! I see you have been stung. Just wash your face with salty water to prevent swelling.' He seemed to have solutions for everything. This remedy did not work – my face was puffed up within minutes. I couldn't open my eyes, and a tablespoon of breakfast porridge could not pass through my lips into my mouth for more than three days due to the intense swelling of my face. 'Yes, I remember the incident. You used to like mangoes too much in those days, didn't you?' he casually responded, forgetting it was he who had sent me up that tree. He also ate the mango I had climbed the tree to pluck!

A few months later, we were having lunch at the Parliament's cafeteria in Lilongwe. I was narrating the story of Cham'godo to a fellow Member of Parliament, Sam Ganda, may his soul rest in eternal peace.

'Yes, I attended a similar magic show in Mulanje only a few years ago. I just do not recall what the chap called it, but it did exactly that, and I was one of its victims.' He promised to try and find the 'magician', but fate intervened too early. He died a few months afterward.

Around the same period, my father employed a Mozambican refugee called John., his job was to draw water for us from a water well which was half a kilometre away and to work in the field. He was the one who replaced Joao. I will tell you more about him later.

John was of medium build and had light-brown skin. I would have described him as handsome if his face were not so pimply.

He was soft-spoken and very religious. He never missed his Friday prayers at the nearby mosque.

Father and Mother had travelled to Lilongwe, where they were looking for a location to build and open another nightclub and restaurant.

One Saturday morning, soon after breakfast, which Modesta, the maid Father had employed a couple of months earlier, had prepared before leaving for Zomba market, John called Chalela and me. 'You two, would you hide in the house just before my girlfriend comes here? I will alert you as soon as I spot her coming through the maize fields. She is very shy.' He spoke with the voice of a man who is pensive.

'Where is she coming from? Which direction?' queried Chalela.

"She is Ashoti's wife. I don't know, but chances are that she will come from the nightclub end,' he answered in a very low hush-hush whisper.

Ashoti was the band leader for the resident music group my father had hired at the time. He was a short bearded fellow with a nasty temper, who frequently beat up his wife in public because of petty jealousies. I, and I am sure also my brother, Chalela, wondered why John was taking such a risk. We also wondered why Ashoti's wife would be having secret canoodles with a farm labourer. On the social ladder, her husband was visibly higher, in our view. It must have been either because she was a loose woman, or it was because she needed a man who did not abuse her. We simply could not make heads or tail of how the adult world worked.

'I will tell you when I am ready,' he said as he entered the kitchen, which was not part of the main house. He took one maize cob and fried the grains in a dry pan until they were completely burned and smoking. He then poured water on the burning maize. He captured the dark liquid from the pan, then looked around for a chicken feather, which he quickly prepared and used as a pen nib. He wrote a few lines in the Arabic alphabet. Finally, he folded the piece of paper into a shape about one inch by one inch. He then put some essence on a piece of burning charcoal and chanted the woman's name. He seemed to warm the folded paper, which he had encased in a piece of cloth. It looked like a tiny pillow. We just stood in the kitchen doorway, mesmerised! 'You two, go into the house and hide.' We did, not because we were doing it for John but rather for ourselves. We wanted to prove John's charms were effective. You can imagine how shocked we were when we saw Ashoti's wife walking towards the house within minutes, camouflaged by the shoulder-high growing maize crop.

We could hear John and Ashoti's wife whispering for some time, and peeping through the window curtains, we saw her leaving John's boudoir at the end of the yard. Still wondering how John had done this, I asked him to help me bring home a girl from school, a girl I admired, Lucy, my Nubian beauty!

'When do you want her to visit you?' asked John.

'How about this Saturday?'

'All right. I will have to make your ink.' I felt reassured, and John did not seem perturbed by the chore I had presented him with. If anything, I was the one who was stressed. What would I do with Lucy should she come over, I pondered. I was doing this because Chalela and I did not believe John had used charms to seduce Ashoti's wife.

The following Friday, John fulfilled his promise and prepared my special charm with Lucy's name in Arabic writing on it.

When we woke up on Saturday morning, I had forgotten all about Lucy. We were playing a game of football with our chums in the mud when I heard a female voice call out my name. It was Lucy with two other girls. She was at the junction to our driveway about twenty metres away.

'I didn't know you lived here.'

'Yes, and where are you going?' It was the only question I could ask her.

'We are just taking a walk. We plan to start walking back now. See you at school on Monday,' she said as the three of them made an about-turn. I was both excited and fearful of what John was able to do with burned maize, a letter in Arabic writing and a little essence!

'So, my charms for Lucy to visit did not work, Davie?' asked John jovially after dinner that evening.

'Oh! They did. Thank you,' I answered and wished I had thanked him earlier.

'But I didn't see her, and I was here the whole day,' he lamented.

I explained to him how the whole visit happened.

'So, you mean I spent all my maize, fire, time, and my knowledge in Arabic charms for a visit which did not last even a minute?' he complained, albeit with a contemptuous smile on his handsome, pimply face. I didn't have a ready response to this question.

'You should have invited her into the house for a glass of water, at least!'

'I promise to do that next time, John.'

I suspect John continued seeing Ashoti's wife for some time after the first time we had seen her at the house. And one late afternoon, we heard a commotion outside the nightclub. There were male and female voices, screaming, wailing, and shouting. We rushed to see what was going on. The mango trees were all pregnant with fruit, which was not yet yellow.

On arrival at the scene, we found Ashoti's wife, half-dressed, wearing only a pink half-slip and a brassiere, on the floor, crying loudly with blood all over her face, with Ashoti standing above her, hitting and stamping on her. People were struggling to stop him from dishing out what was a cruel beating of a defenceless woman.

The whispers from those we found on the scene were that Ashoti had caught his wife in bed with Mr Batani (Button), a six-foot-tall rugged hungry-looking guy, who seemed to look always angry. I never saw him smiling.

'Where is Mr Batani?' asked my brother, Chalela.

'He ran away across the road. Ashoti gave chase for a while, but he soon gave up the chase and returned to confront the wife.'

As we spoke, we saw people who were at one end of the nightclub grounds turn their heads and give way to a running and panting shirtless man. It was Mr Batani. He was growling and snarling, not towards Ashoti but at three nearby mango trees a couple of metres away from where we were standing. He punched the first tree with his bare knuckles, causing quite a good number of green mangoes to fall to the ground. He moved on to the next tree, which he head-butted with a loud thud, and again, lots of mangoes fell to the ground from the impact. He wasn't done yet. He moved to the third tree, which he simply shook with both hands, and on this tree, only a few mangoes remained attached.

'Where is he? Where is Ashoti?' Mr Batani asked disrespectfully as he turned and, still growling and snarling, charged to where Ashoti had been a moment earlier. Ashoti was no longer there. He had legged it! Who wouldn't, I thought. A man who had just demonstrated his prowess in the manner which Mr Batani had just done should not be toyed with. Looking at his hands and forehead at this point, I saw that they bore no marks at all.

A few elderly men present commented that Mr Batani might have had *Mangolomela*. This is a mixture of herbs and roots which are burned and powdered and using a sharp object like a razor blade, small cuts are made on the arms and legs. This concoction is expected to make one extremely strong and, judging from what Mr Batani had just demonstrated, it probably did!

When we returned home, Chalela jokingly asked John when he was seeing Ashoti's wife next.

'Please, please, please do not mention Ashoti's wife to me again. And do not talk to anyone about Ashoti's wife. Ha! After what I saw today, I never will again. I think God has favoured me. I am a very, very lucky man!'

There are a lot of medicines for use in various applications, made of fauna and flora, which the Western world describes as 'witchcraft' and unchristian.

As we watched Mr Batani, I recalled two experiences I had had four years earlier. I had whooping cough, which wouldn't respond to Western medication and was getting worse by the day. Then one weekend, when father had come to the farm in Thondwe and was chatting with two farm workers he had recently employed and like John were also from Mozambique, one of the farm workers observed the whooping cough was not getting any better.

'Boss, I have observed he is in a bad way, but if you would allow me to try, I know some medicine I could prepare for him,' he said unassumingly.

'Is it?' responded father with an air of doubt in his voice. 'Well, I will have a chat with his mother and see how we can handle the situation.'

The next morning, Amini, the farm worker, was given the green light to treat my illness. At this stage, my breathing was laboured and was producing some whistling and frog-like sounds.

Soon after lunch, Amini asked Mother if I could accompany him to the hill to get the medicine he had talked about. With a small hoe in hand, we took off up the hill on a path which led to Auntie Eliza's maize field. Just before getting to the field's boundary, Amini asked me to turn left into the bush. We had only walked for around ten metres or so when he pointed at a climbing shrub. 'Pick five leaves from that plant.' I did and handed them to him. I saw him produce a small pouch from his pocket, into which he put the five leaves. We continued walking slowly. All the while, Amini was looking around for the next medicinal plant. Then, suddenly, 'There, to your right,' he said, pointing and walking quickly past me. 'This one!' he said, holding a short plant with carrot-like leaves. He started to dig, and at about half a foot deep he found the tuber. He cut a finger-long piece of it and left the plant and the remainder of its tuber buried and alive. 'We should leave the rest in the ground to continue growing for the next time,' he said as he gesticulated to me to move on to the next addition to the final concoction.

We were now moving towards the river, Thondwe River, where we picked two more plants before finally arriving at the riverbank. The river had a lot of rocks and stones. It also had several species of fish and crabs, the red ones. People in the area used to eat them, but Mother never allowed us to eat such things. Sitting on one of the many rocks in the middle of the river, Amini pointed at a small rock about half a metre square.

'Feel your hand under that rock and grasp gently whatever you find there.' I hesitantly started to walk towards the rock, stopping several times to look back as I did, and on each occasion, Amini would nod his head encouragingly. I got to the rock. I cast one look at Amini, and he gesticulated to me with a wave of his hand to do as per his instruction. I gently felt with my hands under the rock until I touched something which moved. Startled and afraid, I clasped my hands around it, and shaking, I pulled my hands out of the water. I had just caught a red crab. Amini got it from me and quickly put it in his sash, something like what native Americans call, a bandolier with the rest of the roots and leaves we had collected earlier.

When we got home, Amini asked my mother if he could use the kitchen. He put some water in a small saucepan, into which he put some salt together with the leaves and roots until they had boiled for some time. He then decanted the liquid from this concoction into an empty jam jar. Immediately afterward he put the crab, which was still alive, in the jar as well and put the lid on.

He then asked me to call my mother into the kitchen, and when she came in, Amini opened the bottle and whispered something I couldn't quite catch. He picked a tablespoon from the rack on a table near the door, took a spoonful of liquid from the jar and put it in his mouth. 'This is the medicine, Madam,' he said as he handed the jar to my mother. 'One tablespoon in the morning, one in the afternoon, and one at bedtime for seven days. Okay, I am now off to the field,' he said as he left us in the kitchen, where I took that morning's dosage. On day three the whistling was no longer as loud as it was before. The froggy sounds were also inaudible. By day five I was able to breathe normally, and by the end of the week I was as good as new.

Imagine if there were respect and encouragement from international pharmaceuticals for African traditional medicine – where would we be now? Where would Amini be now?

In the chapter, My Time at Soche Hill Secondary School, I spent one entire year without eating any hard foods, a year spent on liquids, and our family doctor, Dr Antao in Blantyre, had not managed to identify the problem. The other general practitioner in Lilongwe, Dr Kharodia, hadn't done any better either, but this is not a reflection of their medical abilities.

Dr Antao was a Sri-Lankan general practitioner with whom our family was registered. I recall my earlier experiences with him when Father brought me for one ailment or another. There would be mothers, mostly, with their children in the waiting room and one-by-one the nurse would call out a name, and as soon as the mother of the child stood up to go to the consulting room, the child would start screaming, 'I don't want an injection, I don't want an injection …'

The mother would try to comfort the hapless child with a lie. 'No, he will not inject you.'

'I know he will. That's what you told me the last time,' the emotionally charged child would counter. Then within minutes of entering the consultation room, we would hear the screech of a scream. 'You lied to me, Mother. I will never come here again … sob … sob … sob …'

At this point I would look at my mother questioningly, and she would know what was on my mind. 'It will hurt a little and it will make you feel better.' Then, dipping her hand into her shoulder bag, she would produce a few lollies. 'See, these are for you after seeing the doctor. Remember, big boys don't cry,' she would persuasively bribe me.

Sorry, I digress. During that period there was news of a traditional healer somewhere around Kasiya, Lilongwe District. His name was Simbazako. When I came home during that year's summer holidays, Mother introduced the subject of Simbazako in the presence of my cousin, Richard Phoya (now a professor), who was at the time on holiday from his master's programme at Aberystwyth University, Wales, United Kingdom.

Richard did not believe Simbazako was as good a medicine man as people were claiming him to be.

Mother was now pleading with my dad that we should see this famous medicine man, since Western medicine was not working on the ailment I was suffering from. Eventually, Dad succumbed to the pressure and allowed my mother to take me to Kasiya. Cousin Richard offered to join us, and he drove Dad's car. It was soon after the harvest period, and those who had grown sweet potatoes were still harvesting their tubers.

There was a tarmac road from Lilongwe Old Town to what is now the Air Wing, beyond which it was all gravel past Mbabzi, Nakuwawa to Kasiya. I remembered Nakuwawa Primary School because three years earlier, the Njewa Primary School football team had had a competitive football match against Nakuwawa Primary School. At half-time, Njewa was leading by 0–2. Just when we were about to go back on the pitch for the second half there appeared Gule Wankulu, a secret cult, involving a ritual dance practised among the Chewa people in Malawi, Zambia, and Mozambique. It is practised by initiated men of the Nyau brotherhood. Chewas are traditionally a matrilineal society, where major community decisions are made by women. The men find solace in Gule Wankulu as a means of establishing an activity to bond them together as a unitary force against the gender disadvantage they feel is not working in their favour. The Gule Wankulu came from the surrounding villages, a variety of them: Nyolonyo, Akapoli, Phedegu, etcetera. They targeted anyone in green, which was a Njewa colour, whipping us and chasing us around the school buildings. Eventually, peace and order were achieved, but the Gule Wankulu remained threateningly on the touchline. Njewa lost the game 5–2. Talk about football being more serious than a matter of life and death!

After driving for a few kilometres, my mother decided we should stop and ask for directions. Richard agreed, and he slowed down just before a small sweet-potato garden on the right, where a few young girls were digging the sweet potatoes out.

'Hello. How do we get to Simbazako's place?'

'You have arrived. Just turn your car down that narrow road on the right, keep on driving, and you cannot possibly miss it!'

'Is he a good medicine man?' asked Cousin Richard in jest.

'Oh! Yes, he is. We can tell you that in this Kasiya area, there has been no witchcraft since he arrived in this area,' responded the girl who looked the oldest of the three.

'How do you know?' probed Cousin Richard.

'One Nyakwawa, a lower chief, who has been unwell for the best part of the year, consulted Simbazako, who found out through his medicine that the chief's illness was being caused by Traditional Authority Njewa. Simbazako promised the sick chief that he would deal with Traditional Authority Njewa.

'The next day, Simbazako sent one of his helpers to go to Njewa's headquarters, about fifty kilometres away, to deliver Simbazako's message that he needed to see him,' she explained. The story was that Njewa had ignored the summons for a few days, and that's when things became interesting.

Mrs Njewa had prepared dinner and invited her husband, who was sitting majestically on his veranda at the time. It was August, when the weather is not too hot, averaging twenty-six degrees Celsius and rather windy during the day, a time most farmers use as a month of rest. Chief Njewa entered his dining room, where he found there was no food on the table. He angrily called out to his wife, asking her where the food was. On entering the room, the wife witnessed that there was, indeed, nothing on the table, but on closer inspection she found a piece of paper which simply read, *Come and collect your dishes in Kasiya*. It was signed, Simbazako. At this point, Njewa had no choice but to do as per Simbazako's instruction. When he got there, he was ordered to stop bewitching people, and that should he ignore the order he would certainly die. Immediately, the Nyakwawa's health started to quickly improve. A coincidence? Probably, probably not! Don't disregard the skills science has been too slow to appreciate, I say.

We bid the three girls farewell, and within two to three minutes we entered Simbazako's yard, a large clearing in an area as big as a football ground. There wasn't any structure which looked permanent. All of them were built of grass and had grass-thatch. At one end of the grounds, we could see women pounding a variety of tree barks and roots in wooden mortars. We were received by one of the ushers and taken to one end of the grass fence, where we found another expectant crowd waiting for the great man to treat their ailments just like we were.

Looking around, it was like being at a marketplace. The place was a hive of activity. Nearer to the top of the slope were spread ten reed mats. We could see those women who had been pounding tree barks and roots bringing the pulped stuff and heaping it separately on different mats.

I was expecting people to be called one-by-one to see the medicine man. Then, a booming voice came from where the mats were spread. 'Everyone who is here for medical help, come closer, please.' There was a huge push, a stampede towards the area before the mats of the hundreds who had assembled. Some were carrying their sick on their backs. Some helped theirs by supporting them by the arms, side-by-side as they moved as fast as their particular circumstances would allow them. I spotted a few carrying their sick on rickety homemade stretchers. Once we had done as requested, the voice continued, 'The doctor will come out now to deal with your health problems.' The owner of the voice disappeared into a small mud hut around ten metres towards the fence, and within a couple of minutes, he came out accompanied by a young-looking slightly built man of perhaps five feet six inches in height, who was certainly not more than twenty-five. We were later to learn he was twenty-one. This was the famous Doctor Simbazako.

After greeting us, he started to mention different ailments and where those afflicted should queue. Every reed mat with a heap of herbs represented medicines for a particular disease. When my condition was called, the three of us walked to that queue and waited for the next instruction. Our queue was the third to be called, and we listened attentively. One-by-one we moved forward to receive our prescription medicine. Doctor Simbazako wrapped it on a mpoza-tree leaf. I immediately unwrapped the small parcel when I re-joined Mother and Cousin Richard. It was a very coarse tree bark powder comprised of perhaps more than three types of barks, based on the colours I could detect. We were told to add a teaspoonful to my breakfast porridge for three days. If we did not see any improvement after that, Doctor Simbazako told us to return. As I received the medicine, Simbazako whispered, 'Chew the leaf when the medicine in it is finished.'

There was a narrow path from the medicine-dispensing area which was marked 'Njila Yotulukila' ('Exit'). As we walked down the narrow path just before the outside grass gates, we saw a middle-aged woman, who sat on a wooden bench. Next to her was a young boy of nine, so we were informed by one of the ushers. The story was that she had died of a mysterious ailment when she was pregnant. A couple of weeks earlier, her uncle, a maize mill businessman, was summoned by Simbazako, because from his magical research, he had found out that the businessman was a witch, an accusation he denied and braved the summons. Simbazako challenged him that the 'dead' niece, who had died nine years earlier, hadn't died. The uncle had magically put her in his maize mill to assist with the running of the engine and to reduce fuel costs. The niece gave birth while in this magically induced animated life as a maize-mill spare engine. One must see this to believe such stories.

Looking at the woman's waistline, it was hard to doubt the story. It looked like a drive-pulley, around which the maize mill belt rotated. It was shiny, leatherlike, and narrow, reflecting the narrative. They both couldn't speak. This is not a story I heard elsewhere. I saw it and lived through it, and I am not ashamed to narrate it for fear of being seen as a crackpot, which I am certainly not.

I took the medication the following morning and every morning for the next three days. I started to feel less and less abdominal pain on the evening of the second day. By day three I was completely free of abdominal pain. It was the first time I had felt this way in years! My very educated cousin, Richard, was completely gob-smacked. He just couldn't believe this 'miracle', let alone the story about the female maize-meal dynamo.

The sad result of these experiences is that Africa is losing its Cham'godo and Simbazako practitioners, its Aminis, its Man-in-the-Forest and my experience with Mr Thawale at Ryall's Hotel, -(more about him in Chapter 19),ts Mr Batanis, etcetera. Western science has an inbuilt arrogance, which believes, ignorantly, that if we cannot understand an African cure or explain it, it should not be believed. The trouble is that Western scientists do not take the time to understand these wondrous, magical and healing solutions. The tragedy of this conduct is that each time these medicine men and women die, it's like setting a medical dictionary on fire. They are usually very secretive and tend to keep their knowledge locked away in their heads.

Yes, I have witnessed the injurious side of African medicine. I imagine there is some 'clever Dick' who will say, well, it was simply a coincidence! And he could be right, although I doubt that possibility. It is heart-breaking to see respected African professors joining their Western counterparts in collectively degrading African medicine as, mostly, witchcraft. I know it is not! Let me give you another example.

There was a family of five in my village. The children were one girl, a teenager of thirteen, her name was Dorothy (popularly known in the village as, Doffy)and two brothers. One was around three years my senior and the last one was my age. Kanduku Village was bordered by the Khwibvi River, which flowed slowly from the northern side to the west before turning south-west later. As it passed the middle of the village it had a deep area in which we all used to play. I learned my butterfly swimming style in that river. Yes, I am still perfecting it, but it is still effective.

Those of us who had nothing to hide used to jump in completely naked. Those who were transitioning into the adult world used to have their shorts on or, for girls, wraparounds, hiding both areas men find irresistible. Often, Doffy was among the girls in the water. The girls did not come to the river just for a swim. Most of them came over carrying saucepans, clay pots, plates, and dirty clothes for washing. Otherwise, their mothers wouldn't have allowed them to come to the river just to swim!

During one school holiday, my late brother, Chalela, had been shipped off to spend it with Grandmother in Mwanza. Among other activities of interest we were looking forward to doing was swimming with our chums and the girls in the Khwibvi River.

I think it was on day two or three, when went for a soak and a swim, we found, as expected, that the place was buzzing, and there were lots of young boys and girls. Some were washing their utensils, adding to the clatter amid screams of young people simply having fun in the water. Doffy was one of them.

There was a huge tree trunk which had fallen into the river a couple of years earlier. It lay longways on the western bank of the river. We used to run across the river, using the tree trunk as a springboard as we jumped into the three-metre-deep waters.

I followed Doffy as she was running toward the springboard for a dive. My interest was not in the swim but my desire to take a quick look at Doffy's well-rounded derriere. Her wrapper, while covering her embarrassment, was not doing much for the tip of her bottom. What a sight to behold, I thought.

I managed to swim and half-walk to the other side of the river and stood still to await Doffy for the next dive. I waited for two minutes, or a little longer, but she never resurfaced. I raised the alarm, and those of us who were older and better swimmers dived into the river to see if we could find her. Soon, two of the divers resurfaced, pulling Doffy's limp body by her arms. They immediately started to pump the water out of her body and in no time at all, she came to, noisily gushing out most of the dirty water that had clogged up her lungs and stomach.

To our surprise and shock, the beautiful girl, Doffy, had become a humpback. She couldn't stand straight. Her neck looked much shorter than it was before. She was carried home, and within a couple of weeks, she was back on her feet again, joining the other girls in traditional dance competitions.

The next inter-village competition was to be against our nemesis, Hawu Village, across the Khwibvi River.

It was on an early, sultry October evening when the Kanduku team and their supporters left their homes to assemble at the village square before setting off towards Hawu Village. They walked in single file because of the narrowness of the path, and as was the case, they did so noisily!

Doffy was in the middle of this single-file queue, and the report which reached the village was that all they had heard was that there was a shout and a scream from Doffy, something like, 'I have been slapped,' as she fell. At this point, the rest of the group helped carry the unconscious Doffy back to her parent's house back in the village and cancelled the competition for that evening.

Doffy came to later that evening, but she never uttered a word until she died later that year.

The story about Doffy's tragedy was that a man, more than twice her age, had approached her parents to propose marriage. A request was turned down due to Doffy's age and the gap compared to the man's age. He came back twice afterward, and the response was always the same: negative. On the third request, his parting words were, apparently, 'If I am not to be allowed to marry your daughter, no one else will.' Fateful parting words, one might say. Was what happened to Doffy a mere coincidence? I think not. Another example of strange-but-true occurrences in Africa? Perhaps it could be considered in a stand-alone presentation in the future by those interested in understanding some of the mysteries of Africa.

To non-believers, those of you who are 'doubting Thomases', I say the following. Before all these special apothecary practitioners disappear biologically, send research teams to Zomba and Mulanje districts and elsewhere in Africa to see for yourselves what human beings are still capable of before this knowledge completely disappears. Not all witchcraft is harmful. Humanity can learn a lot from it, including time travel!

Chapter 6

DO NOT DRESS UP FOR
THE WEEDY NIGHT BEAT!

Father and Mother started to spend more time in Lilongwe after the first phase of the new Chester's Nightclub & Restaurant opposite the (now Old) Lilongwe Airport gates off the Lilongwe-Kasiya via Mbabzi road.anwhile, in Zomba, Chalela and I were left in the hands of the workers. At this time, we had Modesta, whose responsibilities included cooking and all household chores. She was also in charge of monies for our groceries.

Modesta was not exactly comfortable with her beauty. She had a face one could describe as a square with a nose which was exceedingly big and flat. It looked like a big frog was sitting on the position her nose was supposed to be in and a mouth which one might have found difficult to fairly describe. She was friendly and her cooking was not at all bad.

Each time our parents travelled back to where they were spending most of their time working, they would leave money for groceries with Modesta. Attached to it was a set menu for us, which we later found out was beef twice, fish twice and for the remaining three days it would be either beans or other green vegetables.

From the main house, looking in the northeastern direction, was an anthill on which Mother had planted some creeping bean plant called dzikhwali, a kind of mangetout with a strong taste and smell. They are usually picked before they mature and cooked in peanut powder paste. They are an acquired taste, something one might wish to eat once or twice a year for old time's sake, perhaps. They are something one might eat just to please Grandmother on her short visits! This strain of dzikhwali seemed to be drought-resistant. It continued to flourish long after the rainy season had long gone.

We usually got home from school around two p.m., and Modesta always prepared our food and kept it in the oven as she engaged herself with other household chores or she felt she needed a little shut-eye. The drill was, first one placed one's schoolbooks on the table in the bedroom, took off one's school uniform, adorned home clothes, and speedily went to the Welcome Dover Cooker oven in the kitchen, where your lunch would be waiting, still steaming hot, and at times the nsima would have formed a light brown crust on top.

Since our parents' departure for Lilongwe the previous Saturday, all our meals were nsima with dzikhwali. It was only breakfast that escaped the dzikhwali treatment. I can say that life as we knew it was fast becoming a luxury in the distant past. Simply unbearable!

Our parents came back home two days earlier than expected. They found us just about to have our supper – yes, nsima with nkhungudzu (dzikhwali). Dad walked around the table silently and in a loud, booming voice called Modesta, who was outside. 'MODESTAAA!' Modesta walked in within seconds. 'What day of the week is this, Modesta?' Dad asked with a stern look about him.

'Sunday, Sir,' she answered, looking somewhat perplexed.

'What does the boys' menu say they will have on Sundays?' Modesta did not respond. She simply looked at the floor.

'Chalela, what did you have yesterday for lunch and supper?'

'Nsima with nkhungudzu, Papa.' Father had taught us to refer to him as 'Papa', perhaps something he picked from the Portuguese when he worked there years earlier.

'When did you last eat meat?'

'On the day you left for Lilongwe, Papa,' answered Chalela, and I simply gave a succession of quick nods in agreement.

'How about fish?' Father continued with what had now become an inquiry.

'Not since you left, Papa,' answered Chalela, with the longing for fish and meat only a boy on a continuous diet of nsima and dzikhwali could project.

'It has been nsima with nkhungudzu (the official name for Dzikhwali – the latter being a term of endearment!) twice a day, every day,' I chipped in.

'See me tomorrow morning after breakfast,' Father said, looking at Modesta. The next morning, Modesta was relieved of her duties. She went away with days worked minus all the pocket-money for our upkeep she had been entrusted with but chose to use or keep for herself.

Up to this day, I find a whiff of nkhungudzu off-putting, thanks to Modesta.

We also had Joao and Maliselo, who were charged with the responsibility of working in the fields, drawing water, cutting firewood, sweeping the grounds around the house, etcetera. Joao had been working for almost a year when Maliselo was engaged. Surprisingly, he never seemed to have much to wear both on- and off-duty. He was always in rugs, and my father used to tell him off for this. 'People will think I do not pay you enough. Please buy some clothes?' he would lament. Joao would agree, and each month-end he would disappear from Saturday through to Sunday on drinking sprees.

A few weeks passed and my parents came back to see us. They observed that the residence needed more hands working there, and that's when they employed a young man in his early twenties called Maliselo. He was, like Joao, of medium build and around five feet eight inches tall, and looking at his calves, I could tell he had had a physically demanding life – they looked hard and lean!

Although Joao was hard-working, Maliselo was simply amazing. He drew, every working day, more water than Joao and covered a huge area of tilling in the field. Before long, we noticed differences in the way the two of them were related to each other. Mother was having difficulties trying to resolve their petty but destructive quarrels.

It was now the third month since Maliselo had started working for us. After getting his pay on that Friday, he asked my mother if she would allow him time to travel to Ncheu to drop off some items with his mother. 'What items? You have only been here for three months, Maliselo.'

Instead of answering the question at that moment, he excused himself and returned within a minute or so, carrying two suitcases, which he opened in front of my mother. 'Madam, these are the things I have been buying.' He had blankets, a variety of short-trousers – English and American khaki – and lots of shirts, teacups, plates, pots, etcetera.

'Maliselo, you have bought all this from your two months' salaries?'

'Yes, madam,' he replied, face down.

'Joao! Joao, come here,' she called out, and within seconds, Joao walked in.

'Joao, look at what your friend has done within two months of employment. See what he is wearing. Would you not wish to be like him, Joao? When we have people working for us, we want them to look different from the unemployed,' she said, looking at Joao and Maliselo comparatively. At that point, Maliselo was wearing his English khaki shorttrousers with a light-blue flowery shirt, while Joao wore his patched-up discoloured short-trousers, the back of which looked disorganised and multicoloured with patches. For a shirt, he wore a singlet which had once looked white. He had the unpleasant odour of sweat, while from Maliselo's direction one could pick out the fresh smell of new cotton fabric and bath soap. Joao promised to improve.

Permission was granted for Maliselo to travel to his home village in Ncheu the following weekend. The next day, Saturday, Joao left home early in the morning to go to town. He reappeared just before lunch wearing a flowery cotton shirt and American khaki shorttrousers. Although he looked smart, he also looked a little uncomfortable. Joao wasn't used to wearing stuff like this.

Joao had his lunch, and at about 3 p.m., he disappeared. It was his weekend off. We went to bed at around 9 p.m. that evening. Joao was still not back.

We were awakened at around three thirty a.m. by heavy knocks on the wooden window of the servants' quarters. 'Maliselo, Maliselo, please open the door?' We could hear him talking to himself while Maliselo was about to open the door. 'Chibagela wandimenya apachi, chikhala ngati abaya ndi mpeni ('The punch which landed on the side of my head, feels like I have been stabbed with a knife'),' he flinchingly explained in a Sena accent, and breaking with pain and perhaps a dollop of embarrassment, his voice got fainter as he entered their quarters, which were around ten metres from the main house. We were to learn more about that night's events after sunrise.

In the morning, when we saw Joao, he had a swollen face, and my mother wondered what he had been doing. Joao, who was still sozzled, responded in a voice which was just about audible, 'Madam, you will never see those nice clothes of mine again. They are gone, gone, gone forever ...'

'What happened?' questioned Mother, with a very eager look.

'When I left yesterday, I went to Ku Chikopa for a drink and also to see my girlfriend ...' The tavern got its name from what had been done there in the past. It was a tannery – the word 'Chikopa' means skin – and it had now been turned into a Chibuku (a traditional sorghum-based alcoholic drink), a beer-drinking place.

'You have a girlfriend there?' asked my mother with amazement and disdain, for she never thought there were nice and decent women who frequented Ku Chikopa.

In the meantime, I observed that there was a developing friendship between Ojesi, the Cham'godo teenager, and Maliselo. What was strange was that there were clandestine whispers between them. Chalela and I wondered what the two were hiding from the rest of us.

It was midweek during one of the school holidays when I went into the kitchen to get my porridge, just to find Maliselo and Ojesi putting together a contraption I couldn't make heads nor tail of, and from the look on my face, both of them knew there was a question to follow suit. I noticed they had an open matchbox, which had some herbs in it, the smell of which was a giveaway – marijuana!

'What are you doing?' I cried out.

'You just watch; you may learn something today!' responded Maliselo with a conspiratorial smile. Fascinated by the answer and the other items which were on the table, the porridge my body was craving took a back seat.

There were, scattered around this matchbox, a bottle of Vicks VapoRub, two pieces of hollow dry reed stalk, an empty Castle beer bottle filled with water, and small pieces of old newspapers. The look of guilt on their faces showed me there was something fishy going on. I knew how marijuana smelt because on the way from school, we used to pass through a small village near Three Miles, where young men used to smoke it and those in the know identified it as marijuana.

'Maliselo, this is what you do? Smoking marijuana!'

'Yes. How the hell do you think I manage to work long hours in the field as I do? This is my energy booster,' he answered as he continued to put together his drug-drag-inhaling apparatus. I observed him with a sense of foreboding as he applied the vapour rub to the small newspaper pieces, which they had cut into two-times-three-inch bits. In the meantime, Maliselo had inserted the foot-long reed into the bottle. Three inches above the mouth of the bottle they had bored a small hole in the hollow reed stalk, into which was inserted a smaller and shorter reed stalk. Ojesi got a spliff, which he tightly but gently inserted into the small reed stalk with the finesse of a laboratory technician.

Maliselo then started to roll the marijuana into the vapour-rubbed newspaper pieces. I could see in their eyes the anticipation of what they were about to indulge in.

From the fire still alight on the Welcome Dover cooker, Maliselo pulled out a burning twig, which he used to light the spliff. Quickly, Ojesi's mouth was lowered to the main reed protruding from the bottle, taking in the water as one does from a straw, the difference being that this time it was water and cannabis with acrid menthol-infused smoke in it. Maliselo had his turn before Ojesi returned to the contraption for another water-and-smoke-filled swig. They continued taking turns until the spliff was extinguished due to a lack of oxygen reaching it inside the small reed stalk. Then Ojesi pulled the stub out, unrolled it, and removed the remaining tiny pieces of the drug back into the matchbox.

'I will report you to Mother when she returns from Lilongwe,' I threatened.

'Oh no, you will not do such a thing. Maliselo does not argue or quarrel with anyone when he smokes weed. All he does is go into the field and work like an ox – all for you guys. It would be very unappreciative of his efforts in the field if you reported my friend to your parents,' reasoned Ojesi. I thought, well, if it's an energy booster in our favour, perhaps I should go easy on Maliselo. This was an eleven-year-old's reasoning.

By this point, both Maliselo and Ojesi were full of laughter and movement as they left the kitchen.

'See you tomorrow,' said Maliselo to Ojesi as he picked up his hoe on his way to the day's shift in the field. The latter simply laughed loudly as he took off at great speed towards his family home two hundred metres away.

A few weeks later, soon after breakfast, I heard Chalela telling off Joao for smoking marijuana. He had apparently walked in on him behind the servants' quarters. 'I will report you to Father. Don't you know smoking marijuana is illegal? I will report you.' Chalela looked visibly upset. I thought then that this was as good a time as any for me to mention what I had found Maliselo and Ojesi doing in the kitchen the other day.

'I will tell Mother,' Chalela said with a very resolute tone. I dared not oppose him when he was in that mood. Besides, I did not see my previous position as sustainable.

When our parents came back a couple of days later, they found a raging quarrel going on between Maliselo and Joao. The latter was shouting, 'You drug-head ...' and this and that.

Maliselo responded in kind. 'You too are a drug-head ... and you smoke more than I do ...' etcetera. As Mother and Father alighted from the car, it seemed they had heard a good fraction of the exchange.

'Maliselo and Joao, can I see you in the living room now!' Father beckoned to them as he uttered this question-like command. Chalela and I immediately knew there was trouble!

Maliselo and Joao came out of the house a couple of minutes later. Each one of them was tearful but still pushing and blaming each other for getting one another fired. They were replaced by John, the farm worker and sorcerer whom we have already met in an earlier chapter.

Maliselo moved to the nearby village, where he later began to date our new cook, Derby, who had been handpicked by Maliselo himself during happier times. They later got married. Derby resigned and we never saw the two of them again.

As for Joao, one Saturday we had gone into town, where Dad had stopped to purchase some groceries in Kandodo Shop. While he was in the shop, there was a knock on Chalela's side of the car door. It was Joao. He spotted a crew-cut hairstyle, which we noticed as soon as he lifted his army beret. He was dressed in a very smart-looking khaki army uniform. It was clear he had joined the military. He was almost unrecognisable from the Joao we knew before, and I wondered if anti-drug rules in the army were operational, as they were on the outside.

Soldiers have always got to look tidy when they are on duty. I still wonder how happy and comfortable Joao was in his new career and in the mandatory well-pressed and clean army uniforms. He did look genuinely happy on this occasion, though! Some say that careers in the military can be transformative!

Chapter 7

THE MAKUNGANYA GANG

Our new home, about four miles (Pa Folo Mailosi) from Zomba on the Blantyre Road, was surrounded by several villages, one of which was Nkanda Village. People from this village were mostly Protestants and Muslims. They sent their under-tens mostly to the local junior primary school and later to a fully-fledged primary school, which was Chikowi Primary School four miles away.

From the village immediately to our house's northwest direction was the small village of Kumbengule. Our house was within this village. Although many parents in this area sent their children to Chikowi Primary School, some sent theirs to the Catholic one, which Chalela and I were now attending. Among those attending this school were our new friends, the brothers, Enock and Ojesi. The former was one year older than me, and Ojesi was the same age as Chalela.

From within the Kumbengule Village, there were other boys we were now playing with, and they all went to Chikowi Primary School. These were the two Tsoka boys, Adam and Tilekeleni, and Thomas and Fred, who were also brothers of similar ages as the rest of us.

It was expected during those days in Zomba that apart from having a football team at school, we could also have teams representing our respective home areas, and these would compete against each other mostly at weekends, unless it was during school holidays, when they would play on any other day of the week.

The Four Miles Wolves training ground was a tiny patch of land next to a cemetery. The owner, Mr Logani, was grandfather to one of the players in the Wolves team. It was Thomas and Fred who brought the news that we had been invited to play against Nkanda Warriors the following weekend. The news reached us on a Monday. Since it was during the dry season, our team had been very active in playing competitive games against other teams in the surrounding areas. We had just beaten a team called Stoke City from Ndola Lines. This might have been what aroused the interest of the Nkanda Warriors team. Stoke City had a reputation as a tough under-twelves football team in Zomba Township. This was just as well, because the training ground had been turned into a sweet-potato field during the just-ended rainy season, thus depriving the Wolves of extra hours of training after school. We now relied on the school-hours football sessions only.

On the day of the game, a sunny October day, we gathered near Thomas and Fred's house, for it was the last house in the village on the route to the Nkanda Warriors' football ground. Everyone turned up, and finally we happily set off on the one-mile walk to the ground.

In those days it was easy to pick the good players from any team. Simply spot the ones with a few crepe bandages on the knee, wrist, or ankle – or in all those areas – and who walked sideways like a crab. Up to now, apart from looking mean, I still do not recall why we linked the adorning of these bandages with football prowess, but the sight did create fear in an opposing team.

The game was due to kick off at three thirty p.m., when the heat from the sun had dissipated enough to make our exertions bearable. October is the hottest month in Malawi.

The football field had no grass at all. It was not easy to tell that it was a football field without first noticing the lop-sided rickety wooden goalposts. One end doubled up as the road used by traffic into the village, and at the other there was a small church, the outer wall of which formed part of the touchline. There was also a footpath which passed diagonally across the field. Now and again a football match would be halted to allow a woman to cross the pitch with her large clay water pot beautifully bAaron ced on her head. It seemed some young women would deliberately choose to go for water-drawing during a football game so they could show off their lithesome undulating bodies to the gathered footballers, as well as to the lustier fans around the ground. We did not mind. This was the equivalent of a VAR break in modern football, an unexpected relief and sometimes an annoying break from what is usually an energy-sapping sport.

Markings on the ground had been dug in with a hoe soon after the rainy season, probably between February and March, and they were still just about noticeable. The May and June showers had put paid to their clear visibility. The August-to-October winds were continuing to bury these important markings on this football ground. Still, the referee did not mind, nor did the players.

The church building had large open windows and an even larger entrance. It did not have a door. These orifices must have given those who came to pray a very airy feeling as they worshipped on Sunday mornings. The supply of cool and fresh air was permanent. If the ball was accidentally kicked into the church, and it usually was, the game would be allowed to continue inside, with the two opposing players battling for possession, until one of them, victorious, re-joined the rest of the players outside. Sometimes, one of the players would appear at the church entrance with a bloody nose or some such injury, at the sight of which the referee would blow his whistle and award a free kick right at the entrance, against the other, a member of the unscathed team.

'It is obvious, isn't it?' the referee would sometimes reason. 'He was head-butted!'

'How do you know, Ref?' some smart aleck would ask, and one could easily see that the referee did not like to entertain 'silly' questions!

'There were just two of them in there. Can't you see?' the referee would argue.

'But he could have stumbled, fallen, and hit his head,' the captain from the penalised side would contend.

This would be too much for the referee. 'Now, one more word, just one more word, and you're out. That's dissent in my book,' he would threaten with an air of confidence and authority, in complete control of the situation.

I was the goalkeeper for the Four Miles Wolves, ready with my wrist properly crepe-bandaged. I also had one knee done. I had lent my last crepe bandage to Ojesi, who played in defence, a full-back.

The game was played at a very fast pace, with the Four Miles Wolves scoring three goals in the first half. After the break, we scored two more goals, and I then observed that some of the Nkanda Warriors' most vocal supporters up to this point were, one-by-one, slowly disappearing. I couldn't understand the phenomenon. In those days, disappointed football fans did not desert their team in the middle of a game, no matter what! Yes, five goals to nil was a bit too much, but still, I and every football fan in Zomba did not expect to see what we were witnessing.

The game ended with the Wolves on a high note. We started to walk back home, exchanging different highlights of the game: missed chances, misplaced passes, bad decisions by the referee, and the rest of it, and yes, how rough the Warriors were. 'Apart from the referee, they kicked at anything which moved,' commented Fred.

During this period, 1963 to 1966, young boys up to twenty years of age and perhaps older used to be in gangs. What they usually did was mug people and beat up those who disagreed with their ways or those whose faces they did not particularly like.

Attacks used to happen during daylight and were worse after dark. It thus became fashionable for youngsters to form their own gangs too. These other gangs were not involved in mugging people but in protecting each other from gang attacks emanating from elsewhere. It was like there was no police! People were scared to report this criminality for fear of being victimised afterwards. Besides, the police at the time were deeply involved in fighting Dr Kamuzu Banda's real and imagined enemies. It seemed there was no time for them to allocate to the growing menace of youth criminality at Three and Four Miles and certainly elsewhere.

There were banana and sugarcane plantations on either side of the narrow gravel-surfaced road which passed through the valley like an overfed and tired Boa constrictor crawling reluctantly up the two hills with us, like termites, on its back.

It was as we reached the middle of this valley that we were ambushed by some young boys. Some of their faces resembled those we had seen leave before the end of the game some minutes earlier. One-by-one, they all materialised from behind the banana plants.

I almost started to run backward, a knee-jerk reaction, but Chalela ordered me to stay put. What a man! What a big brother! I reluctantly obeyed.

We immediately realised these guys hadn't ambushed us to give us sweets. We had just vanquished their football team.

'Oh no! You guys must be tired,' started one of the boys. This statement was followed by gales of laughter from the group. I looked at Enock and Chalela and noticed their faces had taken on a different look, that of anger, not fear, a look of defiance, even, which made me even more scared. Surely, they couldn't fight, could they, I asked myself as I stood as far away as possible from their nearest group member.

'You guys, I'm told, have been giving my men here some grief, making jokes about my good friend, Nero. Anyone can lose teeth. I don't see why you find it a joking matter,' said the same guy who had spoken earlier in a voice rising in decibels and lacking in emotion. 'We're all angry because of this, and today, we've decided we're going to fight you, one-by-one. If your side wins you can continue joking about Nero's missing teeth, but if we win, we expect the joke to stop,' he concluded as he moved around, sizing up each one of us like cattle at an agricultural fair.

Nero, Henderson, and the rest were already jumping about, flexing their puny muscles, which to me still looked rather fearsome. The gang member who seemed to have assumed the leadership mantle of their team stopped talking, and he began to pace around us, stopping momentarily before moving to the next boy and, looking at me, he stopped and said, "you're going to fight last, you look so petrified. The first fight will be between Henderson and that guy with lips like a chicken's bum.'" he said, pointing at Ojesi. Ojesi's lips were nowhere near what he was comparing them to.

'Mouth like what?' queried Ojesi angrily.

'Like a chicken's bum, I said. Any problem with that?' the gang member asked as he charged toward Ojesi, who in turn responded by charging forward as well.

'Boys, boys, let us not be violent. These boys are tired. If we whop them, they will claim they were taken advantage of. Why don't we meet them on a different day when we can show them what we are made of?' I couldn't believe my ears. Nero, the peacemaker today? He continued, 'You beat Stoke City last weekend, and today you have put the Warriors to the sword. You must be very proud of yourselves, isn't it so?'

'Well,' started Chalela, 'we are just happy we have won again today. Wouldn't you be happy if you achieved what we have been achieving of late?'

'Very smart, very smart. Now, we are challenging you right here and now to a fighting competition.' At this point he began to match us up. 'This one will fight that one, and that one will fight this one, and this one here will fight with me,' he said as he walked toward Ojesi. Some of us had been left out, unmatched!

Immediately after Ojesi had been matched with the toothless one, he started to pace the ground, growling like a wild animal. He ran forward and reversed just as fast, and then he started to leg it without warning. We all just as quickly followed his cue and dispersed at great speed through the dry fields, which had just been prepared for the rainy season which was around the corner.

The gang pursued us for a while and gave up as we entered our village, our territory.

When we re-assembled deep in the village, Fred and those who attended Chikowi Primary School started to add names to the faces. The one who appeared to be leading the gang was Nero Makunganya. The other guy, who was paired against Chalela, was Henderson Makunganya, Nero's young brother. Apart from these two brothers, three others in their gang went to the same primary school with quite a few members of our team. Fred described them as very serious bullies, who got involved in fights every so often at school.

After hearing the story from Fred, we simply named the group The Makunganya Gang. The path they took from their school crossed at some mid-way point with ours.

I know that Monday mornings are not exactly what most eleven-year-olds going to school look forward to, and after our escape from the gang that Saturday, we were not exactly looking forward to going to school that morning for fear of meeting the Makunganya Gang on the way.

That morning, as we approached the dreaded crossroads, Enock shouted, 'The Makunganya boys!' You should have seen us run away; it was as if we were responding to a starter's pistol. It was both a relief and an annoyance when we realised Enock was only having a bit of fun at our expense.

A day or two later, Tilekeleni briefed us that the Makunganya Gang had a recruit from Ncheu District, the sixth member, and this is how they lined up. Henderson, the squat, square-faced, arrogant one, and his elder brother, Nelson, whom we called Nero (without strength, you cannot protect anything), were the leaders. Mr Makunganya himself was a village headman a few miles from our home. From the way people spoke about him, he must have been a respectable man, but I never met him, apart from his two bother-boys and their gang members.

Each time any one of us, unfortunately, met the Makunganya Gang, we could be assured of a beating. In our gang of 'Yellas', our depth of fear lessened a little when we heard about how Nero lost his two upper front teeth. It was not in a fight against Chief Nkanda's son over mangoes. Rumour had it that it happened when he fell out of a mango tree while being chased by a green mamba. At least he too had something he was afraid of. Nero's face was as welcoming as a heavy cloud shielding the sun at the beach, and the missing two front teeth on his upper jaw did nothing to improve his general looks. If looks could kill!

To avoid confrontations with the gang, our group started arriving at school more than thirty minutes early. We became a shining example to the others, mostly latecomers. Even Mother was impressed by our newly found dedication to education. Our return journey was less impressive, as we walked home as slowly as possible to avoid meeting the Makunganya Gang. After a year of these 'war' games, Enock came back from the long summer holidays a different man. He had had enough.

Drifting back from school after the first day of the new term, the sun had never been so hot, the footpath so dry and dusty. As we slowly walked back home after school, our small feet causing minute craters in the red silt, Chalela started talking about the possibility of being ambushed by the Makunganya Gang, at which point, Enock, like the rest of us, sweating profusely, grew grim and his medium-thick lips set into a powerful and sad curve. He gazed at the sky as if expecting some divine inspiration before moving his gaze towards Chalela. 'I don't know why we should run from those boys,' he announced. These brave words were followed by a stunned eye-popping silence, literally, from the rest of us! It was as if Enock had just climbed onto a diving board at night into a swimming pool to check if there was any water in it. Some call it a leap of faith.

After the shock of Enock's courage had worn off, he laughed sarcastically and said, 'We can't keep avoiding these guys forever, you know. We need to show them we can fight just as well as they think they can if pushed too far.'

'Apart from Nero, the rest are quite tame,' agreed Chalela astonishingly.

Speaking seriously, I do not know why Chalela said this; no one, in my view, looked tame in the Makunganya Gang. Granted, Nero looked the most intimidating and far from tame, but the rest were not far behind him in looks.

'If we were to encounter them today, I would take on Henderson,' Chalela added with an air of defiance and his newly found confidence. Perhaps he was saying all this to impress me, his young brother.

His courage amazed me. Chalela had not won many fights against me in the past, and I was petrified to face even the weakest member of the Makunganya Gang, but there he was, taking a stance like that. Well, I thought, if Chalela can handle Henderson and Enock can take on Nero, I suppose the weakest of the gang can be whipped by yours truly, me. All six of us agreed. The time had come to stand up to these bullies. Our morale was high, and everyone was bubbling with plans on how we were going to vanquish our long-time tormentors. Despite the intense heat and the growing pangs of hunger, our newly found courage put some spring into our steps.

There were many baobab trees along the shortcut we used. Some of them were very old and particularly stocky and very thick-trunked. It was while we were walking past one of the squattest and thickest-trunked trees that the Makunganya Gang, who had been lying in wait, pounced. We have an old saying which goes, 'Never trust the baobab; either its falling fruits hit you on the head, or it helps hide the enemy from sight'. It was just as well the fruits were out of season!

Until that day I never knew how fast Enock could run. He took off like Ben Johnson's drug-induced run in the Seoul Olympics, leaving the rest of us way, way behind, with the Makunganya Gang in hot pursuit. Fortunately, none of us were caught, which gave us time to rebuild our confidence yet again. Enock pleaded that they had taken him too much unawares. The rest of us followers had simply done what was expected of us and followed. We had indeed been taken too much by surprise. Yes, we were!

Cockerels were still sounding their alarms from the neighbouring villages, and our cockerel weakly responded, as if complaining of being awakened from a beautiful dream by his uncouth cousins across the Namiwawa River. From the east, partly emerging above the Ntonya hill, appeared a huge deep orange ball and with great effort, tainted by what appeared to be a degree of reluctance. it finally clambered into the cloudless pale-blue sky of tropical early morning hours. A gentle breeze was blowing, scattering a few dry leaves across our front yard, and from a nearby tree, two doves were singing their morning duet, announcing the start of another day.

While Chalela and I were finishing our maize-meal breakfast porridge before leaving for school, I was silently hoping for another escape from the Makunganya Gang, but hope was becoming too exhausting a novelty to be relied upon for long after so many months of beatings and escapes.

When we met our four friends at the usual junction, about five minutes' walk from home, Enock still looked to be upset and embarrassed over the incident the day before, claiming he had not been given enough time by the foe before the ambush was sprung. 'Have courage,' he added confidently, 'I'm more prepared now. No more running away.' Brave words indeed. I could see our faces transforming into those of ruthless warriors, ready for battle. In Enock, we felt we had found a leader. We did not, however, meet the gang that day.

The road from Nkanda Village passed through a narrow valley between two hills.

If there was a problem in Ojesi's mind, he never voiced it.

'The second fight will be between Nero and the one with the ill-fitting shorts.' That was Chalela. 'Where did you borrow them from? quipped the boy whom we had not seen before this day. hird fight will be between me,' he stopped mid-sentence, then took a few steps towards Enock, 'and you.' This was the day this group of bullies became known as, The Makunganya Gang. We knew the two of them were Makunganya's sons. It was Ojesi' idea later that day.

He went on with the rest of us until he got to me. 'Well, you're in luck. I've decided not to unleash my little brother on you. You look half-dead!'

I almost said to him, I'm glad you noticed!

The first fight ended when Henderson hit the deck and refused to get up. He had a nosebleed and was crying loudly like a baby. I could not believe my eyes and ears; Ojesi had won. He had won! The second bout went on longer than the first, with the two fighters throwing heavy punches from a variety of angles, some of which I never knew existed. After a few minutes, Chalela was still throwing punches at a target which could hardly move, let alone fight back. The new guy, their leader, came between them. Chalela had won!

'I thought you said these boys would be a walk-over,' he complained to his team. 'Let me show you what I can do,' he said boastfully as he took off his shirt and said something incomprehensible. He began throwing a few punches at a banana plant, which keeled over under the onslaught. He reminded me of Mr Batani.

'Don't do it, Jo,' begged Nero. Addressing us, he said, 'You guys had better set off. He never stops fighting until he's seen blood, and lots of it, too.'

We exchanged glances and without warning, Enock was already showing a clean pair of heels. We all followed, with Jo in pursuit, swearing and promising to finish us off single-handedly the next time we met.

'How could you expect me to fight with someone who breaks banana trees with his bare hands? You guys had easy fights,' Enock submitted as he attempted to conceal his shame, which was spiced with an element of jubilation. We were secure in the knowledge there would be no more running away from the Makunganya boys from now on, unless their new leader was in their midst. If anything, it would be us doing the chasing. It was easy to see that the new boy, Jo, was not a pupil. In those days, pupils did not swear. He was a hired hand who knew the best way to beat people was to show them you could eat nails, or in his case, destroy healthy banana trees with his fists, as long as the trees belonged to someone else.

We had gained our peace so long as we did not accept football invitations from their side. Each time one of us was sent on a chore by their family to Nkanda Village, we had to be escorted by two or more of our team just in case we got spotted by the Makuganya Gang plus one. That one!

Chapter 8

WILHELMINA

Grandmother, Amai Marina Kanduku, lived in a typical Malawi village fifty miles west of Blantyre. Five minutes after driving through Mwanza Boma with its pale-yellow-walled red-roofed colonial government buildings, a right turn down a narrow, dusty road led to Kanduku Village, a collection of mud huts both rectangular and round, built in clusters to represent the different families that lived there.

There were a few brick houses, some of which belonged to the chief, and all were inter-spaced with small maize and vegetable gardens connected by a network of footpaths. This was my maternal grandmother's home, and my brother, Chalela, and I was being 'shipped' there for the long school holidays. Although we had not been there for over two years, the memory of the last visit was still fresh in my mind.

Apart from literally eating hundreds of oranges and mandarins straight from the trees every week, I remembered playing 'house' with Wilhelmina. The two of us had been inseparable then, and she had been telling everyone, including her mother, that if she ever married, it would be to me.

Wilhelmina was a beautiful girl. Shehad a longish, delicate face, and her nose, typically African and smaller than most, fitted proportionately well with the other features on her face. Her arrogantly curved, sensual lips made her smile bewitchingly sexy, and I still recall the way she wore her hair short. Wilhelmina was the girl I secretly wanted to, and had to see again.

Wilhelmina hailed from a family considered one of the most successful in the village. Her parents had prospered through their citrus fruit business, owning the largest and most productive orchard of oranges and tangerines in the area.

Like many of her peers, she attended the local Catholic primary school. A Roman Catholic by faith, she was known for always looking smart and presentable.

It was particularly hot that August afternoon when we arrived with our parents at Kanduku Village. The sun struck down on us like a powerful celestial projector, and despite having the car windows open, we were all sweating profusely. Most cars did not have air-conditioning systems in those days.

Along the road the jacaranda trees were in full bloom, giving the surrounding atmosphere a purplish hue and the air a fresh, tropical fragrance. Some distance down the road were flame trees, their flamboyant flowers at full mast, as if in competition with the jacarandas, but the latter were seemingly arrogantly oblivious to the challenge. The few baobab trees, with their squat trunks and large leaves, contrasted dramatically between the two beauties, which upstaged them at every turn.

As soon as we entered the village gates, singing and screaming children, some of them our age, mobbed our car. Chalela was fourteen plus, and I had just turned twelve.

This kind of welcome took me back to five or six years earlier, when my elder sister was to go through an initiation ceremony called Tsimba specifically in the Ngoni culture, and Chinamwali, generally, in Malawi. This is a ceremony which, in my opinion, is misunderstood by the modern world. In the Ngoni culture, when a girl has experienced her first menstruation, she and others who have also had theirs are taken into the bush, usually near a river or a well, for an entire week or two. During this time, the girls are taught about how to take care of themselves hygienically, how to manage a home and a husband and sexual guidance is also given. They are also advised on how to change their general behaviour now that they have become adults. Warnings are also given that should they sleep with a man, the chances of becoming pregnant are high, so they should not do it until they are married. So, they are guided. On the final day of the time spent in a temporarily constructed shade in the bush, the girls, clad in a very short piece of cloth covering only the genital area and the buttocks, are carried back to their respective homes, surrounded by older singing and ululating women. Once home, the girls' bodies are washed and oiled (traditionally it was only handmade castor oil which was used for this ceremony) under the guidance of one or two hand-picked senior women called Anankungwi – cultural advisors.

On the final day, there is usually a huge celebratory party of drinking and eating, where a few animals lose their lives in order for their masters to have their fun. That's one reason human beings keep these animals, isn't it?

The slaughtering of chickens, pigs, goats, and cattle, etcetera – for now, let's call it culinary killing – means the human killing of an animal for consumption. This is also an occasion when young boys are expected to be present and learn a thing or two about how to kill, prepare and cut up an animal before it is cooked. This is where I learnt how to prepare Uchazo (Uwende), animal blood, for consumption. I learned that around an animal's stomach there is a layer of fatty material which is removed while the body is still warm, stripped into small pieces and mixed with the blood for cooking at the killing site. The young boys are given that responsibility. An older boy, who has participated in this honourable and spiritual practice, will guide the younger ones. When the dish is ready, the saucepan is taken to the men, who are now cutting up the carcass to have some of the cooked blood before leaving some for the boys. No woman is allowed to eat Uchazo. Why? Elders used to say that it negatively influenced their menstrual cycle. The bright rays of the American Emancipation Proclamation had not reached Kanduku Village and the entire Maseko Ngoni Kingdom at this point.

Now, back to the arrival in Kanduku Village. My eyes, like security lights, searched every face for that of Wilhelmina, but she was not there, so I turned my thoughts to the next best thing – the oranges.

All the trees, as far as I could see, were awash with fruit and seemed to be struggling under the weight. Well, trees, I thought to myself, your saviour has arrived. As well as oranges, there were mandarins, grapefruits, sugar cane, paw-paws, and bananas. Any of the children could, and did, pick these fruits from anywhere in the village without a finger being raised in protest by the owners. The grapefruits were so plentiful we even used them as footballs.

As Mother and Father sat on the veranda of Grandmother's house, Chalela and I were already off with the others, cousins, nephews, and nieces, for our first attack on the neglected fruits. After a while, we heard Grandmother's voice call, 'Oi, you two girls, come for lunch.' For some unaccountable reason, she always referred to us as 'girls'. I still do not know what long-term effect this has had on my psyche, but so far, my wife has not complained! I was later to learn that Grandmother called us girls because our voices (particularly mine) had not yet broken. We could be trusted to overnight with girls without the fear of any comeuppances!

Mother and Father left the village sometime after lunch but not before the usual lecture for us to be good and on exemplary behaviour while we were in Grandmother's care and forever after, of course!

Traditionally, after supper, which took place at about six thirty p.m., most young people between the ages of eight and seventeen, both boys and girls, would go to the village square, just next to the village court, where my mother's uncle, the chief, presided over minor cases. Ngoni people allowed their children two types of evenings. When the moon was full, they could go to the village playground, where different games were played, and singing and dancing to traditional songs. The same songs my mother had sung during her younger days were still in fashion, but probably the dancing had changed.

Many different games were played out there under the full moon, games such as hide-and-seek, which was particularly popular to those who were, or thought they were, sexually prepared.

Boyfriends and girlfriends would pick each other as hiding partners, and it was amazing how long it took to find some of those hiding. Some who went to hide never appeared again that same night, and the few that did seem to lack the energy to continue playing. Hide-and-seek used to be energy-sapping in my day!

Around midnight, we would start hearing parents calling their children home, but because of all the excitement the various activities had aroused, no one responded. Then the calling would start again, like tormented spirits in the night, from different ends of the village, this time with a few warnings thrown in, warnings such as, 'If you don't come back now, you will sleep outside.' They were idle threats, since this was what most of us wanted anyway. After failing to effect any response, the 'uncles', the ones responsible for our moral upbringing, would be dispatched to fetch us home. They took their job very seriously. Uncles appeared within seconds, big whips in hand, causing everyone to disperse in all directions like mice at the first sight of a cat. It always worked.

It was quite normal at the end of every such evening to expect to be whipped, but it did not hurt, for the joy of being there was far greater. The (mini) boob pinching, the bum pinching, or just touching shoulders with the girl you fancied was exciting enough. For me, the girl I would have climbed any orange tree for, regardless of wasps or snakes, the girl I got whipped for on full moon nights, was Wilhelmina.

On dark nights, as opposed to moonlit ones, it was mostly time for the elders to tell us stories. Sometimes the stories were about their history, passed down in the oral tradition. Sometimes they told us simple fairy stories, and on other occasions, they merely imparted their wisdom to us young ones. This was certainly in the days before television. As it happened, that night, there was a full moon, and Cousin Julio announced that we would be going out into the village square that evening, as there would be singing and dancing.

Supper was not something I looked forward to that evening. My mind was on Wilhelmina, but somehow I lacked the courage to raise the subject with Cousin Julio. Maybe he was already having an affair with her. She was, after all, a stunningly beautiful girl.

Grandmother's thatched mud house was a stone's throw away from the playing field, and when we arrived, around seven o'clock, the place was already packed and noisy. Cousin Julio was in charge. The place he directed us to was under a large and leafy orange tree at the top end of the field from where we could watch the proceedings. It was less crowded there, and Julio added that when the dancing began it would be closer to where we were standing.

The sky was completely cloudless, the full moon, immediately overhead, was directing a supporting cast of a million stars, some of them fallen and about to perform before our very eyes. It was a perfect night. The perfume of the citrus trees which surrounded the field would normally have been very relaxing, but I had still not seen Wilhelmina. I was not relaxed! Then, from across the ground, we saw a group of girls coming toward the playground.

'Do you remember your wife, Wilhelmina, Davie?' Julio's question took me by surprise, and I must have blushed, but my dark-brown skin and the night made it barely noticeable. Cousin Julio had remembered how close to each other the two of us had become on a previous holiday.

'Eh?' I pretended.

'Wilhelmina is a big girl now. Would you like to say hello to her? She is with the girls in that group.'

He had read my thoughts, but before I could answer, Chalela did it for me.

'Certainly,' he said, smiling broadly. 'We might get lucky.'

I did not much like his use of the royal 'we' and gave him a sideways glance, which he chose to ignore. Cousin Julio called out to Wilhelmina.

Under the moonlight, she looked even more beautiful than the last time I had seen her. Her legs had become even more expressive, and when she spoke it was with a voice so serene and warm, so smooth and sensual, a voice even more attractive than all her physical attributes, a voice to make even Mahatma Gandhi throw in the towel.

After greeting us, she said something to the effect that I was growing up fast, and I wondered if it was a compliment. Soon, she excused herself, and as she turned to leave, her bosom gently brushed against my right arm. I am sure it was unintentional. 'My' Wilhelmina was growing up fast, into what could only be described as a voluptuous young lass. Her departure was followed by a little silence between the three of us. Evil spirits passing, as they say!

Soon, the drums began to rumble, and the girls in Wilhelmina's group formed a ring around the two drummers, who were sending out their sensual throbbing notes into the warm African night. Around their waists, the girls wore colourful wrappers which were doubled, sometimes trebled, so that the movement of the waist would be exaggerated as they danced, turning all the sexually active young men wild with desire. We learned they were rehearsing for a competition against the surrounding villages, which was to take place within the following week or two. Their bodies swayed rhythmically in time with the drums as the dancers began moving anti-clockwise, their bottoms wriggling, their heads on one side, and their shoulders shaking up and down. There was a lot of cheering from the crowd, which seemed completely captivated by the spectacle.

An hour or so soon passed and when the dancing had finished, Wilhelmina came to where we stood to say goodnight. Julio and Chalela praised her for dancing and singing. I also did, only the words did not come out. 'See you tomorrow,' were her last words as she ran to join her friends, who were by now far down the path. 'See *you* tomorrow.' I took these words personally. It was me, after all, with whom she used to play 'house'.

We slept in a small hut which Cousin Julio had built next to Grandmother's house. Before retiring, he asked, 'What do you think of Wilhelmina, you two?'

'Well, she's a stunner, isn't she?' answered Chalela with a cheeky grin. 'My kind of girl,' he added devilishly.

'But I thought her eyes were on the younger brother?' Julio queried. 'She never took her eyes off him when she came to greet us. Even when she said goodbye.'

'Oh! Is it?' Chalela mumbled, somewhat subdued.

Cousin Julio's words and observations gave me confidence, although I had not noticed Wilhelmina looking me in the eye.

The following day, Chalela and Julio went fishing at the nearby stream, and while I was attending to some fruits behind Grandmother's house, I heard a voice, someone behind me. It was she, Wilhelmina. She was carrying a large basket in one hand and a yellow paw-paw in the other. If possible, she looked even more beautiful in the sunlight. Her hair was short and jet black and her eyes, large and dark as chestnuts, held about them an element of maturity beyond her years.

'Don't eat all the oranges, Davie,' she quipped. 'I've roasted some sweet potatoes at home. Would you like to come and have some?'

'Yes,' I said faintly, my earlier confidence vanishing. 'I'll see you later.'

'You'd better not be too late, or there'll be nothing left,' she added as she slowly walked up the path towards her house. Watching her rear, the elegance of her body, and the way she walked, was simply too hard to resist. The late afternoon sunshine cast a long and majestic shadow behind her, as if in total agreement with my thoughts. I felt she was the greatest thing in my life at this point. I was at her door within a couple of minutes of her arrival. I could hardly wait.

Sitting with Wilhelmina on the veranda, eating my sweet potatoes and looking across the stream up into the hills and to the blue mountain ranges along the Malawi–Mozambique border to the west, everything looked and felt cosmic. I felt relaxed and at home, because Wilhelmina's family knew me and they, I am sure, did not suspect any romance between their daughter and me. I was still only a child in their eyes, a sinless angel. Not that my loins felt that way. Because all my senses were focused on Wilhelmina, my taste buds were not functioning properly, and I am sure that had I stepped on burning charcoal I would have felt no pain – not instantly, anyway. When Wilhelmina's two brothers, Peter and Joseph, appeared, they assumed I was waiting for them and invited me to join them on a fishing trip in the nearby Khwibvi River. Wilhelmina managed to whisper to me as we were preparing for our jaunt that she had not been expecting the two rascals, and we parted with the promise to meet at the dance rehearsal that evening.

That night the dance was as wonderful as the night before. Cousin Julio insisted it was always wonderful, and at the end, when Wilhelmina asked me to escort her home, he gave me a nod of encouragement, while Chalela gave me a look which said he might just cut his wrists or mine. Talk about taking defeat graciously!

I felt mature, important, and excited, but also afraid and unsure of myself. Wilhelmina, on the other hand, exuded self-confidence, and it crossed my mind that she may have already been de-flowered, whereas I was just coming into bud and very small buds at that.

'You've grown so fast, Davie,' she started as soon as I joined her. 'It's only a year ago we were playing house.'

'Over two years. It's been over two years,' I boldly and proudly interrupted.

'Look at you now. A grown man,' she declared as she reached for and held my right hand.

Nice words! As we approached her home, she asked me to go back.

'My father won't go to bed until I return. I don't think you should go past this point,' she suggested gently.

In some ways this was a relief, for I had done more than I had ever done before, walking a girl home, alone, at night. Just when I thought she was letting go of my hand, she quickly reached for the other one, pulled me towards her and kissed me, forcing her tongue into my mouth. It was my first real kiss, and I must admit I was very clumsy but found myself automatically responding. I had seen lovers kiss before. It was easy and yet momentous. We didn't speak, only listened to the breeze whispering through the citrus trees and the dry grass around us, and yet, there was a language in that silence, and I felt something stir in my heart. Maybe it was love, or something close to it, for a boy of twelve on a journey of blinding discovery. Besides, what is falling in love?

I was still standing there as I watched her walk away, once or twice looking back. What seemed silent was opening to the sounds of crickets, frogs, and all manner of living things making their presence felt around me.

Walking quickly back I could think of only one word to describe how I felt – heavenly! I could still feel the sensation of her sharp-tipped breasts against my puny chest. Back at the hut, it was difficult not to mention the kiss to Julio and Chalela, but I did not want to upset my brother, who was still acting moody. Sleeping was not easy that night. As I tossed and turned, my body, my young body, was biologically in great turbulence, and I felt my romantic geyser bubbling. It was a special feeling! Yes, it was somehow evil – a young Catholic boy should not be having such thoughts; it's a sin! I think the devil had erected a camp in my heart, and I was simply too weak to evict him.

I was awakened the next day by cockerels sounding their early-morning alarms across the landscape. As I lay in the dark, I became aware of a wailing sound which seemed to be coming from nearby houses. We were all awake now. 'Someone has passed away,' said Julio flatly as we all got up from our reed mats spread on a clay-covered charcoal-grey floor. We came out of the hut to see where the wailing was coming from. Although the sun had not yet risen, we could make out in the early-morning slate semi-darkness the figures of what appeared to be two women heading towards Grandmother's house.

By now there was only a handful of stars in the southern sky, and the light was progressively improving, causing the remaining stars to melt away. Soon, a large red ball gently clambered over the eastern mountain ranges, bringing with it greater clarity to the surroundings. Another day. A respectable distant relative of Grandmother's had died in the next village, and tradition demanded that all adults spend the night at the deceased's home. So it was that Kanduku Village became a children's village that night.

In the late afternoon, after the episode of the previous night, I was not in the least surprised when I saw Wilhelmina approaching the house. Her parents had gone to the vigil, and she wanted me to visit her that night, 'Alone,' she emphasised. This was it. A promotion from explorer to discoverer, all in one summer holiday. 'Don't tell anyone,' she added as she disappeared behind the hut.

That night, I excused myself from supper. I said I had eaten too many sweet potatoes at Peter's place. This was not true, and I simply sat there as my brother and cousin ate their supper. I was not feeling hungry at all. My mind was filled with a great deal of excitement and expectation tinted with fear. I was petrified. Wilhelmina did not know that I looked older than I was and at twelve plus I was unwillingly innocent, but pride and sensual excitement drove me on. Another problem I faced was that I could not just leave without telling someone of my whereabouts. It had to be Cousin Julio. He promised to keep the secret, mostly from Chalela, as we both knew how he felt about Wilhelmina. The only trouble was that she did not feel the same way about Chalela, or so I believed.

At about eight thirty p.m., I stealthily set out on my first mission into the unknown.

Walking to Wilhelmina's that evening through the citrus-scented air, my mind was confused. This was going to be my first visit to a girlfriend's home and boudoir alone. Once or twice I almost abandoned the operation.

The other side of my still-developing brain was rowing me forward. I was about to join the grown-ups' club. I felt that my body was in pristine condition and tuned to Grand Prix standards. Normally I would never have walked about on my own at such time of the night, but on this night I felt like a big boy now, simply gliding on the wings of what I believed to be love, true love. I felt I had joined the lower echelons of the adults' league, at twelve – a fully grown and soon-to-be sexually active male. How exciting!

Arriving at the house, I tip-toed to the veranda on which Wilhelmina's bedroom door was. I knocked lightly, as instructed earlier. Her brothers' bedroom was only three doors away. It didn't take long. Wilhelmina opened the door slowly and quietly. She was standing behind it, with just her left shoulder and half of her face showing, and as I walked in, I noticed she was not wearing much, only a flimsy half-slip. She told me she thought I was not coming, and although she repeated this several times, I could not respond. My mind was wandering; no, I think it just froze. This was the first time I had been in the presence of a woman in a state of undress. She shut and locked the door gently. The sound of that lock turning was like an orchestra striking up an overture, a musical introduction to the main act to follow.

I now wondered how to proceed beyond this point. I need not have bothered. She held me, we embraced, saying nothing, kissing, a continuation from where we had left off the night before. I could feel the fast, rhythmic beating of her heart (how about mine?) through my new green flowery Hawaiian shirt. The candlelight, as if for some deliberate special effects, cast our abstract wobbly shadows on the wall as Wilhelmina gently pulled me down onto her bed and started to undo my shirt buttons. I was perspiring profusely, we both were, and in no time at all, I was completely naked. Too forward for a fourteen-year-old, you might say, and I agree with you completely. We were now sitting side-by-side, her hand on my knee and caressing my thigh with gentle upward strokes. My manly response was to put my arm around her shoulders and plant a big kiss on her mouth. She pushed my head back a little and looked searchingly into my face, almost like asking, 'Did you bring the equipment?'

'I love you, Davie,' she said softly with as little effort as the birds singing.

'I love you too, Wilhelmina,' I mumbled, shyly avoiding her eyes.

There was a tear in her eye, which rolled down her chiselled cheeks, stopping for a moment on her chin, attracting the candlelight's reflection before falling onto my foot.

'Come to bed, Davie. Make love to me,' she whispered, her feathery voice coarse with emotion, as she removed her half-slip. She was not wearing anything underneath. I had seen the future, not to mention the small tuft of hairs delightfully covering her womanhood.

Under the sheets, her hands went straight for my wedding tackle. I wanted to ask her to put out the candle as she toyed with me so delicately but somehow lacked the courage. Without finesse, I did the same to her hard and shapely breast, my body responding naturally – nothing to complain about so far. She kicked the sheets off the bed.

'Come in me, Davie. Please, come on in,' she moaned with desire.

Alas, I did not know how to proceed, but she did. She guided me into position, and I continued to kiss her as she struggled to let me in. Somehow my aim was not good, and she directed me with her fingers but to no avail. She was hot, her body wet with perspiration and her face from tears as well. For a moment I could have sworn I saw some steam coming from her groin – a sign of unfulfilled sexual desire, I reasoned.

'Why, oh, why, Davie? What's the matter?' she cried. I could not answer.

Nature had simply said to me, 'Look here, boy, you're not ready yet.' It did not let me past the front door. My manhood dwindled. Disaster! The more we tried, the more she cried. I was gravely ashamed of my inefficiency. I felt sorry for Wilhelmina, to see her in that state and be unable to do anything about it. It was certainly the most humiliating experience in my young life thus far. My time had not come, and neither had I. Well, I had hardly gone! I had let us both down.

At about four thirty a.m. on a sleepless and most shameful night, Wilhelmina asked me to leave. She said this was out of concern for our being found out should I delay any longer. I felt a complete failure. Dressed and avoiding her eyes, which were full of unfulfilled passion and sadness, I shut the door behind me. In the cold morning air, I walked back miserably, using the orange trees as a shield from any possible prying eyes. I do not recall if the sweet fragrance emanating from the citrus flowers was still there; I just do not remember experiencing it this time. I was too distraught to notice, although I could hear the annoyingly threatening laughter of hyenas from the direction of the nearby Khudze Hill. This made me walk and half-run faster!

I let myself back into the hut, trying hard not to wake the other two. No chance. Julio whispered, 'Is everything all right?'

Something in the way I responded told him that not everything was all right in Davie-land, and he quickly lit the paraffin lamp. Chalela was also awake by then and they both looked at me. 'What happened?'

I gathered that Julio had betrayed me. Chalela knew everything. I had to be man enough and bite the bullet. Besides, I was too upset to lie.

'I didn't. I couldn't,' I said with a shaky, emotional voice.

'You mean … the whole night … nothing? You left yesterday Davie! What were you doing all night, then?' asked Chalela in an angry, accusatory tone.

This was too much. I broke down into a sea of tears. Chalela then immediately got up and pulled on his trousers and a striped short-sleeved shirt, almost falling on us as we lay on the mat. He left the hut at great speed, and I could hear his footsteps fading into the muffled stillness of the early air of a tropical morning.

When we saw him soon after eight that morning, he was in a good mood.

'You shouldn't have gone there last night,' he stated. 'You're too young.'

'You mean …?' I queried, the certainty of his smug reply causing a lump to rise in my throat.

'Yes. I did it for you,' he said, the air of satisfaction on his face visible. 'I had to rescue the family honour; can't you see?'

If I ever felt like killing my brother, or anyone else for that matter, this was the moment. I didn't speak to Chalela for a week. I suspected that every day from that fateful night, he continued to restore the family honour and enjoyed every minute of it.

My most treasured possession was still intact, not that I wanted to keep it that way. Wilhelmina had made me feel like a hunter who sees his first animal on a hunt, aims, certain that he cannot miss at that distance, and then the gun jams! Thankfully we only had one week before returning to Zomba, during which time I kept my distance from Wilhelmina – perhaps she from me as well!

Chapter 9

YOU ARE CERTAINLY NOT IN YORKSHIRE

Imagine this: in 1963, in a remote village in Mwanza District, Western Malawi, a newly married man arrives back at his house after a few hours at the river with his fishing rod in one hand. He has five large chambo (perch) threaded through a thin bamboo vine, the fruits of his labours. The hot afternoon sun is now retiring, albeit slowly, and a cool easterly breeze is gently welcoming the truce a couple of hours before sunset.

Between the kitchen and the main house the women are gathered. Some are plaiting each other's hair, while others remove dandruff from each other's scalps. Apart from the laughter, which seems endless, it is difficult to catch what they are saying to one another. They are women, and so they gossip, stuff not for men's ears – I know men do gossip too but perhaps not as much. On the other side of the house, children, both boys and girls, play various games together: football, 'Nsikwa*', and 'Bonkiri**', while others attack the plentiful supply of oranges and tangerines which line the village paths like hedges.

Ever since the husband joined the village, about three months earlier, it had been the same. Whenever he returned home with the fish, his wife never served him a fish's head on his dinner plate.

In Malawi and some other parts of the world, the head of a fish is viewed as a delicacy. One could not honestly claim to have eaten chambo if all they had was the tail-end of it or just the fillet. Wives are aware of this, and they make sure the head goes to Baba (the husband) at mealtimes – men and women do not eat together. The man was at a loss to know what to do. He could not ask why the wife was not giving him the fish-head without being called greedy and becoming the butt of the village jokes, nor could he allow the situation of headless fish on his plate to linger. This time, he determined what he must do. Choosing a spot away from where the women were gathered but making sure they could easily see him; he started gutting the fish and cutting them in half. Calling his dog, he threw him one fish head and then another.

After watching the dog enjoy this rare and generous treat from his master, the wife broke away from the now shocked and silent women and ran towards the husband. 'Baba wa Gumbo, what are you doing, throwing away the fishes' heads?'

'I didn't know we ate them in this village!' came the tactful yet succinct reply.

From that day, this husband had a fish's head on his plate. Fishing became gratifying once more!

In the summer of 1966, as for most summers, Chalela and I had been shipped to Mwanza to visit Grandmother.

It was a must for both citizens and non-citizens to attend a presidential rally taking place in their area. Failure to follow this rule could result in a serious beating or worse. To enforce this rule, the government had brainwashed a high percentage of mostly illiterate youths who were empowered to harass people and beat them up if they felt that way, or if they were feeling mean, and even then they were not answerable to the police.

If, in their eyes, one was showing disrespect for the president in what they said or did, that was enough. There was no need for these guys to be precise. They were protecting the government.

* Nsikwa: A game of spinners made from disks from broken gourds. A tight little stick is inserted in the middle and flung towards an opponent, who has four or more pieces of dry maize cobs of different heights. The idea is knock them down. The distance between the players is usually three metres.

** Bonkiri (Flick): A finger-flicking game usually using discs or buttons. The players compete to see who will get the button into a circle drawn on the ground. Normally the circle is half a metre across; it may also have another much smaller circle inside it. If a player flicks their disc from the starting line into the middle circle, he wins the game and collects one button from all the participants. Otherwise, the game continues with the one whose button enters the larger circle flicking all the other buttons into the larger or smaller circle. It is a game parents discouraged children from playing because it was addictive. First, the child's own clothes would start losing buttons, and in extreme cases, it was the parents' clothes which lost their buttons to the game too.

Apart from the abundance of citrus fruits we enjoyed in the village, I also looked forward to such visits, because it was, for me, a way of escaping the well-defined and strictly applied rules of behaviour at home. True, Grandmother was strict but differently so. Chalela and I knew what chores we had to do, but if we finished them quickly, whatever time was left we had for ourselves.

Our main pastimes were fishing and hunting mice and cicadas. We didn't have any toys to occupy our young minds, and most of the children's parents couldn't afford them. Chalela and I were not allowed to bring any toys to the village. Our parents wanted us to learn about life in the village as it truly was.

However, external political forces had emerged with disruptive tendencies. Every time there was a meeting of the local branch of the Malawi Congress Party, no one could work. It didn't matter if you had an office job or were doing chores around the house; everyone had to attend the meeting. Some families had fields overgrown with weeds and not enough hands to rescue the situation in time. Yet, if there was a public political rally by the ruling party, the whole day was wasted workwise. No one was exempted.

Very close to Grandmother's house there lived a very frail old lady. We used to call her Gogo Nanyambi, which translates as 'Daughter of Nyambi'. She was older than my grandmother, and believe me, that was old! She had no child to help her with her everyday activities and, worse still, had no one to help her in cultivating the fields.

As was the tradition, every year the village banded together to give her a helping hand, yet despite this charity I always saw her walking, stick in hand and with a hoe on her shoulder, every morning, going to work in the field. Although she showed her willingness to work hard in the field for her food, Gogo Nanyambi was well past it. At her age, it was hard for her just to stand up, and yet, she continued to toil.

My first cousin, Julio, my Mother's elder sister's son, had been 'given' to his Grandmother by his mother when my grandfather died. This was to assist our grandmother with some little jobs around the house – those chores requiring a man's touch. Julio was not afraid of hard work, and his mental maturity was way beyond his years, having been brought up by Grandmother and mixing with the elders, who imparted to him a lot of wisdom, including the different ways of trapping mice in the bush. Julio was an expert. He even knew the names of the different species which lived in the area and the many ways of hunting them. One way was to dig for them, but by doing so you risked being bitten by snakes, and you would only ever find one variety of mice in any one hole. Chalela and I found Julio so fascinating with his knowledge. In a way, apart from giving him our company we had nothing else to offer him. I do not know if he minded this fact at all.

It was on one bright, sunny morning when we set out into the bush with one thing on our minds – kuchera Misampha – setting traps, mice traps in this case. The tall grass bent under the weight of the early-morning dew, each drop blindingly crystalised in the sun's rays, and we carried sticks to help clear the narrow path out of the village, which ran along the banks of the slow-flowing Khwibvi River. All around us the birds sang their different melodies, the wind causing the grass to sway in mesmerised appreciation. By the time Julio started to set the first Diwa, a special flat rock, about a foot square and less than four inches thick, we were all completely soaked to the skin, but we didn't seem to mind.

Mwanza is very mountainous and rocky, so it was no problem finding the right stones. The only items we had to carry along with us were small pieces of sharpened bamboo sticks, bits of string, maize grain, and fried maize husks. Julio noticed some tell-tale signs on the ground which made him believe the area was worth a Diwa or two, and he started to set the rocks at an angle of about forty-five degrees, supported by a few pieces of bamboo tied together with a string made from sisal. The fried maize husks were strategically spread in the middle of the Diwa's drop zone. The aroma they produced seemed to attract a variety of mice in the surrounding area to their death. On average these rocks were between two to three kilograms each. When the supporting bamboo was lightly touched, the rock collapsed and the trap was sprung. We covered an area of approximately ten acres in this way and the final total of traps set was a hundred.

On some idle days, we could set out into the forest after the bushfires had gone, leaving the whole forest floor charcoal grey and almost lifeless to the naked eye. Up in the trees, we could see and hear a variety of birds singing, perhaps mourning; we couldn't tell. The cacophony of these birds was made worse by the loud and piercing sound of the cicadas.

Our expedition was to catch cicadas. These insects make a very tasty snack. Not a lot of people know this. Cicadas on a skewer roasted on an open fire – I can almost taste them now. My favourite cicada recipe is fried cicadas in garlic and parsley butter sauce, washed down with a glass of a white South African wine, Marlborough Sauvignon Blanc – these put mussels on a back banner! And it is rumoured, they are equally beneficial to men.

On our way to the forest, the boys in the village who were leading the team led us to several masuku trees which had a mistletoe shrub attached to them. The little red berries are chewed and the rough bits spat out. What remains is white sticky stuff, and we were shown how to attach this glue to the tip of a very long reed which we had harvested along the banks of the Khwibvi River. They were very long reeds; I estimate them to have been around fifteen feet.

Cicadas have a very sharp sense of hearing. The group leader ordered us to shush as he stealthily walked towards a tree, from which we could hear the ear-piercing singing of cicadas. He slowly lifted his long primed reed tip towards the direction of the sound until he finally spotted the cicada and knew that his weapon would reach it. To spot these insects one needed to have a sharp vision. The colour of the cicadas resembled that of the bark of the tree on which they rested. I'm not entirely sure about their vision, but I've learned that cicadas have five functioning eyes[1]. 'I have got it,' whispered Joseph, for that was his name. There was great excitement in his voice and eyes. There were more cicadas which continued to sing from that tree as the rest of us spread toward other trees from which we could hear more singing cicadas.

While we were away, the village had been invaded by the Malawi Congress Party Youth (politely called the Youth Leaguers), forcing the young, the sick, and the old to attend a public meeting which the local party chairman and Member of Parliament was addressing. When we entered the village about mid-afternoon we were met with a ghostly silence, apart from some wailing sounds which came from the old lady's hut. We ran there, Julio leading the way, and as soon as she saw us, the old lady began to speak.

'The little boys spoke to me like I was a young girl. If my husband were around today this wouldn't have happened. They don't show respect at all to the elderly. Even if I went to their so-called meetings, what good would it do me? I can hardly walk to church these days, let alone a political meeting! They stood right there where you're standing now, swearing at me. Maybe it's a premonition. Maybe I've lived too long. I know it's time I left to join my late husband,' she lamented, her dark-brown eyes awash with tears and her wrinkled face completely wet and filled with tension and fear. Here was a woman who had lived through colonialism unscathed, and now that Dr Kamuzu Banda had liberated us from the colonial Yoke, there was no peace in her home.

---

1 Interestingly, they [Cicadas]seem to make themselves easy to catch due to an in-built genetic trait that ensures the survival of the rest. It's quite fascinating!

The poor lady was found dead the following morning by my grandmother. She came back telling us the old woman had died of old age. Chalela, Julio and I knew differently. 'I would say she died of disappointment,' said Julio.

Since, traditionally, children are not allowed to attend a funeral, we three set out into the bush to check our traps. Our success rate was very high, about seventy-five percent, and when we returned home, Grandmother was generous with her praise. 'Three hunters! Three husbands! I am so blessed!' she cried as we showed her our catch. After Julio cleaned and boiled the mice in a spiced mixture of chillies, onions, and fresh turmeric, they were left to dry in the sun for a whole day. The following day, the mice were threaded onto bamboo skewers, also prepared by Julio, and we ate Mice Kebab, or Spiced Mice à la Julio, depending on whether you imagined yourself dining at a Greek or French establishment, for our supper.

Discussing the 'politics of food' with a French priest some years later, I was divinely mocking him for the way his countrymen ate horsemeat and frogs' legs, when, with a twinkle in his eye, he wrongfooted me by retorting, 'We don't eat mice though!'

Wouldn't it be nice if mice-eating people could be able to find this delicacy on a restaurant menu in some Western eateries? That's my prayer. I do not think it is right to eat mice in the privacy of one's home. Food tastes better when shared. I can already see special mice dishes in such restaurants.

Grilled skinless Kapeta* in garlic and basil sauce.
    Sun-cured smoked dried Kapuku* à la Mwanza with spicy salsa
    Smoked Piri-piri Maphanya* on a skewer with a sweet-and-sour sauce[2]
    Etcetera.

---

2 The first thing a mice-eating person learns is how to tell thee different types of mice one can find in a particular bush. Just like different typees of meat at the local butcher's, they taste differently.

I have always been at a loss to understand why a lot of Caucasians and perhaps other groups of people find it hard to differentiate mice from rats. Most Africans, myself included, enjoy eating mice; never rats. Mice found in a house are viewed as rats, and they are not eaten unless you choose to consume them for whatever reason. Besides, to those who know these little animals, a rat cannot be mistaken for a mouse.

I felt good when I went to a garden restaurant in Jakarta, Indonesia one lunch break just to find they had mice on the menu, and, I thought, mice on the menu thousands of miles from Africa! I can see many countries particularly enjoying their mice in years to come. Besides, why is it necessary to judge one's humanity through what the individual eats? I kept my eyes trained stealthily on the heated tray as it slowly became empty. One-by-one, two-by-two the locals proudly served themselves with other food items including a mouse or two. And I thought I could live here! Are we, as human beings, so facetious as to attach great importance to the way we choose to respond to some individuals or groups of people who just happen to eat stuff like frogs, mice, snails, bats, horses, and baboon meat, etcetera, stuff you do not find appetising.

Chapter 10

ELEANOR AND
THE EMPTY MUSHROOM BASKETS

Three or four years later, we moved to Lilongwe. Since our home was literally at the then Lilongwe Airport's gate, most of my friends and classmates came from within the airport area, and their parents worked in a variety of services within the airport itself

The school was just over four miles away. I had just turned thirteen and my best mate, whose father was a meteorological officer at the airport, was called Phillip. Among the girls from our area were two who we thought were rather special. The one Phillip liked was called Maria and for me, there was big Eleanor. She was light brown, of medium height, and for a girl of fourteen, she looked rather mature, and no one could have described her as slim. At her age, she was so shapely and had a rear one could bounce a fifty-pence coin on, a bottom which seemed to magnetically invite a pinch every time I saw her walk. Her round face would have been fairly described as very beautiful if it weren't for the pimples that covered it mercilessly during that period. I did not mind.

She was very playful with me, just as I was with her. She used to tell me how young and inexperienced I was in adult things and that I should be careful with her; she could one day hurt my back! I took this as an invitation to treat, although I didn't have the confidence to treat it after the debacle with Wilhelmina. In my language, Chinyanja, they say, 'Chikakuluma chakuda, umaopa ndi khala lomwe' ('When you have been stung by a black insect, you get scared at the sight of a piece of charcoal'). This kind of talk used to take me back to that night with Wilhelmina, which did little for my confidence. I thought Eleanor liked me though. She used to wait outside my classroom every time she finished her lessons before me and we would walk friskily home together. The teachers knew she was fond of me, and they also knew she was safe – in their view, no harm was expected from me at that age.

As time went by, Phillip and I decided to move our relationship with the girls on to a higher plane. It was Phillip's idea. Maria's home was next to his, and their parents were friends. He told me that the previous weekend Maria had spent a couple of evenings at his house, chatting with his sisters.

'What I found a little surprising,' explained Phillip, 'was that she told me she had fluffed my pillow in the bedroom. You see, she fluffed my pillow! Imagine that! Do you know?' he asked rhetorically and continued, 'She said because she wanted me to dream of her! Did you know that when someone fluffs your pillow for you, they appear in your dreams that night?'

'Nooo!' I gasped, playing for time while digesting the significance of what he was telling me. Up to that day, the only fluffer of my pillow had been my mother, and I couldn't recall ever dreaming of her.

'Yes!' he said affirmatively. 'And the way she looked at me, it was so obvious she fancies me,' he enthusiastically concluded.

'But we know that already,' I commented solemnly, hoping my lack of experience in such matters did not show.

'You know what I mean, Davie. You don't expect diagrams, do you?' Well, I did but didn't want to admit it.

'Ah! It's all very clear now – you mean ... Really?' I said, getting excited. 'Yes, you're right; something must be done.' His next question was a difficult one.

'How do we tell her and Eleanor?' he asked.

'Tell them what?'

'Tell them we would like to take them out one weekend.'

'That's a toughie,' I replied resignedly, hoping to put the ball back in his court for, like him, I also didn't have a clue.

'Mushrooms!' exclaimed Phillip.

'Get them mushrooms?'

'No, silly! We'll suggest to them we go mushroom picking at the weekend. That should do it!' This to us must have been the equivalent of telling the girls we had booked ourselves at some motel that afternoon!

'Phillip, the girls will be suspicious,' I reason with him.

'They know the score. Suspicious or not, they'll come. Look, Davie, a girl who fluffs your pillow doesn't need much tripping. She's fallen already,' he reasoned.

Phillip was right. The mushroom-picking expedition was easily arranged for the following Sunday afternoon.

The Friday before the outing, Eleanor was being her usual self. She finished her lessons earlier than me and was waiting patiently outside the door for my lessons to end.

Heading home, the others left the four of us behind, because they had an idea we were up to grown-up things. Now and again, Eleanor would playfully pinch my bum and I would return the compliment by pinching her bouncy breasts, which were already the size of healthy Jaffa grapefruits at that time. My hands had never been merrier! This courting game went on for the entire distance, and Eleanor would say, 'Don't excite yourself, Davie. You're only a baby as far as I'm concerned. I wouldn't want you to break your tender back.' Then she would give me a daring smile as she once again pinched my now bruised bum. As we did this, Phillip and Maria were also playing their own dating game. For a while they would chase each other across the road into the short bushes and back again onto the road. It was easy to see they were enjoying each other's company. The nearer we got to our homes, the greater the distance between us and them got and the slower we walked.

Eleanor lived a mere five minutes' walk from my home, and as we reached our parting junction, something happened. The long-awaited 'event', the one I thought and felt may never come, came. My undergarment had been indecently assaulted. I had received a visitor. I was finally a man!

I do not know how my face looked at that very moment of realisation, but Eleanor noticed something.

'What's the matter, kid?' she asked. 'You look like you've seen a dead mouse in your water tank.'

'What dead mouse? Where?' I pretended, trying to keep my voice steady.

'Are you all right?' she insisted.

'Never better. Never better, Eleanor,' I whispered. It was more of a mumble than a whisper.

'See you Sunday then, and no excuses, kid. You're not going to fake a headache, are you?' she joked as she walked towards the small parameter fence in which her home was. She turned back to look at me as I just stood there looking at her and fearfully imagining how I was to approach what I had been thinking of for quite some months now. I had no answers. She reached the gate and turned her head back and gestured to me that I should go home. She smiled, and then there it was again, the sexy, bouncy bum. Was I dreaming!

I walked so fast after that. As soon as I arrived home, I dropped my schoolbooks on the porch and ran into the bathroom to see what my body was finally producing. Isn't God great, I thought? I was now in the Man's League. Good timing too, just two days, a mere forty-eight hours, before the mushroom-picking sortie. Yes, come Sunday I would be armed and almost dangerous. I might not have been sure about how best to use my gun, but still, the infantry had to go into battle. This was war! Well, more of war manoeuvres than anything else.

Filled with untold excitement, Phillip and I counted the days, then the hours and the minutes and finally it was Sunday. Phillip, like me, was also going into battle for the first time, so he had confessed to me that week.

It was a typical tropical December day in Lilongwe. The temperature was in the high twenties, and although the skies were clear of any clouds in the morning, there was no telling if conditions would be the same in the afternoon. I did not wish anything to ruin this day. If it had to rain at all, I asked the Lord in prayer, please make it later at night, not this afternoon. Phillip told me when I met him later at his house that his prayers had been along the same lines. His mother was lending a helping hand too. Pointing to a large woven basket on the veranda, she told him, 'Take this one. I saw a few girls yesterday with lots of mushrooms. They were coming from the other side of the airport.'

The arrangement the two of us had made with the girls was to meet at the end of the southern runway, the furthest one from the control tower. As locals, the airport authorities did not mind us entering the restricted areas of the airport if we did not go anywhere near the runway.

When we arrived at our meeting point there was no sign of the girls. Waiting was not going to be difficult, for this was one day both of us were more than willing to wait for as long as it took for the girls to arrive. Then, from the nearby bushes, we heard someone calling Phillip's name. It was Maria. As we gently turned and walked towards her, she told me Eleanor was a few metres away, deeper in the bush. They had thought of everything, crafty girls!

'Come down here, kid,' Eleanor called as soon as she saw me. 'Are you scared or something?' I swallowed hard, petrified. I was on a sticky wicket, so to speak. Knowing, or at least suspecting, I was only an amateur, Eleanor seemed more than willing to show me the ropes, or whatever it is they show mushroom-picking novices, and, by now I was wondering why I was there.

I managed to stammer something like, 'Have you been here long?' before she asked, or more like ordered, me to sit down. I began sweating nervously. Eleanor must have taken this as a sign of intense passion and desire, because she flung herself at me, kissing, groping, and telling me how she was going to teach me a thing or two. 'Oh, God!' I thought.

'Let me remove my–' she started to say when from the clearing a voice from a megaphone boomed out.

'All of you there, will you come out? We know you're in there!'

No, it was not God in answer to my SOS call. We had been spotted by the air traffic control officers, using binoculars, from the control tower. Empty mushroom containers in hand, Eleanor and I joined Maria and Phillip, who had already given themselves up.

We had to vacate the area because an Air Madagascar airplane carrying President Tsiranana, on its way to or from Zaire, had developed an engine fault and they had requested an emergency landing.

The 'arresting officer', who was accompanied by two security guards, happened to be my sister's ex-boyfriend back when they had been in their teens. He was now the airport commandant, and when he saw us, he just burst out laughing. Telling us to jump into his Land Rover, he drove us back to the main office block at the terminal building, where all those on duty, including Phillip's father, Maria's father, and Eleanor's brother-in-law were waiting to see just who these lusty kids were. The shock on their faces when they realised who we were said it all.

'We were picking mushrooms,' Eleanor tried to explain without being prodded.

'And where are they, then? Where are the mushrooms?' demanded her visibly angry guardian and brother-in-law, while Phillip and Maria's respective fathers simply walked away, sucking their teeth in shock and parental dismay.

The girls went their way as Phillip and I went on towards the football ground, which was between the airport terminal buildings and our house just outside the airport gates. We decided it was time for us to do what we knew best – join the boys in a game of good old-fashioned football kick-about. We took our time going to our respective homes, and Phillip seemed rather concerned and reluctant to head home, for he was not sure of the reception awaiting him there. As for me, I didn't know how long it would take for the news to reach my parents; my parents did not fraternise with my friends' parents working at the airport.

'I don't know what my mother is going to say,' Phillip wondered dismally as our dawdling steps finally came to a halt.

'And what about your father?' I less-than-tactfully added to his worries.

'But they know I'm a man.' Phillip tried to console himself. He continued, 'Sooner or later I'll have to go out with girls.'

'Yes, on mushroom-picking expeditions!' I sloppily joked, trying to ease Phillip's worries.

We parted company that evening on a very low note. I was not as worried, because my parents could not possibly know about the incident since they did not mix with Phillip or the girls' parents.

The main thought on my mind was what it was Eleanor had been about to remove when we were rudely interrupted. My imagination ran wild at the thought of it!

Next to Eleanor's house was another house being used as a men's hostel by the meteorological services apprentices. The brother of one of the two trainees staying there was my classmate, Duncan. Every time I wanted to see Eleanor after school I would rendezvous at this house and pass on a letter, or even snatch a few words with her without attracting the attention of her elder sister, with whose family she stayed.

One day as I arrived, I found Duncan playing a game of Bawo with one of the meteorological trainees, who was having a tough time containing Duncan. He was a master Bawo player. When I tried to insolently advise him on his next move, he got upset and slapped me on the left side of the face. I foolishly and angrily tried to hit him back and that's when he got furious. He began hitting me with hard fists around the head. He was about twenty-three plus whereas I was thirteen and a half years old. He was also quite tall and athletic. With blows still venomously raining on me, I decided my only choice was to leg it!

I ran around the house once, and as the trainee was gaining on me, I thought I should swallow my pride and heard towards Eleanor's home, where she was outside on a reed mat with her elder sister preparing pumpkin leaves (Nkhwani) for dinner. I ran right into the house and shut the door before the trainee could get me. I could hear Eleanor's sister asking this man what the matter was. All I could hear was him telling the two women that I had always been rude to him and now he wanted to teach me a lesson. 'He is just a little boy; he should not mess with the likes of me,' I heard him conclude, his voice slowly fading away. He had returned to his house, I thought.

Then a moment later, both women came in, and they looked and sounded earnestly sad that I had been roughed up. They then offered me a cup of tea, and despite my embarrassment, I was hardly able to refuse.Then Eleanor's sister asked me what was going on, and with my voice failing me here and there, I explained as best I could, after which Eleanor's sister could only say, 'Is that it? There must be something else,' she reasoned.

Indeed, a few days earlier, Duncan had told me that the trainee and Eleanor were having an affair! The beating I got was not because of my behaviour towards him when he was losing a game of Bawo, oh no! It was envy! Jealousy. He had gotten the story of our scrambled mushroom expedition at the office! Then, he had waited for an opportunity to present itself for him to exact his pound of flesh. He got more than a pound; more like a kilogram, in my view!

Although Eleanor's sistercould not fully understand my censored version of events, she was sympathetic and seemed to support me as the underdog. 'That boy is no good at all,' she stated. 'He is a bully. I wonder what Eleanor sees in him.'

I wanted to add, 'Ask her, Madam, ask her,' but I decided against it for fear of being reported back to the fuming and jealous meteorological services trainee.

Eleanor finally came to her senses and stopped seeing the trainee. I am sure she believed in the adage that 'The meek shall inherit the woman', or indeed, her sister had managed to discourage her. To my dismay, a month later her guardians were transferred to Blantyre before we could hatch another mushroom-picking expedition plan, and I never saw Eleanor again, except in my dreams. Mother would sometimes give me a funny look when occasionally, following a particularly vivid dream, I would need to rise early in the morning to wash my assaulted bed sheets. In my fantasies, everything was perfect. I decided to remain a secret member of this exclusive men's club for a while yet. It was far safer that way, I thought.

A few opportunities did present themselves from time to time, most of them ending in disappointment. I never gave up though. I felt there was no need to stop marketing the merchandise despite not selling anything yet, it was just that the targeting needed more refinement. The memory of the beating I got from that meteorological trainee usurped my confidence with girls for a while.

Chapter 11

MY TIME AT
SOCHE HILL SECONDARY SCHOOL

There is a minimum of eight years in Malawi primary education. Some students remained at this stage indefinitely because an examination at the end of each school year had to be passed to progress to the next level. This resulted in a mix of different ages in every class, as some learners, known as "Repeaters," had to retake the same grade. From year one, passing the examination was crucial to moving up to the next stage; otherwise, students found themselves repeating the same class, sometimes multiple times.

Finally, at standard eight there was the biggest hurdle in one's young academic life – a national government examination to take the successful students into secondary-school education. At that time the government was the sole authority for selecting learners for various secondary schools dotted around the country. A huge number of learners simply got frustrated, gave up and went fishing forever. Those who stayed the course ended up sitting for government-set examinations called Primary School Leaving Certificate Examinations. Once you had written them, there were three possibilities, as opposed to the normal pass or fail. The third was pass but not selected to go on to secondary school. Out of those who passed, only a minority were selected to continue with their education in various secondary schools. Those who failed were issued with a certificate called 'Completed Primary School Education', a document one made sure was hidden in a very dark place, hopefully never to be seen again.

Data available as of 2017 shows that only sixteen percent of those who sat for these examinations progressed to secondary schools and of those only eight percent went on into tertiary education. In a very competitive job market, I doubt if anyone hoped to get a decent job using this document, and yet with it one was expected to face the job market and the world at large as a serious contributor to society. Looking at the 2017 figures, it seems like nothing has changed much since the early seventies when some of us were selected to go to secondary school.

I had also become a Repeater when I passed my Primary School Leaving Certificate Examinations but was not selected to go to secondary school. In that year, 1970, in a class of forty learners, only twenty-five had passed, and from that total four were selected to continue at various secondary schools. During the first year, when I only passed my exams but was not selected, the only pupil who was selected from the area around the airport where we lived in Lilongwe was Hodges. Hodges was not his real name. Previously, he had sat for these Primary School Leaving Certificate Examinations and was selected to go to Kongwe Secondary School, but tragedy struck! He and two friends had been caught allegedly defacing the Life President's portrait, which was hung in one of the common rooms, as was the custom in all public institutions, come to think of it, even private ones!

The MYP (Malawi Young Pioneers [MYP], close in style to Hitler's Youth, only older and more ruthless) instructor expelled the whole group, and when the rest of his friends protested, the entire school was shut down. The only way for Hodges and his entourage to get an education in Malawi was to change their names. Back then, Hodges' name was Alfred. The secondary school reopened within a few months and took back only those students thought to be non-troublemakers. Two years later, Hodges and one other learner were selected to go to secondary schools. To his shock, he had been selected to go to the same school, and fortunately for him, no one ever reminded him of his previous life as Alfred. His former classmates were then in Form Three, and the MYP instructor had since been promoted to better and higher things, although I dread to speculate what these were.

Going to secondary school was a dream come true for most young people and their families for all that the move implied for one's future, not to mention such places were at a premium since the country had too few secondary schools.

The excitement of hearing of such success helped one forget the dreaded initiation rituals known to be practiced by senior (most Form Two through to Form Five) students at all secondary schools in the country. They was euphemistically known as 'teasing'. New students had been known to drop out of school because of it and, in the worst cases, a few had committed suicide.

As I left Lilongwe for Soche Hill, Blantyre, I had mixed feelings. I was happy to be going to secondary school and yet afraid of 'teasing'[3]. My brother, Chalela, had been selected to the same school a year earlier but was protected by an uncle called 'Quarry' Bamusi N'Nembo. Quarry was a stubby, ragged fellow, about five foot three or so, and he had bushy sideburns which made him look like some historical biblical or Greek wise man. No one at Soche Hill, including teachers, dared mess with him. He was in Form Four that year, and I should add that Quarry was a bit too advanced to be at secondary school at his age. He was not alone though. Most Form Fours were already spendingquite a packet on razor blades. I felt a little lucky that Quarry would now be going into Form Five that year. This meant I would have double protection from my brother, Chalela, and my distant uncle, Quarry.

The school year began in early January, at the height of the rainy season in this part of the world. The bushes along the road were alive with birds, and a diversity of wildflowers were in full bloom. Mangoes were in season, and a few yellow fruits could be spotted hanging invitingly on the branches high in the trees as we hurried past them on our way to school. The road was constructed through an area which had been dotted with villages decades earlier. The mango trees, together with barely visible

---

3 This unwarranted and dehumanising practice was banned by the government in all secondary schools.

signs of where old huts had once stood, were relics of that history. This was now government land.

Soche Hill Secondary School was constructed in the foothills of Soche Hill, southeast of Blantyre. The hill itself is on top of higher ground, which begins to rise from both the Blantyre and Limbe directions, and the slopes look steeper from the former. So, as we approached the school campus, the structures slowly began to materialise in concert with our steps. First, I saw a hedge surrounding a house, which I assumed was a teacher's house. I then noticed there was a row of such houses to my right. There were two pillars at the gate with the words, 'Welcome to Soche Hill Secondary School'. As we walked past this point, I immediately noticed that the schoolyard looked overgrown with grass. It looked most unattractive, and that was before our first experience of 'teasing'. This view blotted the bright image of the school Chalela had given me earlier as we left home in Chitawila.

On this day, the opening day, I wore a new outfit which Father had bought for me as a Christmas present in preparation for going to secondary school. My new shirt bore all the radioactive colours imaginable, neatly bAaron ced by my dark-brown shorts and brown suede shoes. My brother and I were staying with our sister, Naphiri, who was living in this residential medium-density area to the east of Blantyre.

We had left home around six thirty a.m. for the three-mile walk to school, and as soon as we joined the main road, we were joined by other students heading towards the same destination. One of those students was Gertrude, an average-looking girl, who seemed to talk to Chalela as if they were bosom buddies. I wondered. She did have rather a large bosom, come to think of it. Chalela introduced me to his classmate. She was happy to meet me, as she too had a younger brother coming to Soche Hill to start in Form One, and probably he, like me, had heard of the impending humiliating ritual awaiting us. He needed company.

'Where is he?' asked Chalela with a degree of excitement.

The brother was walking right behind us. The expression on his face seemed to suggest he was going to some sad event like a dear friend's funeral.

'Bula,' called Gertrude to her brother, 'meet your new friend. You're both "Nyawans" (new ones, which newcomers were called, among other derogatory terms, although this was friendly fire).

At least you can help each other avoid the ritual,' she added.

I joined Bula behind our protectors.

'So, I hear your name is Bula?' I queried by way of introduction.

'Not really; I am Brian,' he replied assertively.

Too late. To me, he was Bula, period. Bula was handsome, dark brown, of medium height, and when he smiled his beautiful shining white teeth revealed the calm and welcoming soul which lay beneath. I didn't realise that he was to be my closest friend for all the four years we spent in secondary school.

As soon as we reached the school car park, our two protectors gave us a last pep-talk before leaving us alone. I felt exposed. We felt exposed and in peril. As we were walking alongone of the narrow footpaths that joined different school blocks, a rough, unkempt fellow ordered us off it.

'Give room, Nyawans. Go on, walk on the grass.' He pushed Bula, who was in front of me, and was about to reach my chest with both of his open hands when I instinctively stretched out my own hands to push him too. At that moment, Chalela, who I hadn't noticed was a few metres behind us, called my name. I had not learned the lesson of turning the other cheek yet!

Chalela told us we had just met John 'Tinyererana' (Chewa for 'We are going to shit on each other') Phiri. He was a dreaded guy, who had been suspended from school because of 'teasing' the year before. He was now in Form Three. Looking around, we saw a lot of sad little faces being bullied all over the schoolyard. The scene had the appearance of being at Aintree, with bookies taking money from small groups of punters, only this time we were the horses and there was no money changing hands, just teasing.

Bula and I went behind the centre block, where, to our horror, we met a guy who introduced himself as Joseph 'Agaru' Buleya (the middle name here means 'dogs'). He was aware of this hideout for Nyawans, he said, because he had used it the year before and was found by Quarry, who did a few base things to him then. 'And he was thorough too,' he added with a fiendish, lop-sided smile. He took us, well, abducted us, behind a huge leafy shrub. 'Face me, the both of you,' he commanded. 'I'll now grind my palms together, making shutting and opening gestures. As I do so, I want both of you, in concert, to do the same … with your mouths. Okay? Here goes.'

This went on for over a minute, which seemed like forever. My mind wandered to the year before when I was so determined to go to secondary school. And for what?

'Good! Have you done this before, you Nyawans? You seem to enjoy it,' he cruelly quipped. If anything, we did not want to make a mistake in case he got angry and beat us up.

'Now, on your backs,' commanded our tormentor.

'But it's wet,' protested Bula.

'Are you saying I don't know it's wet? Are you saying I am blind?' came his angry response.

We both shook our heads in denial, and silently we got down on our backs and waited for the next instruction.

'Have you ever seen a bike?' Agaru asked with overt cynicism.

Unsurprisingly, we both said we had.

'Well, imagine you're on a bike, cycling towards a zebra crossing, and there are school kids about to cross. When I say one, you start and, two, you slowly stop. Okay?' He paused.

'ONE!'

Bula and I started moving our legs in a peddling motion. Agaru took his time before he said, 'TWO.' Then, as we began to slow the cycling motions, Bula rang his imaginary bike's bell.

'You don't ring a bell at school kids at a zebra crossing! Are you trying to be smart, Nyawani?'

'Bula, don't do that,' I whispered to Bula protectively.

'He didn't say we shouldn't ring the bell,' Bula maintained with a look of seriousness about him.

'He didn't say we could either, did he?' I argued, dismay drying the back of my throat.

140

'He didn't mention the bell, and my bike has got a bell. I must use it,' emphasised Bula.

'Don't be harsh to each other, you Nyawanis. You can go now. Hey, before you go, you tall one, bring me a fart tomorrow, and you, bring me a dead dog. If you don't, I'll tell Quarry to work you over,' Agaru warned confidently.

'He's my uncle,' I replied just as confidently.

'What?' Agaru asked, his eyes popping as wide as china saucers. 'Did you say Quarry is your uncle?'

'We are Quarry's nephews,' half-lied Bula happily, his face widening with a cheeky grin.

'Guys forget all this, please. I didn't know you're related to my friend, Quarry,' Agaru lied. We later discovered he was not even a close associate of Quarry's.

'Do you still want us to bring you a dead dog and ...?'

'What dead dog?' Agaru melted into the schoolyard, never to tease us again. And from that day, anyone who tried to tease us stopped in their tracks the moment we mentioned Quarry's name.

Starting school in January meant that most of the first week was used to clear the surroundings, mostly using slashers. On the last day of that week, our class was given a little patch to clear behind the wood and metal workshops. As we worked, around ten in the morning, we discovered two long pieces of sugarcane which had been hidden there by someone. It was not easy to tell how long they had been lying there. Foolishly and greedily, Bula, Duncan, and I chewed on this unexpected harvest. Later that day, during our lunchbreak, four of us, two boys and two girls, were sitting leisurely at the far end of the school's football field, enjoying our special lunch meal of milk scones from the mobile confectionery and some boiled cassavas. As we did that, we saw Duncan between two mean-looking fellows walking toward us. Behind them was another bearded man who looked like a bearded Mike Tyson. Duncan pointed to where we sat. It was easy to tell from the way they looked that there was trouble ahead. Bula and I were not going to let them humiliate us in front of Elizabeth and Joyce, if indeed, that was their intention.

Duncan (Dunka) was the son of my father's friend in Lilongwe. Our families lived about three kilometers apart, and we often played together. It was very pleasing when we were both selected to attend the same secondary school.

'Which of you is Davie and Brian?' asked the man with thick, well-trimmed sideburns. We thought this was perhaps not the time to give any clever quips, as there were only two boys, but we let it pass. He continued with the command, 'Come with us!'

We quietly followed them, and as soon as I saw them turn towards where we had picked up the sugarcane, I knew what the whole issue was about.

'Have you eaten our sugarcane, you three?' The question was hardly unexpected.

'Yes; we found it,' I answered foolishly and truthfully.

'What do you mean, you found it? Do you think it brought itself here, stupid?'

I kept quiet. What else was there for us to say when three bearded tough-looking and angry men wanted their sugarcane back while calling us stupid?

'Did you find both of them?' asked the slightly less severe-looking one.

'Yes,' exhaled Bula.

'You got them both? Who ate the middle?' he queried.

'I did,' I mumbled.

'Oh, so you ate the sweetest part!' Turning to his friends, he moaned.

'He ate the sweetest part of our sugarcane. And continued, "What should we do with them." Searchingly looking at his friends' facial or verbal responses.

What should we do with them?' he asked his two friends.

'Well, they must replace it. We can't beat them – they're only kids,' reasoned the biggest of the three Form Five students, the main inquisitor.

'Now listen, boys, when they were planting these pine trees around this hill, one old man refused to be moved. His house is right in the middle of the forest, and he grows exceedingly sweet sugarcane. I won't ask you to go there, but tomorrow I expect you to bring us two big sugarcanes to replace those you've unlawfully eaten. I don't care where you buy them, just bring them!'

Looking at these guys, we did not want to put Quarry into trouble, so we did not mention him to them or them to Quarry.

Much to our surprise, the following school day, when we brought the sugarcane, they refused it, asking us, 'How do you know Quarry, you kids?'

'We're his nephews,' came the reply, quickly and proudly, from Bula.

'You can eat the sugarcane. We were only joking with you. Quarry is our very good friend,' they fibbed and swiftly walked back to their class. Apparently, Dunka had warned them after the inquisition that he hoped Quarry would not get to hear about the punishment they had meted to his nephews!

As the year progressed, it was so funny and even sad to hear how most (almost all) Nyawans went through an assortment of degrading initiation rituals involving every kind of base act imaginable, some of them in the toilet bowl. The only comfort was that it would be our turn the following year to tease newcomers, Nyawans! It all seemed normal. Do not ask me how, please. It just did! When our time to tease came, we did our bit. Perhaps we overdid it, because it was just before the next school year that the government took a strong stance against teasing. They banned it, and anyone found and proven to have been teasing would be expelled from school. That did it! Still, too late for those who lost their lives and for those who chose to drop out of school and some more students whose lives were blighted because of this practice. I still wonder why it took the government so long to legislate against this dehumanising behaviour among students in the country's secondary schools!

Chapter 12

BOXING BULA AND COMPANY

Bula was in a very good mood when I met him at Msika Wanjala, near Kamba, that afternoon. He was wearing his favourite yellow jersey and a pair of grey trousers, which were a part of our school uniform. Putting down the basket full of vegetables he was carrying, he called to me excitedly as I entered the market.

'You should've come earlier, Davie. People were punching the hell out of each other down at the UTM (United Transport Malawi) football ground.'

'Why?' I asked, confused.

'They've started a boxing club, and they'll be competing there every Sunday.'

Looking me in the eye, Bula continued, 'Er ... I think we should join the club. What do you think?'

'I don't mind joining their supporters' club, but–'

Bula interrupted, 'Listen, Davie, this is the only way we can learn the skills of the noble art – self-defence against all those bullies at school. Come on,' he pleaded. We had just watched our local boxing hero, King Marshal Jetu, knock out Sandro Zulian in three rounds at the Kamuzu Stadium in Blantyre. The former had sharpened his boxing skills in Denmark, where he grew up, and his return home had breathed new life into boxing.

In public, Bula was a gentleman. However, I knew the private person better. He was, after all, my best friend. Bula was the most childish person I ever knew, and his interest in boxing baffled me. Did he want to go into boxing, albeit only as a part-time hobby, or had the boxing bug sunk into him too deeply to successfully fight it? No answer sprung to mind.

The whole week Bula spoke of nothing else. He even started shadowboxing, stopping unsuspecting classmates along the pathways, lifting their arms into a defensive fighting position, and feigning a few punches at them. Most of them took offence, but that did not seem to deter my friend. I was his safest sparring partner, unwilling but safe. Behind the school dormitories, we could start throwing serious punches at each other, making sure each time they missed their target. The school did not have a gymnasium. This went on for the entire week, and I suppose by then we were both in good fighting shape. Well, we had been sparring a lot, hadn't we?

On Sunday, Bula was ready to go to the boxing training session at the UTM ground early in the morning. The actual event did not start until three thirty p.m., but as a loyal friend, I did not protest. We killed time at the market admiring anything in a skirt, and there were lots to look at. Girls with slender necks, garlanded with multi-coloured beads, thin forearms, and brilliant smiles, most of which revealed beautiful sets of white teeth, and broad pelvises. Thus, one could tell these girls were beautiful from either the front or the back!

A few minutes after two, we started to walk back to the ground, and as soon as we were able to see one end of the field, it was easy to guess that the session would be well attended that afternoon. Everywhere we looked people were gravitating towards the centre of where the action was to be, some simply walking about, others sitting down, and there were also a lot of 'Bulas' around, sparring with each other. As we looked at the far corner of the field, we could see the boxing ring, a simple rectangular structure comprising two sets of strings linking the four wooden pegs sunk in the ground at each corner.

Within a few minutes, there was a whistle blown, apparently an invitation for interested parties to come to the ring. The action was about to start! We rushed to the fore to be able to witness everything from close quarters, and besides, I was going to have the huge task of describing everything in minute detail to our classmates that night in the dormitories and even more so the following day at school to the day-scholars.

In the ring were three squat and mean-looking fellows. One of them introduced himself to the crowd as Justice. He was the captain of the United Transport of Malawi (UTM) Boxing Club. He reminded me of Nero – yes, *the* Nero! Nero of the Makunganya Gang. He in turn introduced the other two as winners from the previous week. Then, briefly, he explained the rules of boxing as he understood them. 'You shall always protect yourself while the bout is going on. Don't hit your opponent below the belt. Don't hit behind the head. When I say, *break*, you break, and you shall follow all my orders.' As he spoke, I looked down at the corner where he was standing, and lying there were two pairs of black, well, black-ish, weathered leather boxing gloves. They had a look of guilt about them, the kind of guilt shown by a bully when found out by a parent in the very act of harassing a harmless child. The gloves were very old, and they looked like they had been through a lot over the years. Only a few areas of original black colour was still visible. They were now almost all dark brown.

'The UTM Boxing Club welcomes anyone interested in the noble art,' pronounced Justice with a raised voice. 'There's no need to register now. What we are going to do is pick those who win their fights here today and on subsequent Sundays. From that group, we will form the core membership of our boxing club. We cannot be fairer than that, can we?' he concluded. I was beginning to see why he was called Justice!

One of the winners from the previous week picked up one pair of gloves and quickly and proudly put them on. Prancing about, he started to shadowbox around the ring, inviting challengers. He looked to be in the middleweight or lightweight bracket or thereabouts, being around five feet seven in height. Slowly, a round-faced slob of a guy started making his way into the ring. The crowd parted in the tradition of Moses' biblical Red Sea, giving way as he passed and then closing behind him. He was somewhere in the fifteen-stone league but probably just as tall as the 'Champion'. There was no trace of emotion, nor any sign of sentiment on his face, only interest in the forthcoming fight he was after. A fight to win. He oozed confidence, touching on the verge of arrogance.

Once in the ring he raised his arms aloft, did a neat 'Ali' shuffle and introduced himself as the 'New Dick Tiger'. He continued to do what I interpreted as showing off, telling the audience he had failed to become a dentist, and in frustration he had taken up boxing to achieve the same goal, in a manner of speaking of course – removing people's teeth but with his fists. 'I enjoy the job immensely!' he said, allowing himself a huge smile, which revealed his own few missing front gnashers.

The crowd, now screaming with excitement and clapping hands, began to sway back and forth as one unitary being, but despite being lifted off my feet by the crush, it did not hurt one bit. Most of them had seen the champion win the previous week and now they wanted to see how good the new challenger was. As for me, I wanted to see how good both pugilists were. As you may have already noticed, there was no weight restriction. You could have a heavyweight fighting a paperweight or a middleweight versus a featherweight – plucking time it was!

I have never seen so many punches thrown in 'cold' within three minutes. It was as if these two boys were sworn enemies, or there were a prize, a material prize, to be won. Not that boxing paid much in my country if anything at all. It appeared as if neither of them were thinking about defence, and every punch thrown seemed to connect. Well, it looked that way from where I stood.

When the bell sounded to signal the end of the first round, it was ignored by the two fighters, probably because they did not hear it due to their emotional intensity and the shouting and screaming from the throng.

The referee had to physically come between them for them to stop throwing punches. He even had to use some choice swear words for good measure.

There was blood coming from the noses and mouths of both guys, and the two corners had a hard time stopping the bleeding within the allocated time between rounds, which was one minute.

The crowd was now just wild, urging the two on with cries of, 'Go on, my son!' or something to that effect. Human behaviour at its blood-thirsty worst. It appeared the challenger had more support, perhaps because of his unlikely build for a boxer, or maybe because of his self-promotion before the fight. Mid-round, the previous week's champion simply could not cope with the stamina of the plump opponent. He suddenly stopped throwing blows, hands down, and then slowly slumped to the ground in a heap.

The crowd was ecstatic. Bula looked stunned. He felt sick and asked whether we could take a walk before the second fight. There was a look of emptiness and awe in his eyes. 'I don't think we're ready for that sort of thing after all,' he resignedly said. It was my turn to be stunned. I could imagine the turmoil in Bula's mind having witnessed the ferocity and brutality of the game in the fight which had just ended. Self-doubt had crept in, leading to a complete loss of confidence, a commodity which, in hindsight, was probably misplaced in the first place.

What we saw later were easy fights for the winners. I remember in one bout the challenger came running out and away from the ring mid-fight, crying. The captain had to run after him to retrieve the gloves. Bula was not impressed with the victor, who was still in the ring waiting for more fodder. 'Go on, Bula, you can take him on,' I shouted jokingly.

'Do you think so?'

'I've seen you spar. I've seen this guy throw wild punches at a little kid who did nothing in the way of defence, nothing at all. At the first smell of blood, he quit. It will be like taking biscuits from a kid. Go on, Bula!' I thought and believed Bula had a chance of victory over this boy.

He smiled at me. 'All right, but maybe next week. If I'm going to make a fool of myself here, I may as well make sure I am still respected afterward, win or lose.'

I have never parried so many punches in my life. For the whole week, Bula was sparring with me, even at night, since we shared the same room in the dormitory.

When we got to the UTM ground the following Sunday, Bula was the first one to walk into the ring. He picked up the gloves and started to shadowbox, walking around the ring confidently. He was of medium build, medium everything really, unless you saw him in the showers, and it did not take long before his challenge was taken up by two guys from two opposite ends of the ring. I was now worried. One of them was Bula's build and height, perhaps an inch taller. The other one was certainly in the six-foot bracket and built like an American Abrams tank. Luckily for Bula, common sense ruled the day, and the bigger guy was ordered to give the other one a chance. Bula and I exchanged glances smilingly, a little relieved. And then I noticed his face had taken on a rather serious expression, just as I imagine Japanese soldiers must have appeared just before launching a Kamikaze attack. Was it a look of resignation now that fate had taken over and reality was looking him in the eye? Almost ready, he walked towards me and handed me his T-shirt and some coins from his pocket, then the gloves were put on the two boxers.

As they stood in their respective corners, I could hear the other chap making growling noises like a wild animal and eyeing poor Bula with squinting eyes. Bula in turn was now hopping on the spot, and probably hopping mad for being in that ring with this guy, and appeared to avoid looking his opponent in the face. I wondered what was going on in his mind!

The first bell rang, and true to his sporting form, Bula began to jump about, both hands up in a defensive stance and on his toes. The other chap threw three quick combinations, all of which missed. Bula would move one way and speedily change direction. He had not thrown a punch yet, whereas his opponent had already thrown quite a few, a few of which had landed on Bula's hands. The longer the round went on, the more confident Bula appeared. He started leading with a left jab, often catching the other fellow. The more the jab landed, the more furious the opponent seemed to get. I became more confident too as I moved to Bula's corner, shouting his name. 'Throw more jabs, Bula! Go on! Yes, that's good – another one!' As he went in with a right for the first time, the opponent connected with a left to Bula's head, but fortunately he did not appear shaken, and when that round ended, he told me he felt okay. I also reminded him of what we had been doing in sparring.

'You throw the right hand just when the opponent's right hand has missed. It's all a matter of timing.' He smiled. I knew he had remembered, proof that his faculties were still intact – I thought and hoped.

Round two started as fast as the first one, with the opponent, now sporting a swelling above his right eye, throwing a quick series of combinations, most of which were missing their target. Slowly, Bula's right hand began hitting home, doubling up, the rib cage and head in one move. It did not take long to notice that the opponent was not moving as fast nor was he throwing many punches, as he had done earlier in the fight. The opponent tried to hold on as Bula moved in with a whirlwind of punches which put him down for the count. There was a lot of excitement among the crowd. As for me, I just could not believe what I had witnessed. Bula was unhurt, and he wanted to fight the bigger chap right away. I stopped him. 'It's my turn,' I told him.

'Oh, yes? Really?'

From the look on his face, I knew he could not believe his ears. 'Don't be hasty now, Davie.' He wasn't comfortable with my idea.

Looking back on it now, I cannot help but accept that my challenge was driven by nothing other than sheer excitement at seeing Bula pull such a wonderful and stylish victory as he did.

As soon as the tall guy picked one pair of gloves and was walking around the ring looking to attract a challenger, I obliged him by picking the other set of gloves. The audience was now wildly shouting in support as soon as I did that and started to walk around the ring, pretending to ooze confidence. Besides, I was a friend and the manager of their new hero, Bula.

It is just possible my opponent was nervous. He had just seen my 'small' companion win with a lot to spare. As we were friends, we must both be good boxers, or so he might have thought. I sensed fear in his dark and now narrowed eyes when the referee was giving us instructions just before the first round. What he might not have known was that I was probably more scared and nervous of fighting him than he was of fighting me.

For some strange reason, the audience began chanting my 'name' – 'Ali, Ali, Ali.' I had become 'Ali' before throwing a punch. I began to float like a butterfly; you couldn't blame me for reciprocating! Not to be outdone, my opponent also started to move on his toes. It was easy to see since none of us wore shoes. His first two jabs landed on my jaw, on the right. I soon woke up to the jab, and the following ones were now hitting the air or landing on my raised arms. I had not landed any punches at all and was missing wildly. Slowly, I could sense the disappointment in the crowd. I knew I had to create my luck by starting to get in close and throwing punches into his midriff. I could just about hear Bula's voice, 'Get low … the ribcage … the ribcage … both hands … go on – get to work, now!'

I landed a few more hard ones on both sides of my opponent's ribcage as advised, but by the end of the first round, my right jaw was getting heavier. The jab had done some damage, albeit superficially.

'You can't beat this guy if you box. Fight, him! You have the punch. He hasn't. Go on, use it!' Bula whispered to me as I stood in my corner, mouth slightly open, attempting to take in enough air before the second round. The bell went. My opponent, noticing my swollen jaw, came in fast, aiming at the same spot. When one or two punches landed on it, I felt more pain than before. Moving in close, I somehow found myself on the floor.

Bula told me later, much later, that I had been hit on the chin with an uppercut. I remember the referee counting, 'Four … five … I did not hear him mention the first three digits.

'Get up! Get up!' shrieked the crowd, with Bula's voice echoing above the throng. I was up at the count of eight. Now, angry and obviously embarrassed, I looked at Bula.

We looked at each other, and although I could not hear the words, his lips were saying, 'Fight him! Fight him!'

It was time for action, and I plowed right into my opponent. I hit him low. I hit him high, the cheers in the audience acting like a drug. I did not stop throwing punches until the man was down. As the referee was counting, I noticed blood on my shorts, and looking down at my opponent, I saw two big cuts, one on top of his right eye and an even bigger one on his cheekbone. There was also blood from my slightly cut lower lip. Bula was so excited. I was surprised when I noticed this injury, because I felt all right and wasn't in any pain at all. The victory amazed me. Bula and I were both over the moon, in a manner of speaking – our boxing careers were off to a cracking start.

The whole week, our dormitory and class heard nothing but the two of us bragging about our unexpected achievements. They were now secretly being invited to accompany us to the fights the following Sunday.

It was on a hot Sunday afternoon the following week when our group of learners, noisy and excited about what they had been promised they would see, left the hill on which our school stood for the UTM football ground in lower Blantyre altitude-wise. They had spent a week listening to ear-bursting bragging from Bula and me about our exploits in the boxing ring, and they wanted to witness our heroism first-hand. Their expectations were raised even higher when arriving at the UTM ground, they heard cheers as soon as the regulars recognised us. There was loud applause, and the names 'Ali' and 'Baby Ali (Bula) were carried on the air. We raised our fists in response as we noticed the evident admiration on the faces of our classmates.

As we chatted, waiting for the competition to start, my mind was gripped with uncertainties. I wondered if presented with a strong and durable opponent I would survive. If I lost, how badly hurt would I be, egotistically and physically? Mind you, there was no ringside doctor, let alone a first-aid expert or equipment around the ring. Once or twice Bula and I exchanged glances. I wondered if he was thinking about the same things that were going through my mind. This was going to be the moment of truth. We had to win, or our classmates would laugh at our expense for the whole school term and beyond. Should the unthinkable happen, they would even laugh us out of school. Mean guys, these, as mean as old Fleet Street hacks, one might add! Ouchy!

The first two fights involved small boys, and they were both stopped when the eventual loser began to cry. I remember the last of them complaining that the opponent had poked his index finger in his nostril. 'But he's wearing gloves!' exclaimed the referee.

'Well, it just feels like it,' said the boy as he took his gloves off and lunged at the winner, who was now smugly sitting just over ten metres outside the ring. A bare-fist fight was underway. They both had to be restrained, but not before the winner had a cut eyebrow on the right side. The earlier result was reversed, unofficially of course, to a draw. Fair play? My mind boggled!

The ring was now empty, apart from the referee, who was soliciting punters. Suddenly, Bula walked in and picked one pair of gloves. He shadowboxed a little, making sure his shoulders showed a lot of movement for special effect, most threatening to any aspiring challenger, he thought. He looked convincingly strong and able, even to me. As a joke, I walked into the ring as if to take him on. There was a lot of laughter among the spectators, including our school group. Bula playfully indicated I was too tall. As I withdrew, a shorter challenger walked into the ring to take Bula on. He was roughly the same height as Bula, but having no shirt on, we could see his body looked a lot more muscular than Bula's.

Turning towards Bula, I could see there was apprehension in his eyes, so I crossed the ring to encourage him, to be in his corner. The opponent, who was introduced as Josafati, did not show any sign of regard for Bula. He stood in his corner as the gloves were being put on, his eyes directed straight at Bula with what was then called the 'eyes-of-a-wolf' look. Like an angry dog or a wolf, the narrowed-eyes stare distorts the bridge of the nose and the mouth at the same time. I had read somewhere that the right thing to do if one were fighting someone like that was to avert their eyes. So, I told Bula to avert his.

'He is trying to psyche you out, Bula. Don't look at him,' I warned. As they were being given the boxing rules, and like the other guy the previous week, Josafati started growling like a dog to more and even louder cheers from the crowd. The bout began with both fighters showing off different styles. Bula was moving from left to right and changing direction quickly to confuse the challenger. The latter was charging forward with his head held very low and swaying his upper body from left to right like a chameleon, only faster, a lot faster. There were more cheers of appreciation and encouragement from opposing fans even before a punch was thrown.

Bula threw three quick punches, missing two, the only good one glancing off the top of the head of the challenger, who looked up at Bula and smiled as if to say, 'Do you call that a punch?' This was greeted with more cheers from the crowd. Then he threw a short jabbing left, which landed on Bula's jaw, and he followed it with two, left and right, to Bula's body. Following another hook and a body shot from Josafati, Bula looked a little worried and responded with his uppercut, which missed by a mile. It was easy to see the frustration in his eyes.

I shouted some words of reassurance. 'He doesn't eat nails, Bula. He's only human. Go on, keep moving!'

He looked at me as if to say, 'I would rather go home.' I avoided looking at our class classmates at the other end of the ring. Things were looking bad. The round ended with Bula on the receiving end of the challenger's long, piston-like jab.

My advice to Bula was to concentrate on defence and hope to catch up with his tormentor in the third and last round when hopefully he would be slower and a tad more tired. Bula just looked at me, but there was some hidden determination in his eyes – if only he could use it. Round two started with Bula moving fast towards Josafati, with hands held in front of his face. I realised he had decided to fight inside (close range) to nullify Josafati's damaging left jab. In no time at all, it was Josafati who looked uncomfortable. 'Baby Ali' was in the ascendancy once again. Again and again, the referee had to separate them due to the challenger's holding tactics. Bula's round.

The third round followed the same pattern as the second. There was one important difference though. Bula's shots were now snappy and aimed with much more accuracy. There was a head-splitting roundhouse, that started from Bula's waistline and thundered onto the temple of the challenger, putting him flat on his back. Embarrassingly, he tried to get up at the count of seven or eight, but his legs had had enough – they could not support him.

You should have seen Bula – the excitement, the bragging, telling me and all the others that he knew what he was doing all along. I believed him. After all, he seemed to have ignored his manager's advice, my advice, and still won and won well. How could I argue with a boxing genius?

The excitement which Bula's endurance, his boxing, and his round-house punch had aroused took a long time to die down. It was easy to see that Bula was on cloud nine. The eternal smile on his lips spoke volumes.

There was now another aspiring boxer in the ring, a heavy-weight of around fourteen stone and at least six feet in height. He looked hungry and angry. He had the kind of looks we associated with charcoal salesmen: torn clothes, unkempt hair, and generally dirty. Such people carried two-hundred-pound bags full of charcoal on their backs as they went from door to door on their selling rounds. They were strong men.

The longer he walked around the ring, bashing the two gloves against each other as he did so, the more his eyes turned to me. I felt exposed.

'Made to measure for you, Davie?' Bula asked rhetorically. There is no avoiding this one, I thought. I faked a few steps forward to loud applause from the crowd. Even Josafati looked glad to see me take on the 'charcoal' man. Deep down, I was petrified. I was not sure whether my first win was a fluke or not. The confidence simply was not there. I did not have a battle plan. I had not had the advantage of watching this man fight before, but neither had he seen me fight before, I hoped. This gave me a little more confidence. If I am a little afraid, I thought, so is he.

'Come on, Davie, loosen up,' instructed Bula in a low voice, now standing by my side as the winner of the previous fight. 'Boxing is seventy percent psychology. You know that. Dance around and look menacing. Give him the evil eye as the gloves are being put on. Make him feel he is nothing! Put the frighteners on him. Think of him as you do of me. Only this time, make sure you take his head off!' I still ask myself who told Bula that boxing was seventy percent psychology! He concluded his pep-talk just as the referee called us for the usual talk before the start of a fight.

Bula came to the centre of the ring, gently massaging my neck and shoulders from behind. 'Give him the evil eye now,' he whispered to me again. I did attempt the evil eye, but there was no sign of fear in the eyes of my opponent. Maybe he thought I always looked like that. I was already perspiring. I felt uneasy. A man who earns his daily crust by lifting two-hundred-pound heavy charcoal bags was not to be taken lightly.

'Ali! Ali! Ali!' chanted the crowd as the first bell sounded, signalling round one.

'Pace yourself, Davie,' advised Bula from my corner. 'Pace yourself, and keep your arms higher. Keep moving.'

My first punch, a jab, landed on the face of the Charcoal Man, but he hardly acknowledged it. He replied with a straight right to my chin. I was slightly hurt but stayed on my feet as I held onto him. The referee split us. 'Stay close to him, Davie,' I could hear Bula call behind me. I threw three quick punches to the Charcoal Man's ribcage. A fourth one landed below his belt, which the referee warned me for. I moved forward with hands high, shielding my face, and as I did so, punches began raining on those areas of my head that remained exposed. Some land-ed on my gloves and arms, and the pain was growing with every punch which landed. I do not think I threw more than a doz-en punches in the entire round, compared with my opponent's what seemed a hundred-plus. The round ended with me on the receiving end. There was a little swelling just below my right eye and grazing above my left.

'You're showing him too much respect. For every punch he throws, respond with one or two of your own. He can't go on at that speed for the remaining two rounds,' Bula reasoned.

The crowd was a bit subdued now. Ali was getting whopped.

Round two began as the first one had finished, with the Charcoal Man throwing wild punches, only now I was bobbing and weaving better, causing him to miss with most of them, and those which landed were without much power. My jab was now back on duty, occasionally stopping the Charcoal Man in his tracks as he moved forward. He was slowly getting disconcerted and exasperated. He threw even more wild punches, one of which landed on the side of my head, sending me sprawling onto the floor. I was not badly hurt and was up at the count of four. There were some whistling sounds in my ear, which felt heavier than usual, proof that it had swollen from the impact. It was now my turn to get angry. As soon as the fight resumed, I charged forward, throwing 'bombs' with both hands, most of which landed. The round ended with me on the attack. The crowd was once again cheering me on wildly.

'One more round to go,' said Bula. 'Just one. The last one. Are you okay?' he asked. I was and responded with a nod. 'He looks tired. You can take him out, but don't get careless. Okay, let's go,' he ordered as the bell sounded for round three.

I had fought flat-footed all along but now I was on my toes. Time to show the style. I was floating like a tiring butterfly and mostly stinging like a bee. I kept my distance, taking advantage of my long reach. As the round wore on, the Charcoal Man, who was by now bleeding from the nose rather badly, caught me with another punch, an uppercut, to the chin. I went down to a count of six. When the referee asked me whether I wanted to continue or not, I soundlessly indicated my desire to go on. Charcoal Man having taken his best shots already, I decided it was time to throw caution to the wind. Toe-to-toe, we exchanged punches non-stop. The screams from the crowd were now at a fever pitch. The 'Ali! Ali!' chant was all but drowned out by shouting and hand-waving fans as the non-stop bruising action continued. The Charcoal Man was now on the retreat, moving backwards into the crowd after the ring ropes had given way under his weight. I was in hot pursuit, unleashing more punishment at an opponent who had become defenceless. The referee ended the fight when my opponent stumbled and fell on the uneven surface, and being too weak to get up, he was counted out. His face was a mask of blood and mine puffed up and bleeding from the mouth.

The spectators, most of them, like me, bare-footed and dressed in khaki shorts, the cheapest available clothing material on the market, and a variety of coloured shirts at varying stages of wear, were drenched in sweat. Their feet and legs were spattered with red dust, and to crown it all, almost literally, their heads did not escape the red-dust treatment. They looked wild as they ran towards me after watching me win a tough fight.

When the Charcoal Man eventually managed to convince himself that his legs could give him the needed support to stand erect and walk, he came to where I was, still surrounded by adoring, screaming fans, shook my hand, and hugged me. 'You have won today, but next week, I want to fight you again. Congratulations!' he said with a forced smile on his swollen lips, spitting blood and wincing with pain as he said this. The crowd continued to cheer and applaud – for both of us. They waved their arms and yelled, the patter of their feet raising more red dust. We had both contributed to a good fight. The evening sun, streaming through the nearby leafless autumnal trees, turned the red dust which engulfed us all to a rich gold hue, which for that moment looked like the colour of our little world, normal and endearing.

The walk back to the Hill must have been a joyous one for Bula and the other guys. It was hard going for me though. The three-mile walk seemed like a slog. What was making matters worse was the fact that I was unable to move my jaw freely, so I was not contributing to the chat. The nearer we got to Soche Hill Secondary School, the steeper the climb got. There were heavy rain clouds gathering in the northern sky, and above us the sky was pale slate grey. The sun had just gone down.

'When is the next fight then, Champ?' asked Snowden, holding my right hand playfully.

'What do you mean, when's the next fight? Next weekend, of course,' added Ivor. I tried to laugh. It must have sounded as if someone had described to me what laughter was but refused to give a demonstration. I was in a lot of pain and was still swallowing blood from a cut on the inside of my right cheek Ivor and Snowden were my classmates, and we grew closer as the months went by. We were a group of boys who worked hard in class and laughed just as hard outside of it.

Bula must have noticed there was something wrong with me.

'You look so tired, Davie. Are you all right?'

'I'll be okay,' I responded softly.

His thin eyebrows resembled two steps of doubt leading up to a bewildered frown as he listened to my response.

'Has the bleeding stopped? Let's see,' he said as he reached up for my chin, causing me to take evasive action with a little scream.

'You're not okay, are you, Davie?'

My lower jaw was not moving with its usual freedom, but not wanting to alarm the others, I still insisted everything was all right.

During intervals on Monday morning, the whole school heard of our heroic exploits the previous day. I could see we both felt good getting all the attention and adoration. I only wished there had been a less painful way of gaining it.

The Christmas holidays were around the corner, and I had sought permission from Father to spend one week at Bula's home in Ntenjela, near Lunzu, in Blantyre. He had invited me, and both his parents were aware of my visit.

We got off the bus at Lunzu Market, and Bula and I, with heavy suitcases and holdalls in hand, started to walk towards Ntenjela. Bula had given me the impression that Ntenjela was just behind Lunzu Market. It was anything but. We must have walked for around four miles when Bula said, 'Do you see that house on the left ahead of us? That's my home.' We still had around two hundred metres to cover.

The house could not be described as small. It was built of burnt red bricks and had a corrugated iron sheet covering it. As we turned into the driveway, I could see between the small rocks a crop of pineapples on both sides of the path, and there were different colours of bougainvillea flowers around the house. They were red, white, purple, and yellow. The red soil grounds appeared well looked after, and the house felt homely. It had been constructed on a knoll, and as I stood on the front porch I could see in the receding distance several villages to the east and south.

Bula's mother was a nurse at Mlambe Hospital, a private Roman Catholic hospital located at Lunzu, and she was off-duty that day. The father, Mr Chiwaya, commuted to work in central Blantyre every day on his bike, a forty-kilometre round-trip of cycling, five days a week. He worked as a manager at one of the clothing companies in town. He wasn't home when we arrived.

Bula and I were to share a bedroom that had two entrances. One could access it from inside the main house or by using the other entrance on the side of the veranda. Dinner that evening was nsima with charcoal-grilled baby pigeons, and there was mpilu as our vegetable. In the local culinary culture, it is a great honour to be offered such a delicacy as your first meal in someone's home. As I greedily demolished the two baby pigeons, I could understand why this delicacy was preferred to chicken by many people. Years later, I enjoyed for breakfast this special dish once again at the Addis Ababa Hilton Hotel. It brought back good memories from Ntenjela.

The next day was a Saturday, and Bula had whispered to me that there was a dance in a nearby village. An old primary-school friend had invited him. Obviously, Bula's mother couldn't allow him to go to such an event at night, so we had to sneak out after dinner that night. I felt rather uneasy cheating his parents in this way. What if they found out? What if something untoward happened to us there? Finally, we agreed to use a different lie, which was that we were going to my cousin's birthday that night and that we would not be long. Permission was granted by the parents, and after dinner that night they wished us well and said that they were looking forward to our safe return.

When we arrived at the dance-party at around eight p.m., the place was already buzzing. There were two large loudspeakers and a disc player. In those days, it was mostly vinyl LPs, singles, and cassettes being used by DJs. We were welcomed by the owner of the dance-party, whose name, I was informed, was Weston. Jovial, short, with a dark mahogany look, Weston seemed to be smiling each time I saw him walking around the dance floor. He explained to us that, 'This dance-party ndi yo becha,' meaning that, if you want to dance, you pay five tambala to the DJ, who will announce your name and the disc you want played and whom you would like to join you on the dance-floor. In case you are wondering how this arrangement worked, well, I will tell you. This meant that only those invited by the sponsor should be on the floor and dancing, and everyone else should not be seen bobbing their heads or stamping their feet in response to the song. Those who transgressed this rule were warned, and if they didn't listen, they would be roughed up. That night, over three fights were emanating from such lapses. Most of them were under the influence of alcohol.

Later that night, two guys arrived and went straight to the DJ, paying him for two songs to be played consecutively. When the songs were played, the two guys waddled onto the dance-floor and sat down back-to-back, looking around to make sure no one was moving in any noticeable way to their songs. Of course, no one was! This conduct was called a power play. Stronger DJs usually did not allow power play.

Bula and I were invited to dance by several sponsors throughout the night. We were back home just before one a.m.

We spent the next few days visiting Bula's relatives, whom he hadn't seen for years. We did a spot of fishing in the nearby river. I found Bula's parents very supportive and loving of their children, including Bula. They had six children in all, three of each gender.

Bula saw me off at Lunzu Market, where I boarded a Lilongwe-bound United Transport Company Leyland bus.

When we got home in Lilongwe, my brother, Chalela, had unwittingly told our houseboy Eliya of my boxing skills. Eliya did not look at this information as a secret to be kept away from my parents.

One day, as we were pushing my cousin Edward's car, which had failed to start due to a weak battery, Eliya shouted, 'Let Davie push it on his own. After all, he is a boxing champion in Blantyre.'

My dad, who was within earshot, responded with a question. 'Is he?'

Eliya, now looking at my dad, continued, believing he was giving Dad some good news. 'Yes, he is a member of the UTM Boxing Club in Blantyre. Master Chalela told me last week.'

'Davie, is that true? I send you to Blantyre to study and you join a boxing club? Chalela, is that true?' I could see Dad was fuming!

'Well, he has not joined a boxing club. It's just a place we go as students to watch boxing …'

'Davie, I do not want to hear that you are taking part in this kind of sport. Do you want to become punch-drunk? Do you know that with one punch you can kill someone or indeed get killed? I do not want to hear this nonsense again,' he concluded as he disappeared into the house.

The following school year started the second week of January, and I only had one pressing issue on my mind, and that was how to tell Bula and company that I had now been forced into early retirement from boxing by my angry father.

***

Life at Soche Hill was always full of fun and excitement. We had the usual mix of eager students, show-offs, resident comedians, and bullies. We even had academics. The last weekend of the month was the most exciting, because many students would have received their pocket-money from their parents or guardians. It was the only weekend we were allowed time to go into the local town of Limbe for shopping. To those who hadn't received their divvy at this point and their home was not too far, it was a window to use to go home and collect some extra foodstuffs and other everyday toiletries, and if they were lucky, some came back with a little pocket-money as well.

Boarding-school food was carbohydrate-rich, meaning that there were too many mealie-mill dishes throughout the day. There was a maize-flower porridge for breakfast, and there was a hard maize-flower porridge (nsima) for lunch and dinner. For protein, there were usually red kidney beans crudely cooked. Once a week, there was beef served with nsima. However, one had to search on one's plate for the piece of beef mentioned on the menu. To enhance the stew, the cook used to mix it with cabbage. The dish should have been called beef-spiced cabbage stew, in my view. This was the immediate reason learners looked forward to the month's end; it was a time to augment the dire diet the school was providing.

We were all expected back on the school campus by five p.m., and there was a punishment for not being back in time, just as there are punishments for all manner of transgressions in schools. So from around three p.m. to four-thirty p.m., most of those who had left the campus early in the morning could be seen waddling back with their holdalls in their hands or on their backs.

Some boys who came from relatively well-to-do families would return wearing entirely different attire from what they had worn that morning. Boys usually came back from town at around three thirty p.m. to four thirty p.m. in the afternoon, carrying their holdalls full of a variety of items, mostly foodstuffs, and those with real money used the day out to make an addition or two to their wardrobes. We used to collect cuttings of flamboyantly attired African Americans, mostly show-businesspeople, from magazines like *Ebony* or *Eleganza*. All that was required was to show a local tailor called Jimmy, located in Limbe, whatever style you thought would look good on you, give him the material, usually bought at the Pound Shop near the rail-crossing in the same town, and within a few weeks you would be wearing your own *Eleganza* outfit. Any secondary-school guy worth his salt knew Jimmy. He was a brand name in our fashion stakes.

If I have said I have not seen any young people dressed the way we used to, I would not be exaggerating, and I am being very modest about it. Guys like Ramsey, Aaron, Duncan, and Bula were our fashion-setters. Duncan had asked Jimmy to tailor for him a jumpsuit with a huge butterfly collar, from which his head appeared to pop out like a tortoise's head from its shell. And from the way Duncan swanned about when adorned in this attire and a pair of platform shoes, it was easy to conclude that the boy was feeling he was on top of the world. Bula had a beige military jacket which his brother had brought back from Sandhurst Staff College in the United Kingdom and which he treasured greatly, because it was the clothing item he wore to school dances or when he was on a special date with his girl-friend, Edith. His favourite trousers were one of Tailor Jimmy's creations – a pair of black crimpling corduroys with very wide bell bottoms, of which the front zip went all the way from the crutch to just below the breast line.

Bula was one of the top guys in fashion, and he used to call himself the soul brother number one. He modelled himself around Wilson Pickett, the black American rhythm-and-blues artist. There were times some of us would be honoured to inad-vertently watch Bula walk from the dormitories to the school blocks around the car park, adorned in the attire I have described above, including the expected pair of platform shoes. Witnessing this was to witness a young man in total control and at peace with himself and his surroundings, and if he were an ice cream cone, he would have licked himself to nothingness! He walked like he was floating on thin air; quite a picture to behold with great admiration!

On weekdays, except Wednesdays, we were restricted to wear-ing school uniform, which consisted of a white shirt and a pair of grey long- or short-trousers. One Wednesday, Bula and I wore long-trousers, which had been suitably adapted to meet our need for self-expression, the hems of which had been unstitched and the threads frayed out to give a fluffy look just above the shoes. We thought we looked hip and unique, and we were right, for during prep, the art teacher (who was also the boarding master),, whom we had nicknamed Mphaka (a cat), because of his stealthy movements when tracking down students suspected of breaking school rules, noticed Bula's trousers and promptly ordered him to report to the headmaster's office. 'Go and ask him if this kind of dressing is acceptable at this school.' Instead of going straight to the office, Bula went behind the school buildings and removed the offending frills, using a flattened Coca-Cola bottle top as a blade.

When he finally stood before the headmaster, he explained that he had been sent by Mr Nampeya to find out if the school allowed his kind of trousers. 'Ah, I see,' said the headmaster. 'No, we don't. You see, they've got to be grey.' At this point, he picked up the telephone and ordered the general office to bring him a colour sample of the school uniform. When Bula arrived back in class, we all, including Mr Nampeya, naturally assumed that it had been the headmaster who had cut off the offending frills. Teacher Nampeya felt better for it, that the headmaster had upheld his position!

In the evenings, after the lights were off in the dormitory, entertainment was brought to us by Nelson (surname withheld). He was a quiet, lanky young man, who used to read fake news. The 'bulletins' contained all the local gossip, including who was going out with whom, who had been ditched, who ate what and how much in the dining hall, and he always exaggerated. First, he would mention the name of an imaginary city followed by a brief report. The funniest place, the city for hard-hitting and amusing stories, was one he called Lokoshoni. Somehow, by association, because he used to bounce his jokes off me, I was also stuck with the name Lokoshoni. The trouble was that, unknown to us, whatever was happening in our dormitory, the girls would also know about it, because, secretly, Nelson was a clandestine newsreader for them too, mostly at weekends.

One weekend, we went to Chiradzulu Secondary School, about twenty miles away from our school, for a competitive football match in the WenelaWenela is Malawian shorthand, meaning the Witwatersrand Native Labour Association – a recruitment organisation in charge of recruitment of workers for the federated Chamber of Mines, based around Johannesburg, who looked to centralise recruiting and therefore drive down labour costs. Despite being banned in 1913, Malawians retained a presence in the mines throughout the 1920s and 1930s through to the late 1970s. Cup competition, and as it was going to be my first game with the school's main football team. I was very excited and nervous. Apart from this big chance to prove my sporting prowess, I had just started going out (perhaps I should say, seeing, for we never went out that much) with a lovely girl called Jo, who was the captain of the school's netball team and one of the most elegant girls in the school.

The girls played their game first, and having won and knowing ours was about to begin in a few minutes' time, the girls came over to stand along the touchline to watch and cheer us on. Jo was surprised to see me on the pitch, for she knew I played volleyball but not football. Wearing the number six jersey (defensive midfielder), I was to play just in front of the defence, and that day, I played out of my skin. With a new girlfriend watching, I could not afford to do anything less. The strikers had a tough time breaking through the opposition's defence, and at halftime there were no goals scored by either side.

With ten minutes to go before the final whistle, I unexpectedly found myself in possession of the ball. Running so fast with it, I crossed the centre line, trying to pass it across, but there was nobody from my team ahead of me. I was so scared I might lose it when suddenly I came face-to-face with their charging goalkeeper. I just kept on running, yes, past him and straight into the net. How? I do not know to this day. 'Lokoshoniiiii' excitedly sang out the girls, including Jo, of course.

My teammates could not contain themselves either. Although the goal was most certainly a fluke, they knew it might see us through to the next round of the cup. As soon as the final whistle was blown, I saw Nelson surrounded by the girls. He could not look me in the eye. His secret was out. He had told the girls our private dormitory names and from that day onwards the whole gang was known by our nicknames.

Brian 'Bula'
Brighton 'Scoop'
Duncan 'Dunka'
Aaron 'Loony'
Clement 'Ment'
And yours truly, Davie 'Lokoshoni' Katsonga

All Jo's love letters to me were now being addressed to Loko. These were days of great fun and innocence, lots of the latter, although the impression given to one's chums was one of the great secret canoodles in the Soche pine and guava forest, trips which were indeed taken but mostly for the fruits. Once in the forest, I simply did not know how to set the ball rolling. Come to think of it, I doubt if any conquest narrated by anyone in our group had any truth in it. The idea then was to impress the others.

At weekends, those with girlfriends practiced their skills in dealing with women. We could either go into the forest for guava picking, or for those who were feeling particularly energetic, there was always hill-climbing or walking in the nearby villages. One evening, during a study period, Bula and I arrived early for prep, and I wrote on the blackboard the line, 'Something is worrying me', which was the title of an Otis Redding song. Why I wrote it down is hard to say; I just do not know. On the following day, a Saturday, Jo suggested we go guava-picking in the forest. It was on a breezy, hot day, and I thought I was looking particularly striking in a purple T-shirt and a pair of blue denim bell bottoms. Jo looked lovely in a flowing, light-blue cotton dress. After picking and eating quite a few fruits, she startled me with a question.

'What's worrying you, Davie?'

I was not worried and did not know why she thought I was. 'Nothing,' I replied, puzzled. 'Why?'

'Yesterday, on the blackboard, that was your handwriting, wasn't it?' She had recognised my handwriting because of the frequent, almost daily, notes we secretly passed to each other. I could have easily recognised hers had she left a message on the blackboard.

'Ah! That!'

'Yes. Davie, what's the matter?' she insisted.

Other than telling her the truth, which was not in the least bit interesting, I decided to sweeten the issue.

'Well, Jo,' I started while trying to organise my line of response, 'I've been told that Ramsey and you are in touch and things are getting serious, and as you can imagine, I'm worried,' I concluded with what I thought was a convincingly sad look on my face.

'Who's been telling you this, Davie?' she demanded.

'People who know,' I said, not giving anything away, not that there was anything to give away.

'Do you believe them?'

'Of course not, but I can't help getting worried about it,' I answered coolly, getting into the swing of things.

'Listen, Davie. You should know that Ramsey is my past. You're my present. People will always spread rumours to destroy us. You're the one I love, and that's all there is to it,' she concluded, planting a kiss on my cheek. 'Let's sit down; I'm beat.' I obliged. She sat on a guava-tree branch while I sat on a rock about a metre or so from her. In the distance, all the majesty of Mount Mulanje, with its mist-covered peak, was in evidence as the breeze whistled musically through the pines around us. The sun's exquisite heat-induced drowsiness seemed to coat our love and the moment in a granite cocoon, unshakeable and everlasting. I was certainly not worried anymore. A few years later, I wondered what she meant when she said, 'I beat; I want to sit down.' Was she trying to tell me something? Nah, silly! Just growing pains, I guess.

After several memorable guava-picking expeditions, I saw Ragu, who had written his Ordinary Levels and was awaiting results, at the girls' hostel. He had come to see Jo. I could not believe my eyes. Jo had assured me he was her past. When I confronted her later that evening, she denied anything was going on. 'He wants to; I don't. I have moved on.' The academic year was melting toward our Ordinary Levels, and I did not see or hear anything about Ragudzeni and Jo.

Ragudzen was arguably the best-dressed and most fashionable guy in our school. Although he was a year ahead of me, he was approachable and friendly to those of us in the lower grades. The girls liked him too. Ragudzen was also a brilliant dancer. You should have seen him in his platform shoes and bellbottoms at the school's Friday night entertainment hall. Quite a picture!

After writing the examinations I moved to Lilongwe, while Jo remained in Blantyre, where Ragudzeni stayed. It didn't take long for Jo to dump me. Soon after, I heard from Brighton that he had met Jo and that she looked positively pregnant. I later learnt that it was Ragudzeni who had knocked her up! As was the norm in such cases at the time, he denied responsibility until the day of the court hearing for damages. Do not ask me what had been damaged – mostly pride, I would have thought. The two families contesting the case knew each other well, and the magistrate knew both sides too. This magistrate was notoriously, some would say famously, tough in such cases, because, it was alleged, his daughter had suffered a similar fate at the hands of some peasant from Manyowe, a Blantyre suburb. To escape without punishment, the man had to be white, blue-eyed, blond, and hopefully gay, and the offspring completely black, since most cases involved Indigenous Malawians, otherwise the defendant never stood a chance.

These modern ways of proving paternity had not arrived over the local borders. My friend, Ragudzeni, came to court dressed in a very fancy purple shirt with collars like jet-fighter's wings and a pair of purple bell bottoms. The entire ensemble was tastefully rounded off by a pair of beige-and-brown platform shoes. Generally, this style of dress was frowned upon by parents, including his own, let alone the magistrate. Others would say he didn't dress up as a young man seeking sympathy from this judge.

The moment he set eyes upon the judge who was presiding over the case, Ragudzeni simply froze. Soon after the deliberations had started, the magistrate called for the baby, held it, examined a few details, then beckoned Ragudzeni and gave him the baby to hold. This must have been too much for Ragudzeni to take, so he decided to end it all. Turning his face to the dock, the infant in his arms, he said, 'Sir, I don't know why this matter has come this far; this baby is mine! I have told Jo before that this is the case.' A small, slow-flowing stream of reluctant tears began rolling down his cheeks and gently dropped onto the collars of his reproduction *Eleganza* shirt. The case was dismissed, to be resolved later by the two families. No, there was no marriage, and there were no more court appearances s. They simply resolved the matter between themselves.

Losing Jo was very painful, and it took me a while to recover. I think the blow of this loss was cushioned by the fact that Jo had been Ragudzeni's girlfriend before she was mine. Ragudzeni was simply re-claiming something that was his. I was just the other boy.

My group, which had now assumed the name 'Scoop', was comprised of boys who acted tough and streetwise and were 'ones for the girls', who did not do badly in class either, or on the sports field. We were all-rounders, if you like. As boarding-school scholars, we used to go for the official prep, after supper, for two hours between five-thirty p.m. and seven thirty p.m., during which time we had to study under classroom conditions, that is, in dead silence. Everyone who was not officially ill was expected to attend these study periods. One fateful day in March, when the maize crop surrounding the school was around two metres high on average and we were all in our different study rooms, Brighton came to me and tried to interest me in leaving the school campus to go and buy mandasi fritters at a nearby house from a lady who made them on most days. Brighton did not have to try too hard. I was a pushover for these fritters. Besides, school food was, as I have already pointed out, so awful, and we regularly used to supplement our meals in this way on most days. I excused myself, telling the prefect in charge of the study room, Newton (the Newt) Banda, that I was going to the toilet, but as we reached the school campus boundary, we heard a voice behind us.

'Brighton and Katsonga, where do you think you're going?'

We knew it was, the dreaded Malawi Young Pioneers P.E. teacher. He was neither young nor was he a pioneer. The MYPs were the Life President's crack troops, his eyes and ears, whose presence was felt in all corners of the nation, Every primary and secondary school had its own MYP instructor, and this one was ours.

Without giving a reply, we quickly legged it into the nearby maize field at break-neck speed, knowing we were in trouble. We had had several brushes with the MYP Instructor before, from which we had managed to survive, but we knew, somehow, he was not going to let us get away with it on this occasion. Getting together at the end of the field, under the cover of darkness, we planned our defence. Brighton would admit that he went to buy fritters, and I would stick to my story that I had been in the toilet. The teachers knew I was suffering from a stomach condition at the time, and I had also told Newton I was going to the loo.

Brighton re-entered the school campus by the east side and was a long ten minutes ahead of my entry from the west. By the time I got back, there had been a huge fight, during which Brighton had beaten up the MYP Instructor, who in turn had called on the help of the school's two nightwatchmen. When the headmaster and several other male teachers arrived on the scene, Brighton had beaten them up with a broomstick too! Together they all managed to restrain Brighton and bound him with the rope we had used earlier for tug-of-war. There he was, alone in his room, tied up like a sack of potatoes. I remember someone remarking, 'We knew something like this was *bound* to happen, sooner or later!' When I was questioned by the headmaster and the MYP Instructor, I denied everything and was allowed to go, to report back the following morning after Assembly. That night, the whole dormitory was buzzing. Chins were wagging.

Any boarder will tell you that as students, lives are usually highly controlled. Any time someone does something as audacious as we had done, it puts their spirits in over-drive, something to whisper about for days on end.

The following day, during Assembly, the whole Scoop team was summoned to see the headmaster immediately. We all moved forward in front of the whole school, all, that is, except Brighton, who was still locked in the dormitory. No one was in any doubt about the seriousness of the offence. Beating a teacher, or in this case, teachers, was taking things to the extreme. Although Brighton had been the main protagonist, the rest of us, I suppose, were guilty by association. While our classmates were struggling with tangents and congruence in geometry that morning, we were being marched back to the dormitory, where we all looked unsettled by this turn of events, having been expecting to be taken directly to the headmaster's office. It was a very sombre occasion. I could almost hear a funeral march, the Russian one, things felt that bleak. As we assembled in front of the dormitory building, the boarding master, Mr Mphaka, his bloodshot eyes filled with hatred and negativity called Duncan into the dormitory and straight to his dormitory compartment. We could see them through the louvres as they headed there. After ten minutes or so, as we waited in total silence, petrified as to what fate awaited us, the door opened again, and Mr Nampeya called in the next person until we had all been inside.

We learnt later that after the previous night's fracas, an emergency staff meeting had been called by the headmaster to discuss the activities of 'The Scoop'. Before this incident, at least one of us was being punished for some offence or other, at any one time, for various transgressions, some of which were, in our developing brains, so minute and not deserving of punishment. Were we guilty, though? Not always. There was a certain degree of vindictiveness and pettiness on the part of some of the teachers. Our behaviour, on this occasion, they reasoned, could only have been induced by drugs, so they instigated a surprise search of our dormitory lockers, as witnessed earlier.

They found nothing until, that is, they searched mine. In it, they found some tablets my father had bought for me at Lizulu[4] on the Mozambiquan side of the market. They were for a stomach problem I had, and the school authorities already knew about my condition, but the headmaster seized them as proof of his worst fears – the Scoop Gang was taking illicit mind-altering drugs!

That morning, Brighton was dispatched to the hospital to be evaluated for his mental condition. They reasoned that even if my tablets were for a certain ailment in my body, if taken by a different person, they could induce a varied and unexpected reaction. Brighton was found to be normal, and no illicit drug was apparently found in his blood. When he returned to school after two days, he was suspended for three months for violent behaviour and leaving the school campus without permission.

They accused me of smuggling the drug from Mozambique, ignoring the raising of the national flag, and disrespecting the National Anthem, although I had been punished for the latter two offences already.

They told me that they were sending 'Exhibit A, the stomach-ache drug' to the customs department, who told them the tablets were not sold in Malawi, positive proof, in their view, that I had illegally brought them into the country. I do not know whether they even bothered to have them analysed to prove the drug's usage. The writing on the packaging was all in Portuguese.

That afternoon, I was ordered to hand in all my school textbooks to the headmaster. When I arrived at his office, the headmaster and Mr Zambezi were there, and Mr Nampeya joined us within a few minutes of my arrival. The riot act was read to me because of what they stated was my total lack of respect for

4 Before the liberation war led by Samora Machel spread throughout Mozambique, Lizulu was a bustling commercial center. It featured wine shops, pharmacies, restaurants, and various other establishments typical of a rural trading hub. People from both sides of the border freely used either currency for their purchases. It was in this vibrant setting that my father bought the medication for my persistent stomachache.

my country and thus the president, Ngwazi Dr Kamuzu Banda. And, of course, there was the other very serious offence, that of smuggling. Oh dear, oh dear. Lack of respect for my country? Well, I will plead guilty on this one. There were times when I did not feel I should stand to attention when the flag I despised was being raised. So yes, I did ignore it a few times. The last punishment I had received for such behaviour had been to clear a football ground, one hundred metres by fifty metres, overgrown with grass up to my knees, all alone and with nothing but a garden slasher. To add insult to injury, I had to do this from the last Friday of the school term. While my friends were dancing with the girls, I was slashing away on my own. I did not finish until the following Monday. This time my punishment was worse. I was told I was being *expelled* from school. The Ministry of Education was advised of the decision and so were my parents.

My father was the one person I did not want to know about the troubles I had found myself in, certainly not this kind of jeopardy. He was such a strict parent and very harsh, particularly if he thought I was out of line. Ignoring the national flag was suicidal. If anything, I was putting the whole family in danger, politically speaking. I decided to go and stay with my aunty at her house on the outskirts of Blantyre. She was the only person who could stand up to Father, even more so than my mother. After hearing my story, she decided first to go to the school herself and try and make peace, but she failed, and she was a good negotiator too. Only then did she speak to my father, who was surprisingly cool about the expulsion and asked to speak to me on the telephone. He wanted me to go home at the earliest possible time, and two days later I was back home, in Lilongwe, 205 miles north of Blantyre.

I explained the whole incident to Father, who listened dispassionately and without interruptions, for it was he who taught us children that a primary sign of good brains is a willingness to listen and analyse other people's ideas, even if you do not agree with them. He listened very well. The way he responded was out of character. Short of a slap or two, I was expecting at least a very long and loud lecture.

On Friday afternoon, he took his copy of the letter from my school to the Ministry of Education, which luckily was only thirteen miles away, where he had arranged over the telephone to meet the permanent secretary. After the meeting, he told me that the matter was being passed to the minister himself, who would be making his decision the following Monday. On Sunday we went to an early-morning Roman Catholic Latin Mass, and at the end of the service, as we headed towards the car park, we saw the education minister and his family leaving as well. The two families greeted each other, and as we talked, the two gentlemen, who had known each other professionally for a long time, excused themselves for a few minutes. There was no question in my mind about their conversation's subject.

Driving home a few minutes later, Father told us that the minister felt there was something more to my expulsion than the school was telling us. He promised my father he would get to the bottom of the matter. I thought the minister was openly showing his disapproval of the system which he was part of. The following day, I received a telephone call from Mr. Malunga, the permanent secretary, ordering me to return to school immediately. He also asked to speak to my father – the minister wanted a word. He then told Father he had personally spoken to the headmaster and that a strongly worded letter had been posted, expressing his annoyance at their vindictive behaviour towards an innocent student.

Father did not want me to go back to Blantyre alone, so on the Wednesday, we set off, southbound, arriving at the school at two forty p.m. precisely. I remember this so vividly, because we used to have various sports and games on Wednesdays at two forty-five p.m., the last lesson of the day. Our classroom had louvres facing the main car park, and recognising my father's car and its passenger, most of the class ran out to meet us. Father told me to wait inside the car while he alerted the headmaster about my return. As he walked toward the office, the whole square began to fill with cheering students. I was dragged out of the car, and someone opened the boot, took out my suitcase and other items, and carried them to the dormitory. Before I could start to think about what was happening, I was in the air. They had lifted me and carried me to the dormitory, a good seventy metres. The noise made everyone want to see what the occasion was, and the crowd swelled. Father had to tell somebody to ask me to telephone him at our farm fifty miles away that night, which I did. I felt a hero that day, albeit a hero without a cause.

The headmaster, no doubt under pressure, had allowed me back. He was unable to show my father the offending tablets. They were 'lost', he had apparently informed him. Although I had only been away three weeks, my friends (some of whom I did not know I had before this) were able to tell me lots of stories about how the MYP Instructor had been bragging about my fate and warning anyone who misbehaved that they would end up like me. I spent the next two months or so being ignored by the three Willy, the boarding master and art teacher, never came to check my work the whole of that period. The Malawi Young Pioneer instructor would not talk directly to me during Physical Education, fortunately for him, the headmaster was able to keep out of my way – all out of shame, perhaps, with a tinge of guilt, I thought.

During the same year, the Minister of Education, John Nsonthi, was expelled from the party. Everything he held in his post was taken away. He was disgraced. That night, the MYP Instructor came to our dormitory as we prepared to go to bed. Walking past our room, he began to talk to the chaps in the next compartment about John Nsonthi's expulsion. 'I wonder where some people are going to take their complaints now that their champion is gone?' This was intended for my ears, and everyone knew it. I just had to bite my tongue and pray he did not come to my bedside. My temper was not something I trusted to respect the authority of any kind when provoked, and this time, they would have an irrefutable reason to expel me from school.

Chapter 13

NO PERCY SLEDGE; SUPER DIANA, YES.
THIS IS CERTAINLY MODERN DANCING WITH
POLITICS SPRINKLED ALL OVER IT

Every year, the Malawi Congress Party held their annual convention, and being a well-bAaron ced and fair-minded political organisation, they held it on a round-robin basis. Each of the three regions was given the honour of holding this jamboree once a year. In 1972 it was held in Lilongwe, the headquarters of the central region.

As a teenage student growing up in Malawi, the party convention meant very little to me, except for the fear of hearing the Life President using disparaging remarks against my father in his speech, as he had done in past years.

Chalela had taken and passed all his eight O Levels and was in no doubt which career he was going to follow because Father had already told us that our destiny lay in the family business. 'No one ever got rich working for other people,' he had told us on several occasions.

Any attempts by us to stay longer in Blantyre after school broke up for the holidays were thwarted by Father. He believed in the adage that a change is as good as a rest. He made sure that the day we arrived was the only day of rest. We had to help in the family's catering business.

Nevertheless, our real intention for staying longer in Blantyre was to attend a live concert by the legendary American rhythm-and-blues singer Percy Sledge, who was scheduled to perform at the Kamuzu Stadium on the 16th September 1972. Instead, we spent the whole holiday working behind the counter at Chester's Nightclub Lilongwe.

As the 16th September approached, the advertisements on the radio promoting the show were broadcast almost every thirty minutes. We were so depressed that weeks before the day of the concert, Chalela started to turn off the radio every time an advert for the concert came on the air.

The day after the show, we were expecting photographs in the national newspaper (we called it *The Paper*; it was the only daily publication in the country at the time) showing our musical hero on stage, but the sun rose and set on the 17th August without even a mention of the performance on the national radio neither. Instead, the newspaper's front page printed pictures of people preparing for the MCP Annual Convention.

The leader, Ngwazi Dr. Kamuzu Banda, Life President of the Republic of Malawi, never addressed the nation in the vernacular. Instead, he always spoke in English. A lot of years in America and Britain had taken their toll on his Chewa knowledge. His people, us, we did not doubt him. We had no reason to. It is perfectly understandable that people who stay away from their original countries for as long as he did would forget the entire vocabulary of the native language. Kamuzu had left Malawi when he was only a toddler – ten, to be exact, so he told the nation!

The first man to make a name for himself as an interpreter was John Nsonthi. He was then the Minister of Education, and he was very good at interpreting English into Chichewa at Dr. Kamuzu Banda's rallies. He had such a wonderful way with words that people would go to a mass rally just to hear Nsonthi at work. Had Shakespeare written in Chichewa he would have been proud to have Nsonthi perform his work! Following Nsonthi's fall from grace, the job of interpreter was given to Mr. Chikhakhalala, who failed to live up to the standards set by his predecessor, and from the responses his speeches received, I am sure the president was aware of this. For some reason, the Ngwazi could not fire Mr. Chikhakhalala. It was rumoured that the reason for this was simply that Mr. Chikhakhalala was uncle to Lady Bhekimuzi Mukarakate, the official government hostess. Years later, I proved this link as fact. Her late mother, Anatembo, was Mr. Chikhakhalala's sister, who had served in Dr Hastings Kamuzu Banda's government in various capacities since 1964. He was a man physically slight in body, fastidious, and has been described by those who knew him well as, 'cunning and politically dangerous'.

This powerful politician was elected to the legislative assembly of NyasAaron d in 1961, three years before the country gained its independence and became the Republic of Malawi. He was the second Minister of Finance in Malawi after independence, succeeding Chalela Phillips (later Sir Chalela Phillips) in a post for which the intended candidate had been Dunduzu Chisiza (Chisiza died in 1962 in a car crash). Mr. Chikhakhalala was the only cabinet member not to resign in the notorious cabinet crisis of 1964, after which most of the president's closest lieutenants, their opposition to his policies thwarted, fled the country. (Chinua Achebe in *A Man of the People* admits having used a real situation gleaned from the Hansards of a certain African country to portray his main character, Chief Nanga, the heckler in parliament who hounded out the 'offensive minister' who had just resigned.)

Mr. Chikhakhalala's relationship with Dr Kamuzu Banda might not have been all that rosy, and if it weren't for his blood relationship with Lady Bhekimuzi Mukarakate, he wouldn't have survived in Dr Kamuzu Banda's administration, so it is alleged in the public media and among the academia. Sadly, for him, he is said to have been prone to taking some unilateral decisions, for example, the '1974 Youth Week Inauguration' venue saga, when Mr. Chikhakhalala decided, apparently without Dr Kamuzu Banda's permission, to stage the event in Lilongwe to coincide with the 'New Capital City' inauguration gala Dr Kamuzu Banda had yet to sanction. Dr Kamuzu Banda found this offensive, and he, apparently in the presence of Gwanda Chakuamba, dressed down Mr. Chikhakhalala before instructing Gwanda Chakuamba to rearrange, at a very high cost to the government, the Youth Week inauguration back to Blantyre.

Despite Lady Bhekimuzi Mukarakate's intervention, allegedly, Dr Kamuzu Banda proceeded to remove Mr. Chikhakhalala from the National Celebrations Council and placed him into a politically minor post of Reserve Bank Governor and the ceremonial chairman of the University Council. The Dr Kamuzu Banda–Mr. Chikhakhalala relationship deteriorated further, and it became an uphill struggle, even with Cecilia's active support for Mr. Chikhakhalala to regain his position of prominence. His role as the Chichewa interpreter to Dr Kamuzu Banda was, allegedly, so engineered to make sure that Mr. Chikhakhalala always stayed within the president's line of vision. And when Mr. Chikhakhalala suggested, during one of Dr Kamuzu Banda's speeches on ubiquitous and 'invisible enemies', that ministers and those around the president should carry automatic weapons to 'defend' Dr Kamuzu Banda, Mr. Chikhakhalala was swiftly rapped on the wrist and a temporary replacement interpreter was arranged.

As confidante to the president, Mr. Chikhakhalala was used as Dr Kamuzu Banda's Machiavellian bludgeon during the latter part of Dr Kamuzu Banda's thirty-year tyrannical rule. Mr. Chikhakhalala came to personify the negative actions which Dr Kamuzu Banda carried out.

There was quite a good number of Malawians who thought that Mr. Chikhakhalala had made himself a man without whom nothing in Malawi politics could happen. He behaved rich and looked rich. He made consequential decisions. He was, in the eyes of many Malawians, the government!

The greater majority in Malawi came to hate Mr. Chikhakhalala for the excesses which ideally should have been aimed at Dr Kamuzu Banda himself. While most people became resigned to the 'life presidency' issue (wait until the old man departs), a determination, especially after the Mwanza Assassination, emerged that Mr. Chikhakhalala would never rule Malawi. Yet, in a move demonstrating that Dr Kamuzu Banda embraced democracy much earlier than portrayed, Dr Kamuzu Banda released Mr. Chikhakhalala from his duties as governor of the Reserve Bank and sent him on a two-year sabbatical to the U.S. Congress to study the workings of democracy. When Mr. Chikhakhalala returned in 1989, Dr Kamuzu Banda appointed him as Minister

Without Portfolio, much to the furor and great agitation of multiparty democracy.

When Malawi became a republic in 1966 after attaining independence in 1964, Mr. Chikhakhalala was appointed as Minister of Finance. In 1971, at the Dowa MCP Convention, Mr. Chikhakhalala was the 'primary' sponsor (while another two seconded) for Dr Kamuzu Banda becoming the Life President of Malawi. Dr Kamuzu Banda rewarded him with postgraduate studies in central banking in Britain and France. Later, he was to use his knowledge as governor of the Reserve Bank of Malawi, a post he held for thirteen years.

In January 1995, some months after Dr Kamuzu Banda lost the election to Bakili Muluzi of the United Democratic Front (UDF), Mr. Chikhakhalala, 'Lady', [Bhekimuzi Mukarakate] and others were put on trial for the murder of the four prominent Malawi politicians in 1983 (the so-called Mwanza trial). The two who pleaded not guilty were both acquitted.

People used to call Lady Bhekimuzi Mukarakate, in whispers, the president's 'wife'. This was also denied silently. Well, let me add, that the questioning was just as silent. In Malawi at the time, it was the only way to ask such questions to those who had the kamikaze courage to discuss such matters.

Anatembo (may her soul rest in eternal peace; she died in 1978 or early 1979) was Lady Bhekimuzi Mukarakate's mother. When I officially asked for the hand of Allena Allena Mukarakate in marriage, at the time I learnt that Lady Bhekimuzi Mukarakate's mother's health was failing, although she was not yet admitted to the hospital. She and her husband, Mr Mukarakate, were very fond of me, and on most occasions when we met in the Old Town, Mr Mukarakate would bid farewell to his uniform-clad Malawi Young Pioneer driver to join me in my car for the rest of whatever he happened to be doing on that day. He was a very chatty man with whom I struggled to initiate any conversation, because I just couldn't pick any theme to engage him with. He was officially and practically on the side of Kamuzu Banda's regime, whereas I was reluctantly in it and struggling to hide the emotion tightly within myself.

So, I always let the old man Mukarakate lead the conversation, always prolonging my responses to erode the minutes we were going to be together on that day. Despite that, I found the time spent with him culturally enriching. He never discussed politics! And when Anatembo was finally admitted to the Kamuzu General Hospital, I would arrive there and hear from family members visiting her that she hadn't spoken a word that day. As soon as she heard my voice she would open her now sallow-looking eyes and stretched out and clasp my hand and in a hardly audible voice say, 'Muli bwanji?' ('How are you?') She would ask me how business was progressing, how my parents were, etcetera. She seemed to wish to engage me in conversation although her body was struggling for the energy to continue with such an exertion.

Anatembo and her husband, Mr Mukarakate, were two very loving and humane individuals. This is how I will always remember them.

On one occasion, the Ngwazi was in Lilongwe, addressing his loyal subjects at a rally within the city with Mr. Chikhakhalala one one side and his beloved companion, the Official Government Hostess Her Excellency Lady Bhekimuzi Mukarakate, on the other side. Also seated somewhere on the platform among his cabinet ministers was the previous interpreter, the honourable John Nsonthi.

Kamuzu started to speak and then, suddenly, he stopped abruptly in mid-stream, so to speak. What exactly was being said by the Life President, followed by an interpretation from Mr. Chikhakhalala, I do not recall, but suddenly Dr Kamuzu Banda said, 'No, no. John? Where is Nsonthi?' This surely disproved that the Life President's knowledge of the local language was not up to scratch!

When Nsonthi humbly stood up and made his way to the front of the platform there were loud cheers from the audience, screams, people waving their hands in the air, drums beating, and whistles blowing for well over a minute, or so it seemed. Mr. Chikhakhalala sheepishly walked to the chair he had occupied before the start of the president's speech. The first sentence *he* interpreted was greeted with the same prolonged applause and handclapping.

When the meeting was over, all the fifty thousand-plus people had nothing else to talk about but Nsonthi. Those who were in the know did not like what they saw. As an executive chairman of the Grain and Milling Company, Nsonthi still enjoyed many privileges, including a direct line to the president, but not even he had been fooled by this appointment. He even confided to his private secretary his fears and the way he felt he must conduct himself in public, always implying that the man behind his downfall had been, allegedly, Mr. Chikhakhalala.

Now that Mr. Chikhakhalala had been humbled in front of the nation and his very powerful niece, Lady Bhekimuzi Mukarakate, how was he going to react?

Perhaps the agony of lost power or responsibility is something that should not be underestimated in all leaders, even the most judicious ones. There is a natural reaction which is triggered when this happens, and that is to fight the source of that agony!

A few months later, when this occurrence had been almost forgotten and life was back to normal, well, as normal as life could ever be under the Ngwazi, Nsonthi paid a visit to his home district of Nchisi. I am unsure of the preceding events, but the result was that Youth Leaguers beat him up rather savagely, and a few months or so later Nsonthi was dead. There is no evidence to show the beating contributed to his eventual demise. There is no evidence either to prove who had sent the Youth Leaguers to commit this crime. Both the president of Malawi and Mr. Chikhakhalala did not attend the funeral, which was just as well, because some people in Nchisi, John Nsonthi's home district, had allegedly threatened to kill Mr. Chikhakhalala if he dared show his face there. The fact that there was no sign of the president at the funeral either was surprising given the number of years Nsonthi had loyally served him as his minister and interpreter. I must also add that there was no evidence directly linking Mr. Chikhakhalala to the beating. On the day of the funeral in Nchisi, it was reported that there was a gun battle between the eloquent Chichewa interpreter, John Nsonthi's family members, and supporters against the supporters of Mr. Chikhakhalala.

Getting back to the rally, this time, in his opening speech, the Ngwazi praised himself and his wise leadership and his courage in destroying 'the stupid Federation' nine years earlier. He also mentioned the importance of decent dress among 'his' people. He repeated his dislike for seeing respectable women in mini-skirts and men in bell-bottom trousers and unshaven. He stated, 'I am sure the Convention will look into these matters and make all the necessary resolutions.'

The maxim, 'The president's word is law' was at its truest in Dr Kamuzu Banda's Malawi.

Even before the motion was debated in the conference hall, Youth Leaguers and Malawi Young Pioneers were already on the streets and everywhere else, cutting short bell-bottom pairs of trousers worn by any unsuspecting or rebellious, foolhardy young men into short-trousers. Those trying to resist were beaten up. Women were harassed by being asked to bend over so the chaps could see how much their dress was revealing. Talk about being thorough! After feeding their cruel and lusty eyes, the tormentors would then let down the hem and send the offender on her way with a warning about her future mode of dress.

It was a terrible day when news spread that the motion had been passed, not that there was any doubt that this was the trajectory. We knew it was coming, but we still hoped for a miracle. Father was quick to obey the new law. During those days, whatever the Malawi Congress Party convention or the president wanted parliament to pass, it was first decided at their convention or at a public rally by the president. Parliament was there only to rubber-stamp such decisions. Father ordered us to take all our bell bottoms to the tailor and have them altered into ordinary trousers. I felt like crying. How could I give up my favourite pairs of trousers? How could I wear platform shoes with regular pants? I would look ridiculous. I thought of the British rock band Slade, who wore their tight pants and platform shoes and looked hip. But they were not me. I loved my bell bottoms and my high-soled shoes. They were part of my identity. I hated the MCP for taking them away from me. I was miserable that holiday and in the years that followed.

Although at fourteen I was underage, I did not look it. Chalela and I often worked behind the counter at the family nightclub despite our age, and for some strange reason, the authorities chose to look the other way. In nightclubs and pubs in Malawi, there was also a tendency to employ young, beautiful (this being in the eyes of various beholders) women to serve drinks and clients, although the latter was unofficially. Their quarters, where they could earn extra money for themselves, tax-free, were to be found behind or within the complex where they worked. They spent most of the daytime sleeping. Only a few would be on duty during the day. They were allowed to come on duty for the evening shift at nine p.m., three hours later than the rest.

Although Chalela and I had an idea of what some of these women did to earn extra income, we could only joke about it between the two of us. Father never discussed anything to do with sex with us. I suppose, like for most parents in the country at the time, it was a taboo subject to discuss. Most of these young women looked respectable, and some were even motherly to Chalela and me.

Chester's Nightclub was very popular for several reasons. There were ice-cold drinks and imported liquors and hot meals under one roof, a clean environment, very good service, even if I say so myself, and, above all this, late opening hours. We used to stay open until three in the morning, whereas other establishments in central town shut at ten thirty p.m. This meant that from eleven thirty to midnight there was always an influx of customers from town, most of them already tired and emotional.

One weekend, as was the usual arrangement for Friday and Saturday nights, we had a live band playing, and on this occasion, it was a band which was popular nationwide. It was called The Strings, featuring the famous States Samangaya. Tickets could be bought at the door for one kwacha single and one kwacha fifty tambala double. We expected a full house on both nights. Picky.

The Right Honourable Justin Malewezi, Malawi's former vice president, once shared with a few of us his observation at the night club. 'Do you know Mr Chester Katsonga was quite an audacious man? In his nightclub, he had a huge portrait of himself on one wall and a small one on the opposite wall of the president of Malawi.' Isn't this tempting fate, I remember thinking at the time. 'I am sure the subtlety had not been picked up by the ever-picky intelligence police.' He had shared these anecdotes with me in the presence of the honourable Salim Bagus and Clement Stambuli over lunch at Mudi House in Blantyre in 1999. The jukebox filled the air with music as the early birds arrived. They were eager to see The Strings perform. Around eight p.m., Peter, the club bouncer and my father's bodyguard, came in with some empty bottles hipped on a tray. He put them in the crates behind the counter, slowly and thoughtfully. I noticed Chalela and him exchanging some secret hand signs, but I didn't pay much attention. Father walked in wearing a white shirt and a paisley necktie. He ordered a double red-label whisky with ginger ale and sat on a bar stool. He sipped his drink and looked around, taking in the growing crowd. He loved his whisky, and he drank nothing else, except for some water when he took his anti-malaria pills or gargled. He always made a face when he did that, as if he hated the taste of water. He just sat there nursing his drink, occasionally turning his head around like a searchlight to appreciate the increasing numbers in the dance hall and around the bar. Peter reappeared yet again. He tried to catch Chalela's eye once more as he walked away. It didn't take long before he came back with more bottles. I was now curious and asked my brother what was going on. He pretended not to know. It wasn't Peter's job to collect empty bottles in the nightclub; there were others whose responsibility that was. Something must have been afoot, and I thought I should know. My brother feigned ignorance. He denied there were any hand signals and winks between Peter and him.

Since the band had started playing and the place was almost full, Peter was supposed to have been at the door controlling the inward traffic. Now, casually and without warning, he started to move in tune with the song the band was playing as he slowly passed by my father. 'Makono, Kubvina Kwa Makono,' he uttered, which meant 'Modern, Modern Dancing'. He repeated it twice, with a wicked lingering smile on his face and a sideways glance towards Chalela.

'What's all this twaddle about, Peter?' demanded Father.

'I was simply showing Master Chalela modern dancing,' Peter replied humbly and still smiling as he made his way back to the main entrance, exchanging one or two conspiratorial smiles with Chalela as he disappeared back to his station at the main entrance.

Two minutes later, I saw five rather beautiful girls walking in, accompanied by Chalela's friend, Rankine, and after Father had gone back into his office, which was next to the main entrance, Chalela explained he was 'seeing' one of them. She and her younger sister worked at a night pub called the Modern Inn, which was located around fifteen miles away on the Lilongwe–Salima road. The message Peter had problems communicating to Chalela in the presence of Father was that his girlfriend from the Modern Inn was at the main entrance, and Peter was seeking permission to allow her sister, her friends, and her to enter the hall free of charge, a request my love-struck elder brother was not about to turn down.

Peter had not said there were six of them, though. Not that it would have made the slightest difference, judging by the grin on Chalela's face. When Chalela introduced me to the girls, he added in a whisper that the younger sister had come specially to meet me. You could have heard my heartbeat from yards away. I was, as usual, petrified. The merest thought of the idea, the expected possibilities, was simply terrifying. The poor girl tried everything to interest me that night. She bought me about four bottles of Fanta Orange, one after another, and then suggested something more 'serious', something alcoholic, so I served myself a cream soda just to break the monotony. After that, she invited me to dance, but I told her I was not allowed. This wasn't a fib! Eventually, Chalela came to my rescue by telling my keen and willing friend that we were going to visit them the following day in the afternoon. Somehow, I just could not imagine Chalela with 'Modern'. I do not know why; I just could not. Maybe it was due to the fact he was only two years older than me. My Chalela, going out with a woman like that! Oh no, surely not, and yet there he was, positively glowing before his conquest. What would his mother say, I wondered to myself, not to mention his Father! Sunday came and I faked a headache, put down to over-indulgence the night before – all those cream sodas! The later-than-usual closing time! Chalela could tell I was not up to it and decided not to force the issue. I just did not find the idea interesting.

When Chalela and I resumed our places at Soche Hill after our summer holidays, the bald heads of the returning students and their drawn, sombre faces filled with resignation resembled those at a funeral wake. There was no point discussing the politically enforced change in our mode of dress. We knew and accepted where the problem lay, and politics was not something Malawians enjoyed discussing. Chalela and I sought out our number one soul brother, Bula, to tell us how the Percy Sledge concert had gone. We wanted to know everything. 'It was a wonderful day, Davie,' Bula started.

'Percy Sledge had made a grand entrance, waving from a top-down Land Rover as he drove through the main gate. The Kamuzu Stadium was packed and roaring with excitement. He wore a dazzling white outfit and greeted us with his 'warm and tender love'. He kicked off the show with his hit song of the same title. He had us hooked with his soulful voice and smooth moves. He sang 'Come Softly to Me', and we just melted before him. Then a girl with red roses approached the stage to present them to him. He received them with a broad smile, microphone in hand while still singing. He then momentarily stopped singing while the band continued to play and planted a big kiss on her cheek, and she swooned. After that, more and more women rushed to the stage for their share of his kisses. He welcomed them all, but when a man tried to join them, he responded, "No, not me, brother, women only," and the man retreated in shame. He was on fire, singing one hit after another. But then, suddenly, the show was over.'

We listened intently as Bula continued, 'The following day, we were told that Percy Sledge had broken one of the major rules of Malawi. Only the president was allowed to use the main gate to enter the stadium in a convertible. Percy Sledge was charged with the offence of impersonating the president and was given forty-eight hours to leave the country. Small wonder Chalela and I had found nothing in the papers the following day after the concert. Why Percy Sledge did not simply walk into the stadium like everyone else, I will never know!

During the next holiday, my school friend, Ivor, accepted my invitation to spend Christmas with us. On Christmas Eve, The Strings were playing, and I was sure Ivor, being a year older than me, was already familiar with modern dancing. In Lilongwe, there was one well-known prostitute who claimed to be a university graduate, although I never asked what she majored in. 'Super Diana' was a snappy dresser and she also spoke very good English. The moment Super Diana set eyes on Ivor, it was like a magnet. She pulled up a bar-counter stool and sat next to him. 'Hello, my name is Diana,' she said while ordering what we had come to know as her favourite drink: Bulmer's Apple Cider, 'What's your name?' she continued, her eyes fixed intently on Ivor's, although the latter was struggling to maintain this eye-to-eye approach Diana was employing.

She bought all of us drinks before she hurriedly responded to a song playing on the jukebox in the dance hall. She must have proceeded to go to the restaurant, because a few minutes later she returned, eating a chicken's very spicy drumstick. She got to the bar counter and picked up Ivor's Sprite for a quick swig to douse the heat of the Piri-piri. 'Sorry. Don't worry; get him another Sprite, Chalela,' she ordered. From this moment onwards,

Diana did not let go of Ivor. We noticed Super Diana was singing along in Ivor's ear as they danced cheek-to-cheek, with one half of Ivor's sweaty face buried deep into her huge Afro wig. An alien from outer space would have been forgiven for thinking human beings had two heads with a very strange hairstyle – one head with lots of hair and the other almost bald, and that they also had two pairs of legs and hands. Ivor and Diana were dancing very, very tightly. For a minute or two, I worried whether Ivor was still able to breathe. He seemed comfortable though! He appeared to have gotten lucky, very lucky that Christmas Eve. They later sat very close in one corner of the dance hall, arms entwined, gazing into each other's eyes and drinking from the same bottle, although Diana was double-dipping, drinking her cider and swigging from Ivor's Sprite bottle. The intensity of their passion added to the heat in the fulfilled nightclub that night.

It was the best Christmas present Ivor had ever got thus far, so he confessed the following morning.

When we returned to school the following term, Ivor spoke of nothing else. The poor boy was besotted. If my memory serves me well, the word marriage did pass his lips on several occasions, and he only stopped talking about Diana when no reply came back to the love letters he had written her.

As we shared all this holiday trash-talk, Dunka decided to share one of his own. His father was the human resources manager at Wallace Estates, who specialised in tobacco farming in Lilongwe. Most weekends, piece-croppers with grievances against the company or with each other used to come to the Tung'ande's residence, which was located on the borders of the Wallace Estate in Mbabzi. This is where he held court.

One day, there was a case from a piece-cropper, from Mulanje, originally, who had been severely roughed up by an angry husband who had accused him of having an illicit sexual relationship with his wife. Dunka had seen the man arriving and wanted to know what the issue was. At the time of the narrative, he had strategically started to wash the family car, which was parked in front of the house, a couple of metres or so from the veranda where the case was being held. He pretended not to be paying attention to the talks because he knew it was wrong to eavesdrop on matters like that, but still, having picked up the nature of the opening lines of the complaints, my buddy simply couldn't help it. He wanted to hear more.

The piece-cropper was on his way to the farm, taking the usual shortcut through the fields, when he felt a sudden blow to the back of his head. He stumbled and turned around, only to see the enraged face of his co-worker, who accused him of sleeping with his wife. He denied the charge, but his words were drowned out by the fists and kicks which rained down on him. He tried to defend himself, but he was no match for the furious husband who had been cuckolded. He felt his teeth crack and his eyes swell shut as he lay on the ground, bleeding and bruised. He would have been killed if not for the intervention of some other farm workers who heard the commotion and pulled the attacker off him. He was barely conscious, barely alive, as they carried him to safety. He had been the victim of a false and potentially fatal accusation.

It was now time for the estranged husband to speak, and I paraphrase. 'I have been told by friends that this man,' he said, pointing at the complainant and then continuing, 'has been having sexual relations with my wife for some time. I decided not to ask her, because I knew she would deny it, so, I decided to catch her myself. There is a huge and leafy mango tree in the field close to the front of our house, so, on some mornings I would climb up and sit on one of the branches to see if the stories I was getting were true. On this day, as I sat up in that tree, I saw him walking towards the house and giving my wife some hand signals while my wife beckoned him to follow her into the house.

'Within seconds, I saw my wife's wrapper she was wearing being draped on the front window hook. I waited to allow them time to get started. I them came down the tree and slowly and quietly opened the front door, which was not locked. At that point, they must have heard there was someone in the house. He came out running at great speed, and because I needed to know if the rumours were correct, I entered the room and demanded from her an answer about whether he did it or not. She denied everything. I didn't believe her, so I demanded a quick inspection of her privates and, there it was! He had done it!

The narrative in Chichewa with a Lomwe accent sounded both funny and vulgar, but all he was doing was trying to make a case the only way he knew how. This is the Chichewa version, and it's not for the faint-hearted.

'Wathila? Wathila?' he asked her.

'Iyayi hanathila,' she replied tearfully and looking petrified.

'Tione!' he angrily demanded as he roughly and disrespectfully forced his wife's legs open. "Ah! Haa! Wathila?, Wathila?" he cried out as he set out after the adulterous man.

. The sight of what he saw made his blood boil to temperatures he had not experienced before in his life. He ran out of the house to follow this man. The moment he came eye-to-eye with him, the imagining, the image of the man on top of his wife would have turned him into a killer that day, he concluded, with tears rolling down his dark-brown well-chiselled sun-hardened face.

Judgement was to follow a week later, Dunka concluded. As fourteen-year-old secondary-school kids, we found the story and the wild imagination, though uncomfortable, hilarious. The cruelty of young minds, one might say!

Six years later, the quick-witted and humorous Ivor was still single, and he had enrolled in Soche Technical College for a diploma in car mechanics. He was later to work for a Mercedes franchisee in Malawi, Stansfield Motors, as a workshop manager, so I was informed by friends twenty years later.

Chapter 14

JOB HUNTING,
COMPLETELY WITHOUT A BLESSING

I had mind and decided to work in Blantyre after my O'levels for a while before joining Father in Lilongwe. I thought it would be good for me to gain some experience and independence. I wrote to him about my plan, but I didn't wait for his answer, which never came. As soon as I finished writing my examinations s, I moved out of Soche Hill and stayed with my cousin and her husband. They lived in a nearby neighbourhood called Kanjedza.

In my youthful optimistic mind, I was certain that my uncle, who was a former mayor of the city of Blantyre and was now the executive chairman of the Malawi Housing Corporation, a parastatal, would not deprive me of a job. So, I called his office, requesting this of him, and he did not disappoint. He gave me an appointment for seven thirty a.m. the next Monday.

I was sure that my uncle,, would help me get a job in this organisation. I phoned his office and asked to see him. He agreed to meet me the next Monday at 07.30hrs. I put on my best clothes – a crisp white shirt, a black pair of trousers, and a sky-blue velvet necktie which Dennis Kambalame, a patron of my dad's nightclub, had bought me from Esquire men's shop. I looked and felt very smart.

My uncle was in a good mood and listened to my request. He picked up his phone and called the head of recruitment. He told him to find a vacancy for a young Form Four student. A few minutes later, a man came in, breathing hard. 'Your Worship, these are the suitable vacancies as per your request, Sir,' he said, placing a file on my uncle's desk.

My uncle opened the file and glanced at it. He said, 'We will give you a job. Can he start tomorrow?' The head of recruitment nodded eagerly. My uncle turned to me and told me to come to work the next day at seven-thirty a.m. I was overjoyed. It was like a dream come true. I went back to my cousin's house, feeling elated. I had landed my first job.

When Monday morning arrived, I put on my best blue trousers, which Jimmy the tailor had conjured up for me, and a white shirt which was part of my school uniform. I felt well-dressed and smart as I arrived at MHC at seven o'clock. My uncle had not yet arrived, and it was thirty minutes later when I was called in by his deputy to be told a mistake had been made and that the vacancy they had offered me was not available after all. 'Try us again in a month,' he told me, and I went home a very sad man. I refused to eat. How could I possibly have an appetite when I had been fired before I had even had my feet under the desk? Still, I was determined not to give up.

I had always felt like the shadow of my father, not a person in my own right. Being a Katsonga had its perks but also its limits. I couldn't enjoy the freedom of my friends who had no famous fathers. I wanted to be myself, to start from scratch, to be an individual. So, I went to my uncle for a job, using the very privilege I wanted to escape. But he turned me down. I remembered my mother's words. 'Good things come to those who wait.' I decided to keep looking. That night, as I tossed and turned in bed, unable to sleep, an idea popped into my head. There was a company run by the Life President, Ngwazi Dr Hastings Kamuzu Banda, the Messiah, the man I detested. It was called Press Holdings Limited, and the personnel manager was my father's friend, Mr. Mbilizi. I resolved to visit him.

When I arrived at his office the next day, the receptionist told me the personnel manager did not see people without prior arrangements. 'Tell him Mr. Katsonga's son is here to see him,' I announced confidently, using the privilege the name carried. A few seconds after the receptionist had disappeared into what I guessed was Mr Mbilizi's office, the door opened and there stood the man himself, his arms outstretched in welcome. His dapper black pinstriped suit made him look the spitting image of Sydney Potier, the film actor.

'Ah, Davie, come in my son.' I thought he looked pleased to see me. The interior of his office was most intimidating. Two telephones were looking lonely on an otherwise huge uncluttered shiny mahogany desk, behind which hung an enormous portrait of the Life President. Its eyes seemed to follow me as I walked into the inner sanctum. Mr Mbilizi motioned me to sit down at the far end of the office in one of the two armchairs, cosily positioned next to some healthy-looking pot plants, as he ordered tea for two from his pretty and buxom secretary, whose quick steps belied her ample body.

When I explained that the reason for my surprise visit was to ask him for a job, Mr Mbilizi deliberated momentarily. 'I know ... I know ... er ... er ... I will put you in the main PTC supermarket,' he declared. 'That's it. Security section. With your height, you should do well there, son!' This was music to my ears, and I beamed in appreciation. Behind the smile, though, there was a slight nagging doubt. My girlfriend, Madalo, also worked there, and I did not know how she would handle the situation, but I gave myself comfort by looking ahead to the day when I might be promoted to become head of security or security executive.

'When can I start?' I asked enthusiastically.

'How about Monday, son? Take these forms to fill in – it's just a formality. So, see you Monday,' he said warmly as he stood up to register the end of our meeting, even before the tea arrived! Executive behaviour, I wondered!

I told all my friends about my new job in the centre of town. Most of them were consumed with envy, which I fully understood. There was always high unemployment in Malawi, even during this boom time. When Monday morning came, I set off in a white shirt and charcoal-grey trousers, with my broad expensive navy-blue velvet neck-tie dangling merrily from my neck. This was the same necktie I had worn when I met Uncle Duncan Phoya at Malawi Housing Corporation two weeks earlier – the very picture of a working man. As I walked up the steps at the front of Chibisa House, the headquarters of Press Holdings Corporation, to start my new career, I could sense eyes focused on me. I was sure the girls were saying, 'What a guy!' Maybe not, but still, I felt that good.

It was thirty minutes before the official starting time, and the personnel manager was already at his desk. The thought crossed my mind that conceivably this was the reason why he was a manager, being punctual and dedicated to the job, or then again, perhaps he was just avoiding a nagging wife at home! Not that I knew he had that issue. There was even a cup of double-fresh steaming tea and a jam tart awaiting me. Almost as soon as I sat down, Mr Mbilizi brought me down to earth with the words, 'I don't know how to tell you this, son. The job was taken on the same day you came to see me. I didn't know they needed someone that urgently. I'm so sorry. More tea?' He filled my cup before I could answer. 'By the way, how is Daddy in Lilongwe?'

Ah-ha! I should have guessed – that question, 'By the way ...'

Was I being sabotaged by my father? I somehow suspected it. Both places I had been would have given me a job, possibly even creating a vacancy where there was, hitherto, none! These were my father's good friends, and one was my uncle. They had both changed their minds unexpectedly. Both had let me down, albeit as gently as possible. When I arrived back at my cousin's house, I found a message that Father had telephoned to say he wanted me to go home urgently. I found it hard to convince myself that the timing of this message was a pure coincidence.

The following day, I saw an advertisement for hotel management trainees in the national paper, and on the day I left Blantyre I posted my application, giving my family home address in Lilongwe.

Surprisingly, Father did not shout at me, as I had feared he would. He simply told me that I should have come home first to get his blessing before going on my 'fruitless' job hunt. There was no point in asking if he was behind the sudden withdrawals of the job offers; he would have simply blamed the Spirits. So, for the time being, and with suppressed disappointment, I went back to the nightclub to work as a bartender.

I was summoned to his office three weeks later. Father had just come back from a meeting in Blantyre, where some top officials from Malawi Hotels and Tourism had whispered to him that my name was among one hundred candidates shortlisted by Goodwood Hotels for management trainees. He wanted to know why I hadn't told him. My excuse was that I had applied to so many companies and I did not see any need to tell him until there had been some progress. To Father, this was simply another example of my disregard for him and the Spirits. He wanted to show us he was there for his children, he told me. If we wanted a job, he had thousands of friends he could talk to. He did not want his son working for just anybody. He wanted to vet any future employer. He felt there were few employers worthy of our labour.

Although I said very little, he knew I was determined to go on with my plan to get a job elsewhere. I was eventually called for an interview, which was followed by two more. Finally, I was one of two picked from nine hundred and fifty-five applicants for training in hotel management. I still suspect my father had put his thumb on the scale in my favour despite my apparent single-mindedness and the disregard he thought I had shown for our ancestral spirits.

Chapter 15

LEARNING THE ROPES – LIFE AT RYALL'S, MY FIRST PAID JOB

I was so excited when I landed a job with the Goodwood Group of Hotels. Among their hotels in Malawi were Ryall's Hotel and Shire Highlands Hotel. I had *successfully* applied and went through an interview conducted by the then Director of Tourism Mr Jack Mwamba and supported by the personnel manager from Ryall's Hotel. This was on the top floor of Kanabar House in Blantyre.

The government of Malawi had just formed a parastatal called Malawi Hotels, which owned most of the hotels in Malawi and was now training black Malawians to take over the administration of these institutions from the expatriates.

Ryall's and Shire Highlands were among the biggest hotels in the country and certainly the oldest. They still carried the colonial stench about them. It was not a decision which was voluntarily taken by the Goodwood Group but rather one which was forced upon them by this government policy. After the interviews, only two candidates were deemed to have been successful: Noble Litete (the second-born son of the author of the popular Chichewa book entitled *Nkwatibwi Okhumudwa – the Disappointed Bride*) and me. We were to be trained in hotel management.

After the initial induction meeting, during which it was explained that both of us recruits would eventually be sent abroad for training, the manager of the hotel, a Scottish man called Mr Kennedy Andrew Nicholson, took us through all sections of the hotel, introducing us to different heads of department. At the end of the tour, we were told where we should go to collect our uniforms. Uniforms! I thought they had designed a special trim to show we were management trainees – not on your nelly! My colleague, Noble, was going to begin his training in the kitchen, and I was put in the Dugout Restaurant, where, to use Mr. Nicholson's own words, 'You will be meeting the customers face-to-face.' At this point, Mrs Chawula, the kitchen supervisor, provided us with two new sets of uniforms relevant to our allocated workstations. I was mortified!

As a management trainee, I had not expected to have to wear a uniform. What I thought was that an official badge pinned on my lapel, saying something modest like 'Mr Katsonga, Management Trainee', would be issued. Alas! The manager explained that it was normal procedure and practice to wear a uniform representing the section you were deployed in; that way your understanding of the psychology of the department you were deployed in would be better appreciated.

I felt like a fish out of water, carrying a tray of food and drinks for strangers. This was not the kind of training I had signed up for. I wanted to be a manager, not a waiter. But I had no choice. This was the first step of the ladder I had to climb. I was later to learn that being a waiter was not a shameful job in the West. It was a respectable profession, unlike in Malawi, where it was seen as lowly. It was hard for me to adjust, especially coming from a family business where I was used to giving orders, not taking them.

After I had put on my round-necked brown jacket with black trim and a black pair of trousers, I was handed a beautiful silver tray stamped with the name 'Ryall's' in the middle and a traditional dug-out canoe below it. I was also provided with a cloth serviette 'proudly' draped on my bent arm. Mr Katsonga, trainee waiter, was ready for duty.

The hotel had three restaurants. The Dugout (named for dug-out canoe) was mainly for snacks and quick dishes. It had a bar, and most of the tables were set out around the swimming pool. Then there was the main dining room, which served table d'hote meals, mostly to residents staying in the hotel. The flag carrier was the 21 Grill. It served à la carte meals, and during the time I was there, it won the Department of Tourism-sponsored Golden Spoon competition on three consecutive occasions.

Clients for the Dugout were mostly young middle-management clerks who worked in the Blantyre city central, and tourists. At the month-end, courting couples, men and women about town, used to assemble there, spending their hard-earned wages as if there were another paycheque coming tomorrow, arguably simply showing off.

The head waiter, called Maizoni, a stubby square-faced fellow, similar in looks to Benny Hill (without the sense of humour), showed me how to use my order book, which had to be filled out in triplicate, and within a few minutes, I had my first customers. Fortunately for me, they sat very close to the bar counter, so I did not have to parade my indignity around the swimming pool. By twelve thirty or so, all my tables were busy, and the head waiter was by my side making certain I was all right. The whole place was buzzing with the beauties

Blantyre had to offer, and to hide my embarrassment, I made sure I concealed myself by standing behind one of the columns around the bar. I did not want to be spotted by any one of them. In no time at all, most of my customers began calling for their bills. I even got a few tips and, as advised by the head waiter, I had to remember to say the customary 'Thank you, Sir' (or Madam), even when the tip was a meagre penny. And then, it happened. One of the waiters came to me with a grin as wide as Wembley Stadium. He told me about some girls at the far end of the swimming pool, who wanted no one else but me to serve them. I had been spotted! My colleagues thought this was a great honour; they could not begin to know how I felt.

'Well, that's a good start, Mr. Katsonga. Girls, eh! You'd better take a bigger tray, then,' said the head waiter, smiling, handing me his own. Some honour!

I have never felt my legs so heavy. I somehow managed to cover the fifteen metres or so to their table, which seemed like miles, without stumbling and falling into the swimming pool. My fast walk was in slow motion. spoke first, was particularly amused by my undisguised discomfort.

'Ah, good afternoon, Waiter!'

'Good afternoon, Madam,' I responded, my heart beating a little faster as I faked a smile. I took their orders and had to cover the whole length of the swimming pool again as I proceeded to the kitchen with the food order. I felt like every diner's gaze was on me! One of the girls even had the cheek to call me back twice just for water. After the main course, she paid the bill for the group, and I hurried back to the head waiter, who kept the cash box. There was two pence change, which I took back to them, together with the top copy of the bill.

'Keep the change!' The girl spoke loudly as she pocketed the bill and rose to leave. I felt like a punching bag, taking blow after blow of insults and mockery. I had never been so humiliated in my life, never. The next day, the Dugout was packed with more customers who came to see me in my lowly state. There were the same girls who had laughed at me, and they brought their friends and boyfriends to join the fun. It was like a nightmare which wouldn't end. But I held onto my dream. I knew what I wanted and nothing, but nothing, was going to stop me. Not even a bunch of sneering pretty girls and their boyfriends!

Three years later, on a Sunday morning, the same girl, the one who gave me a two-pence tip, accompanied by her boyfriend, came to the hotel to attempt to cash a personal cheque. They knew the hotel sometimes offered this service to their regular and *trusted* customers when the banks were closed and, in answer to their question, the receptionist told them they would have to see the manager about such transactions. It just so happened I was the junior assistant manager at the time and duty manager for that weekend. As such, I was responsible for everything around the hotel.

I was sitting at my desk – well, Mr Nicholson's desk – which was right behind reception, when I heard a light knock at the door. Before I could answer, the door opened, and as if in slow-motion two figures materialised: a young woman and a man of approximately the same age as her.

I offered them seats and after greeting them, they explained the reason for their early Sunday morning visit.

Revenge is sweet, so they say, and my mind was made up even before she concluded her last sentence. Just her face, her presence, brought back the rudeness she had enjoyed dishing out to me three years earlier. I had not forgotten nor had I forgiven her. Yes, it was she that June month-end day three years earlier, when she treated me like a figure of fun while I served her food at the Dugout restaurant.

I pretended to work on some important and urgent papers scattered on the desk. Then I told them that indeed we did have registered customers who were allowed to cash cheques at the hotel but that only my boss could deal with issues like that. I was, therefore, unable to assist them. As if to emphasise the point, I stood up and walked towards the door. Reluctantly acknowledging the strongly silent message, they followed, and as I went to shut the door behind them, the young woman turned back and gave me the kind of look which seemed to say, 'I know why you are doing this, you mean so-and-so.' Looking back now, my actions seem rather petty and harsh. Still, I enjoyed the moment while it lasted! As a committed Roman Catholic, I did go to Confession the following Sunday!

***

After pocketing my two-pence tip, things quietened down, and I was looking forward to going off duty at four p.m. My career in the hotel industry had well and truly begun. Within a week, Madalo had to explain to the whole of Blantyre City that she was dating a waiter. Bad news travels fast.

I had met Madalo two years or so earlier while we were both in secondary school. She was most pleasant and pretty, but she never allowed me to get physical with her. She told me it was better that way, at least until we got married. What an incentive, I thought! She said I was allowed to get physical with whomever I wanted to, as long as I did not fall in love with them. That was the general idea, and I was happy to go along with it. Show me a man who would not!

Until I could find accommodation of my own, my sister and her husband helpfully agreed to let me live with them in Soche East, a mid-density residential area in the south-eastern part of Blantyre. When I arrived home at the end of my first day, I found a note from my school friend, Ivor Mlenga, saying our football club, NOIL, had been drawn against Bata Bullets in the second round of the Kamuzu Cup and that I had to collect my training kit from our team captain, who lived nearby. The training was to start the following day. Unfortunately, the captain was not at home when I arrived there, and as I pondered whether to leave a note under his door or wait, my thoughts were interrupted by a tall, dark, smiling girl from next door.

'Are you looking for Bob?' she enquired.

'Yes. Do you know what time he normally gets home?' I asked.

'Well, it depends,' she replied thoughtfully. 'He's usually back by now.'

The late-April southern--hemisphere sun had just gone down, and it was getting rather chilly. The air was thick with different cooking smells and the noise of hundreds of insects and birds, accompanied by screaming children. I decided not to wait.

'I was thinking of leaving him a note. It's a longish one. Do you have a pen and paper I could borrow, please?'

She hurried into her flat and came back quickly with the two items I had asked for. As I wrote the message for Captain Bob, we chatted about our jobs. She told me her name was Elizabeth and that she worked as a credit controller for a marketing company called MSM. I thought she was attractive, and she also spoke English with a rather posh accent, the kind of accent we called 'the nose brigade', because the voice seemed to come through the nose and the mouth at the same time. I also noticed she walked in a lady-like fashion, making sure her feet stepped straight, one behind the other, almost in a single file. I thought it was a sign of good breeding. She was not the sort of girl a second-ary-school leaver like me would have the courage to go for. She was the kind of girl I could only admire from afar. Come to think of it, I had reached a point in my life where I was admiring all women from a safe distance. My body was biologically ready-ish, but my brain was still doubtful!

The following Monday, a week after the day she and I met on her doorstep, Elizabeth telephoned me at the hotel. She wondered, she said, what time I finished work. It so happened I was finishing work three hours earlier than her that day. She suggested I should pass by her office, and we would walk the three miles home together.

When I arrived at MSM, Elizabeth seemed pleased to see me, and we had hardly covered twenty metres when she took hold of my hand. I was very nervous, but it felt good. For the first time as a working man, I was walking and holding hands with a *city* girl. As we walked, she did most of the talking. She told me about her son, who was six years old at the time and going to school, which put me off a bit, but I tried not to show it. When we arrived at her flat, she invited me in for tea and biscuits, and we decided to meet the following day after work, at her flat. She knew this would be around midnight, because I told her I was on night duty. This was just as well, for I would have found it hard to find an excuse to leave my sister's house at that time of the night. My brother-in-law would never have allowed it.

The following night, I asked the driver from work to drop me at the girl's place and waved him to drive off before I knocked on her door. I did not want him to know where I was headed.

When Elizabeth opened the door, I noticed the bed-seater was lit by one huge candle, the kind you might expect to find in a Roman Catholic church at Easter, and when she hugged me with one arm while closing the door behind us with the other, I noticed she was wearing nothing much under her dressing-gown. My heart skipped a beat or two! I was overcome with the same old feelings of fear and nervousness. No chance of a landing aeroplane coming to my rescue this time! I remember sitting on that bed, as usual not knowing how to proceed and yet smiling confidently, trying to look experienced in *adult* matters.

'You don't go to bed fully dressed, do you?' she asked as she stood up to bring me two wire hangers. She was standing right above me, and as I nervously rose to my feet, she gave me a peck on the mouth. Helping me undo my necktie and remove my shirt, in no time at all she was reaching for my belt. My mind went back to Wilhelmina. As I got into bed, Elizabeth excused herself and disappeared into the bathroom, returning a few moments later wearing absolutely nothing. What a woman! The end is nigh (or was it the beginning?), I thought, as she slowly and seductively lowered herself into bed and between the sheets.

By now, I had heard a lot of stories about what to do in such circumstances, read a few books, watched eighteen-certificate movies, and listened to my experienced peers as they graphically bragged about their conquests, both real and imagined – I couldn't tell which was which though! I need not have worried. I must have been very orthodox, but I do not think it mattered much. Youth was on my side, and lots of it too. When, at about two a.m., I told her I had to go, she complained, 'But you've only just arrived.'

'I'll come again tomorrow,' I reassured her.

'Do you love me, Davie?' She surprised me with the question.

'Yes, I do, Elizabeth,' I answered without thinking.

'Same thing tomorrow, you said?'

I agreed, and we were to see each other almost every day after this. As I slowly walked home that night, accompanied by a symphony of sounds from a variety of frogs and insects, I thought of all those close encounters which had ended in disappointment. What had I been afraid of? Everything had been accomplished naturally, and I was now a fully-fledged member of the exclusive club which age confers on its members. The mystery had been solved, at last.

Tired, knowledgeable, and happy, I slipped unseen into my sister's house and slept like a baby. My sister soon heard about our affair, and she once joked, 'You're being overworked at the hotel these days, aren't you?'

'Yes,' I replied, avoiding her eyes.

'The one down the road, I'm talking about,' she teased.

I didn't comment.

A month or so after these most exciting days, the *Hotels and Tourism Monthly* magazine printed an article entitled 'Two Bright Sparks at Ryall's Hotel', featuring the two new trainee managers. Call me biased if you like, but I thought it was a well-written article! At about the same time, I rented a house which belonged to my brother-in-law, in Kanjedza, about five miles from my sister's house. It had two bedrooms, a good-size living room, kitchen, and bathroom. It was a dream start to my working life, and I asked my fellow trainee to share it with me, but during the first few days after settling in, something went wrong.

After work one evening, at about ten p.m., the driver pointed towards the top of Hannover Avenue, where a group of prostitutes were still hoping for some late customers and made some remark about, 'Those girls never giving up'. To my surprise, Nobby, my fellow trainee, suggested we pick them up. I later got the impression it was not his first time dealing with this kind of woman, as he did most of the talking. The Ford Transit van dropped us in front of the house, and the four of us were involved in Ugandan talks that night. I was learning fast, somehow, a little too fast. The following day, Elizabeth came over and stayed the night. On the third day, I began to experience some strange sensations in my body. When I spoke about my problem to our football coach, who was a full-time medical assistant, he gave me an appointment to see him at the hospital where he worked the following day. A serious urethral infection was diagnosed, and I was given a penicillin injection with some antibiotic capsules to take for a week. My main problem was how to tell Elizabeth. Being young, foolish, and embarrassed, I started avoiding her. I stopped taking her telephone calls at work, never went to her house, was no longer the lover-man in her life I had quickly become. I simply dropped the whole affair.

One morning, she came to the house at about six a.m. to catch me before I left for work. She knocked on my bedroom window, calling my name, but I did not respond. I could hear Nobby telling her that I had gone for outside catering the previous night and was not back yet. They left together while I hid in the bedroom. When Nobby saw me at work later that day, he told me Elizabeth too had felt something strange and her doctor wanted to see me. She had told her doctor about my recent strange behaviour. The doctor's response had been, she said, that I was avoiding her for one of two reasons: either I was upset with her because of the infection she had given me, or I was feeling guilty for giving it to her. Nobby assured her it was the former, which only served to confuse matters further, as poor Elizabeth had not been with anyone else since we had met; this she assured Nobby. Elizabeth's doctor's response and Nobby's subsequent comment gave credence to my lie, somehow., somehow. The doctor had also explained to Elizabeth that these illnesses are known to lie dormant in the body, mostly in women, and that I was, therefore, possibly the victim.

I owe her an apology. Elizabeth and I reconciled our differences, and she did her best from then on to show me there was no one else in her life. Next time I see Elizabeth, I will apologetically tell her the truth.

In Blantyre, as in most small cities, guys who are considered 'groovy' tend to be known to everyone else in their circles, and Elizabeth's ex-boyfriend and the father of her son fell into this category. His name was Robert. One Sunday morning, at about seven a.m., as we were having a lie-in at her flat, there was a knock at the door. Elizabeth reluctantly got out of bed and looked out of the window.

'It's Robert,' she whispered to me.

'You're not opening the door, are you?' I asked, suddenly nervous. Remember, I was the master of not answering the door!

Elizabeth's face changed, her eyes narrowed, and her lips pursed tight, and they looked like a chicken's bum as she grabbed her dressing gown. Angrily, she opened the door just enough for Robert to be able to see me having an afterglow in what used to be his bed.

'Do you want to come in?' she shouted.

The man simply turned and walked away. Robert worked for Air Malawi, and although his office and mine were next to each other, and we met on our way to work almost every morning, we had never spoken to each other. This situation continued until I left Malawi, although the affair itself died a natural death within a year. Elizabeth had become so demanding of my time. Losing my freedom as well as my virginity, and becoming her son's stepfather all within a year had been more than I had bargained for. Remember, I was only nineteen!

After a month or two of training in the Dugout, I was moved to the main dining room, where I learnt how to set tables according to what was on the menu, how to do the 'Silver Dish' service, what sauces go with what, etcetera. I still used to try and avoid being seen on the main veranda leading to the Dugout for one reason or another, and it was a further two months before I was allowed to serve the à la carte menu to customers in the 21 Grill, and, as they say, soon, I would be opening tins!

Serving food in the 21 Grill was a ritual. It was a place where, even if one were inexperienced or simply under the weather, no mistakes were tolerated by the head waiter, Barnett. The uniforms were a striking contrast to the ones in the Dugout and the main dining room. They were dark-orange jackets with black trousers, and they had to be crisp and clean every day. The first thing I had to learn was how to walk like a proper waiter. I thought I knew how to walk, but Barnett showed me that I had to keep my arms close to my body and not swing them. It was a challenge for people of colour like me. He said I should hold my head up and swivel it from side to side, like the all-seeing sweep of a security camera. Added to this, my steps should be short, keeping my knees as low as possible, and in other ways, I should try and make myself small in stature and inconspicuous. After all, he reasoned, that is what the customer expected of a waiter, for him to be there but unseen when not needed and unobtrusive but also alert to their every need. I thought Barnett knew more about catering than the general manager. He was the first black man to be on the wine-tasting panel in then-racist South Africa, or so he told us. He even spoke English like a Boer, and it was easy to tell he was proud of it.

The restaurant was fully booked most nights, and unlike the other two restaurants, tips nearly always came in banknotes, cheques even, never in small change. Although we had allocated workstations, there was a policy to assist anyone who was busy when you were not. Because of this, it was only proper to pool all the tips together and share them at the end of the shift. This was a fair policy, one might say, except for two waiters, Hopewell and Maizoni, who were rather greedy. The former had two wives. The second wife hated the idea of saving money, so every time Hopewell got paid, she made sure she spent it all for him. The latter, Maizoni, came from Lilongwe in the Central Region and had six children, a wife, and a mother-in-law to support. They both needed money, and the idea of sharing their hard-earned tips with the rest of us was something they wanted to avoid at all costs.

In the evening, the electric lights in the restaurant were dimmed so low that the room seemed to get all its available light from the candles on the tables, creating a relaxed and romantic ambiance, like eating under a star-strewn sky on a moonless night. Bills were presented on a tray, in a time-honoured way. When the opportunity arose, Hopewell would take the bill, mostly to those tables at the far end of the room. When this was happening, his partner in crime, Maizoni, would follow him discreetly halfway, touching a thing or two on the tables as he passed, straightening cutlery, lining up condiments, all the time with his eyes on his partner, the crafty Hopewell. When a diner signed the bill and dipped his hand into his pocket to produce a banknote and put it on the tray, it was clear for all of us to see. Yet when Hopewell returned to the cashier, to everyone's surprise, there would be nothing on the tray. He would then deny receiving a tip at all.

Hopewell and Maizoni had a clever plan, that worked. Having received the payment, Hopewell would swiftly and skilfully tilt the tray, causing the tipped banknote to fall off the tray, where Maizoni, loitering behind him with intent, would pick it up and pocket it. They would split the money later on their way home.

But the head waiter caught onto their scheme and stopped giving them any bills to collect. So, they had to look for other ways to make some extra cash.

One afternoon, around two o'clock, my Scottish boss called me into his office. He wanted to know if I had noticed anything strange in the behaviour of the regular waiters. I told him one or two things I had observed, and he said he too had been keeping his eyes open and that he was certain Hopewell was stealing from the kitchen. 'I'm told he never leaves the premises empty-handed,' he said. 'Can you imagine how much the hotel is losing? What's more, I'm sure he is not acting alone.'

He then said he planned to ambush Hopewell when he left the hotel at the end of his shift. It seemed Mr Nicholson had lost confidence in his senior subordinates to do an honest job of apprehending the pilferers.

Mr Nicholson parked his car behind a big truck near the hotel gate, watching for his prey. He saw Hopewell walk by the guard, who let him go without checking the bag he was carrying. Mr Nicholson jumped out of his car and shouted his name several times. But he ran away like a thief, without turning his head or acknowledging him. He came back to work for the six p.m. shift that day and was summoned to the manager's office immediately. He denied hearing anyone calling his name. 'Then why did you run away?' the manager asked.

'Boss, I live five miles away from here. I always rush to the bus stand after the afternoon shift, so I can get home faster and rest before the evening shift. That's my routine, boss.' He escaped with a warning, but the boss was not convinced by his story. Without any proof of what was in the bag, he could only tell him to watch his back. But the guard was not so lucky; he was sacked on the spot. You know how the Scots are, right?

I had an idea that pilferage in hotels was a problem, but not to the degree which had been hinted at by Mr Nicholson. I was to learn later.

I used to enjoy making Crêpes Suzette and other flambeé dishes at the table when the restaurant was buzzing with tired and emotional diners, some of whom had worked their way to the bottom of the menu, and the moment I added Cognac to the dessert and set it alight, there would be screams, usually from the ladies, followed by some wisecracks from their husbands.

'Mind my wife's wig!'

'My wig? What wig? Say that again and I'll order the waiter to empty the Crêpes Suzette pan on your crotch!'

After that, most other tables would order a similar dessert, and the merry banter would be repeated.

Rarely would a Dugout restaurant diner materialise in the 21 Grill. This was a room for employers of people, company owners, and directors – the well-heeled classes. They came to the 21 Grill because the food and service were first-class. Some came because they wanted to impress colleagues. These were the Châteauneuf-du-Pape, Pouilly-Fuissé chardonnay classes, not the Dugout restaurant's Pink Lady or cold duck crew!

Chapter 16

DANNY, SALT OF THE EARTH

If anyone wanted to see Danny at his happiest, all they had to do was visit him on a Friday, for it was on these days he put his social plan for the weekend in motion. Being a regular social drinker and serious-minded about his work, he never mixed the two.

Danny stood at about five feet ten and had a sturdy build. His ready smile and easygoing attitude made him a natural at making friends. These traits also served him well in his professional life as a sales representative for domestic appliances, including vinyl records, at HomElectrix. The company was located on the ground floor of Kanabar House on Victoria Avenue.

Although he was initially my brother's friend, Danny and I became very close when he came to live with me in Kanjedza, Blantyre.

'Should the two of you not hit it off, you, as my young brother, will be the one to blame,' Chalela had said in his letter to me, which Danny had brought with him from Lilongwe, and, he had added, 'Danny is simply a great guy.'

Danny arrived on a Sunday afternoon, and after inducting him into his new home I prepared dinner, and that's when Danny could not stop cracking jokes, or rather, telling me funny stories. I began to understand what Chalela had said about this man.

The very first Friday after Danny's arrival, I knew my life in Blantyre would never be quite the same again. I arrived home at around six thirty p.m. I found three crates of Carlsberg on the kitchen table, a goat tethered to a kachere tree behind the house, and a note under my bedroom door which simply read, 'Barbeque tomorrow, ha, ha, ha!'

I never saw him that night, but at around nine o'clock the following morning, my bedroom door gently opened and there was Danny in his pyjamas, carrying a tray with two large mugs of coffee.

'Good morning, Danny,' I said, the last word cut short prematurely because of a huge early morning yawn.

Danny sat at the foot of the bed before answering and resting the tray on the bed next to him.

'When are you getting up? It's the bar-be-que day today, remember?'

'What are we celebrating, Danny?' I asked, raising my upper body and resting my head on my hand supported by a bent elbow.

'Good health! Isn't that worth celebrating, Davie?' he replied chirpily and proceeded, 'I've invited Augustine and Geoff to help with the slaughtering and general preparations of the goat. They're very excited about the whole idea, and they're so happy that they'll be eating at Ryall's Hotel's à la carte on the cheap. Naturally, I took the liberty of telling them all the cooking will be done by you. You don't mind, do you, Davie?' This was the moment I observed that although my brother, Chalela, was away, his double was right here next to me! Danny was also the same age as Chalela, who was two years older than me.

I introduced Danny to Augustin and Geof the second weekend after he arrived in Blantyre. We met at Chisakalime Night Club in Limbe. Augustin and Geof were my former schoolmates from Soche Hill Secondary School. Geof was my brother's classmate, and Augustin was a year ahead of them. After that initial chance meeting, the three of them hit it off like the proverbial house on fire.

Well, what could I say? 'So, what time did you agree they would be here?' I asked, getting out of bed and putting on my dressing gown.

'They should be here by eleven this morning, and after breakfast let's walk to the bottle store to buy a few extra drinks and maybe extra spices for the goat.' My life with Danny had truly begun!

I do not recall a weekend when Danny did not go out for a drink. Occasionally, whenever my shifts at work allowed, I would accompany him, and as was his way of doing things, often we would not be home until dawn. And since he was the only one with a car in our immediate group, I was forced to tag along with him no matter how tired I would be. Besides, it would have been viewed as extremely selfish to curtail colleagues' weekend fun by forcing them to return home prematurely!

One Saturday evening, our friend, Eddington Chipendo, was getting engaged to be married, and both Danny and I were invited to join the celebrations at the Migochi residence at Railways' senior staff residence in Limbe. The girlfriend, Isabel, was one of Mr Migochi's daughters.

Despite being on duty on this evening, I was determined to make myself available to attend this momentous occasion. Both Isabel and Eddington were our friends. I was working at Ryall's until ten o'clock at night that day. Saturday evenings were busier than most. As it happened, I was heavily involved in managing private dinners until around nine thirty and did not have time to eat, so I asked Thomas, the sous chef, to prepare some food for me to take away and made sure I was sitting in the hotel van when the clock struck ten.

The driver put his foot down hard on the accelerator, and we were in Kanjedza within around fifteen minutes. Quickly dropping the food I had carried from the hotel in the sitting-room, I rushed back to the van for my short trip to the engagement party, which was only three kilometres away.

As the driver pulled away for his return trip to Ryall's, I was already getting myself in the mood. Danny, Kelly, and the rest of the guys were there and well into the swing of things. I felt a bit out of place, so to make up for a lost time, I gulped the first drink which Cedric, Eddington's young brother, had served me. I knew from the taste that it was alcoholic. Within a few minutes, he came with a bottle of Carlsberg (Elephant) Special Brew, which I again quickly dealt with. This was my first time taking an alcoholic drink! Cedric, seeing me empty-handed, quickly brought me a glass filled with what looked and smelled like whisky and a bottle of ginger ale.

'Anyone who is going to leave this party sober will have to be a witch!' he said as he quickly disappeared onto the dance floor.

The place was buzzing. I was buzzing, and my feet were becoming lighter, at which point Cedric reappeared. 'Another drink, my brother?'

'Whisky,' I answered.

He returned with a glass of brandy. 'Whisky has finished,' he contritely explained.

One sip, then another, followed by a gulp, and like a thick cloud I could feel my inhibitions evaporating, and as if on remote control, my feet were now stomping the floor rhythmically to the beat of the music in the room.

Up until this point, I had never felt comfortable with my dancing abilities, but now, I felt I would have made even the great King of Soul jealous. Isn't it amazing what effect alcohol can have on our brains?

Confidently, I joined the others on the dance floor, and who was there to welcome me? Cedric, with his over-used line, 'A drink, my brother?' Not even waiting for my response, he momentarily vanished and like lighting reappeared, this time holding a glass containing something which, under the dimmed lights, looked like water. 'It's gin and tonic, brother. Brandy has finished. We must make do with what's available, isn't it, my dear brother?!' I sipped the liquid and although I was not too keen on the taste, I was enjoying the effects, so down the throat it flowed.

I had just started to dance when I saw, right next to me, a man I did not recognise threatening the elder sister of the girl who was getting engaged. Without thinking and without considering my safety, I came right between them, my hand reaching for his throat. As he pushed me away, I took up a Bruce Lee kung fu stance. At that moment, Kelly came along and so did a few other people who must have witnessed what was transpiring just before my brave if somewhat foolhardy intervention. They threw the guy out and the girl thanked me for defending her. Kelly took me out on the veranda and said, 'Nkulu Waledzelatu.' This translates as, 'Dude, you are drunk.'

He knew I was drunk although he had never seen me in that condition, because until then I was a teetotaller. It was only when Kelly said those words that I realised I was indeed drunk. Until then I had just felt relaxed and in control and self-assured. Now I felt somehow embarrassed. I had always despised those who got visibly intoxicated in public, and I thought I would do better than that, that I would be able to handle alcohol in a gentlemanly fashion, but here I was, almost legless and showing all the signs I despised in drunken people.

It was now after two in the morning. Danny, who had been away dropping a few friends off at their respective homes, had just returned and was parking his car in the car park. He had not witnessed my little contretemps. I could see Kelly whispering to him as they both walked towards where I was standing on the veranda. Danny's first words to me were, 'I think you are tired; we should be going home.' I knew right away Kelly had told him of the fracas and the fact that I was drunk. I felt ashamed and did not utter a word.

Within a couple of minutes, Danny was ready to take me home, and this time there was one other person in the car. He was to be dropped at B&C Quarters, less than a kilometre from Ryall's Hotel. This meant that we had to drive through where I lived and through all the streetlights in Blantyre central.

The dazzle of the streetlights as we drove along simply added to my misery. I know those who have reached a certain level of intoxication will agree with me about the effects of walking like a person who has taken one drink too many. It is simply hell! I could hear the witches' cauldron in my stomach bubbling like a distant sound of thunder. I could hardly keep my neck upright. Things around me seemed to be off-bAaron ce and they swayed from side to side. I remember the chap saying when he was dropped at his house gate, 'I suggest you drive him straight home and give him the salt treatment. He looks in a bad way. Some people cannot control their drinking!'

He spoke like I wasn't there, exceedingly adding to my discomfort. I did not comment. I could not comment. I felt (I cannot use the word 'thought' for the fear of over-stretching its meaning) that if I opened my mouth, everything inside me would just gush out like a volcanic eruption. I hated the idea of vomiting, and worse still doing so in public, so the strategy was to keep my mouth firmly shut to control the 'event' until we got home where, in the privacy of my bedroom, I would be able to loosen the brakes. However, my stomach had other ideas, and as soon as we passed the junction to M'jamba Park and the Malawi Housing Corporation on the Kanjedza Soche road, the inevitable happened. Danny applied the emergency brakes, and I clumsily opened the door and managed to put my feet out. Although I hadn't caused much mess in the car, outside the passenger door and all the way on the left side of the car to the back was a site I wasn't comfortable looking at more than once. I could not stand up. My mouth was like a fully turned-on tap on those Roman statues' mouths, evil-looking, the ones where water gushes from their mouths and the facial expressions show they are not enjoying the experience. Involuntarily, I opened my mouth so wide that I felt it would split in two. My chest was hurting, my head was spinning and death, if not imminent, seemed slightly preferable.

'Are you all right, Davie?' asked Danny without expecting a reply, I guess. Although I tried to answer, it was not words which came out of my mouth but the gush of a ponging concoction of what had biologically become a nasty stale mixture of a variety of liquors, rice, and different types of meats. Not very nice!

'Oh, dear!' That is all I remember him saying as he disappeared into the nearby bushes to spend a penny. He was back in no time at all and immediately started the engine and we were off again, but a few metres down the road the car coughed and spluttered to a halt as Danny tried unsuccessfully to give the Austin Mini more throttle. We had run out of fuel!

Malawi, along with several other nations, was rationing petrol because of a civil war raging in Iran, where the Shah of Iran had been deposed by Ayatollah Khomeini, and Iran being one of the major exporters of crude oil, the conflict affected supplies worldwide. In response to the shortages, Dr Kamuzu Banda's regime introduced fuel rationing whereby it being a Saturday, there was no fuel station open in the country.

I do not know whether Danny was saying a silent prayer or not as his head rested on the steering wheel, engrossed in thought about how we were going to get home. There were no mobile phones then, and finding a public phone booth, and a working one for that matter, was not a very practical expectation in that vicinity. My divine spirit, having been drowned in the bottled variety, was unable to join in, but just at that moment, a car going in the opposite direction stopped. It was being driven by a chap named Pearson Phiri, who had been at the party earlier and recognised Danny's car.

'What's wrong?' he asked Danny as he crossed the road towards our stricken chariot. 'And who is the guy on the other side of the car?' he continued. Danny explained the situation and that I was the other guy.

'I didn't know he drunk at all,' commented Pearson as he walked towards me, where I was barely conscious.

'No, he doesn't,' answered Danny warily.

'You mean he didn't,' quipped Phiri, and they both laughed. 'So, he has just de-flowered himself!' He continued with his quips as he walked towards his car on the other side of the road to make a U-turn and take us to Kanjedza. I am sure I was more appreciative of this gesture by Pearson than Danny might have been, because I didn't think I was in any condition to walk the two kilometres home in the state I was in – I could hardly stand up!

I spent the night failing to sleep because of a bed and a room which seemed to be oscillating, forcing me to change my sitting and lying positions again and again, and as if that were not bad enough, the throwing up continued.

I managed to steal some little sleep a few hours later, and when I woke up there was vomit on the bed and on my jacket, which I had not taken off. I also noticed my Ryall's Hotel kitchen boots were still laced on.

I gingerly struggled to make my way to the shower room, using the walls for support as I did so. I found the idea of even touching any part of my clothes or body repulsive. I stood under the showerhead fully clothed, letting the power of the flowing water remove from my clothes and body all the muck which had stuck on me. Only then was I courageous enough to have my clothes off and shower properly, notwithstanding one arm supporting me against the wall.

I think the noises I must have made while having the shower must have awakened Danny, because I heard the opening and shutting of doors as soon as I returned to my room. My little battery-operated Seiko clock on the stool next to my bed showed that it was six fifteen a.m., too early for us to begin our off-day, particularly after the kind of night we had both experienced, albeit somehow in various ways.

There was then a slight knock at my bedroom door, and the door slowly opened long before I could answer. It was Danny. He had two coffee mugs in his hands and, stretching his right hand to offer me one of them, he spoke.

'Oh! What a mess, Davie, and what a night! What were you drinking last night?' I just looked at him like a zombie with an embarrassed smile on my face.

I took a sip from my coffee mug, and it tasted awful. It was like there was no sugar, and it was very strong! 'Danny, you forgot to add sugar to my coffee?' I queried.

'Oh! But I did. Still, let me bring you the sugar bowl.' He did that, and even after I had added two extra teaspoons of sugar, the taste was still unpleasant.

'I know; it's the alcohol. It does temporarily kill one's taste buds! I think you need to replenish your body with some food. When was your last meal, Davie?' I explained when to him.

'Ah! That was well over twenty-four hours ago!' With those words, Danny disappeared into the kitchen, where he warmed up some food from the previous night and brought it to the bedroom. He left me alone as I tried to eat.

The food and the coffee seemed to make my condition worse. I resumed the throwing up, causing Danny to take some quick evasive action! I reached a point when I felt my intestines were going to come out too, and my chest bones were now feeling dislocated. I was in unbearable pain, and I could hardly sit or lie in one position without feeling some invisible force was tipping the bed over, at which point I would turn to the other side where the same feeling would start all over again. I was now certain the four horsemen were drawing close, and with great effort, I crawled to my bedroom door, which I managed to open. Danny, who had left his bedroom door ajar, came out, took another look at me and thought it was now time for the salt treatment.

From the kitchen, he brought a mug full of brine and extra salt on a side plate. He ordered me to drink the brine as he washed my bare feet with warm water. He then applied the salt to my wet soles. It took less than five minutes for me to start throwing up again. The sun was now about to rise, and the sounds of singing birds could be heard from the kachere tree behind the house. Looking back and hearing from people who understand the salt treatment better, Danny should have performed that on me the previous night, when some of the alcohol was still in my tummy and not yet fully absorbed into my bloodstream. The throwing up after the salt treatment had nothing to do with the treatment, apparently! But it does work if applied in a timely fashion.

I yet again dozed off and only got up after two in the afternoon. By this time, Danny had tidied up all the mess in the house and my filthy clothes had been washed and were drying on a line behind the kitchen.

'I had to hire the neighbour's houseboy to perform the chores. By the way, the guys are here. Augustine and Jeff have brought us some pork, which we are already roasting on the veranda. Come and join us when you are ready, man!' It came out like a friendly order.

The smell of charcoal-roasted pork was irresistibly wafting through the whole house, and I thought this could be the solution to my wonky taste buds!

I slowly made my way to the veranda. I was still suffering from vertigo and feeling thirsty and very hungry. Danny was sitting on a little bamboo chair, and as soon as the boys set their collective eyes on me, they all busted into uncontrollable laughter.

'Davie, you needed to manage a tricycle before a bicycle, a motorbike, a car, and then an articulated truck! You do not go straight for an articulated, as you did. Do you want to die young? What did you think you were doing, man?' That was Augustine, nicknamed, endearingly, Mugabe! By the way, we all had nicknames. Danny's was Kabomba (a small bomb – I don't know why – he never made bombs), and Kelly was Mungo, after the Caribbean musician, Mungo Jerry. Kelly was a big fan. He used to like Mungo Jerry's 'In the Summertime' rather a lot!

Danny was now telling us his new girlfriend would be joining us soon, to help with the cooking, he said.

Janet was shapely. She was short and of medium build, and every part of her anatomy which was supposed to bulge, bulged, apart from her tummy, that is! She spoke with a voice so soft that listening to her was such a soothing experience, even when she was angry. Her eyes were big and chestnut-brown. Danny had told me these were what had attracted him to her in the first place – eyes, he said, which projected kindness and sad innocence at the same time. They were mentally very calming facial attributes, he had told me.

Danny had met Janet before he moved to Blantyre from Lilongwe, and they had been seeing each other now for well over six months. Judging from the way he spoke about her, one could easily tell he loved her deeply. He was utterly bowled over by her.

For well over a year, this was going to be my new life with Danny, but slowly I could see the effect of Janet's presence in Danny's life. Out were those nightclubbing days and in were the wining and dining evenings, topped up with even more bliss at KJ241, the official house number for our house in Kanjedza.

Very often I could guess whether Janet had stayed with Danny by the sound of him playing a tune on his box guitar for his lady, serenading her. He wasn't bad with it either. I sometimes listened closely as he played the classic 'Eluby' repeatedly, and I thought of Janet, lying there on his bed, not completely dressed, as she was being serenaded. Just a wild imagination of mine! As I drifted in and out of sleep, there was a little envious smile on my face, not envious of the two but rather of my failure to play the guitar or any other musical equipment. This was despite having guitars and a variety of musical equipment in our house, where my father had various musical equipment for his bands at the nightclub. Despite that, he had always discouraged us from playing any one of them, because he had reasoned that only crooks played such instruments. Certainly, Danny wasn't a crook! He had also played the church organ when we were growing up. We simply obediently obeyed that instruction!

'Davie, I've been thinking,' Danny started one Sunday afternoon as we were relaxing on the veranda. 'I've taken Janet to all the good restaurants in town, but so far, I've been avoiding the 21 Grill at Ryall's simply because of the price! People say I might have to sell my jalopy to afford a meal in the Grill Room!'

'Do they? They may have a point, but they also do exaggerate a bit,' I said. 'But I don't think selling your jalopy would raise enough cash for a proper romantic dinner for you and Janet in the Grill Room,' I teased him. 'No, seriously, it's not as bad as that. I'm sure you spend more money when you go to a disco than you might spend in the 21 Grill with your beautiful lady.'

'You're not just saying that to boost sales for Ryall's, are you?' retorted Danny.

'Danny, Danny, Danny, giving you a table in the Grill Room would be a financial loss for the hotel. People who dine there do not count their pennies, like you. These are top executives, man! Chief executive officers, Malawi Congress Party's top brass, intelligence chiefs, serious tourists, etcetera.'

'All right then, I get the point. How much are we talking about on average for a meal for two?' he asked, with his large dark-brown eyes focused on mine. His eyes and general looks always reminded me of The Temptations' Melvin Franklin (real name Davie Melvin English).

'Let's see,' I said. 'What is Janet's favourite dish?'

'Prawns,' he answered. 'The large ones, you know, tiger prawns, grilled and out of the shell.'

'Now, those don't come cheap, my man Danny,' I advised.

'It's for Janet, Davie. You must understand. I love that woman, man!' he replied resignedly.

'And how about you? Your favourite – should I take it to be the usual?'

'Yes – grilled chicken with Piri-piri, extra hot.'

'Any wine?'

'Yeees – what do you recommend, Davie?'

'Well, that's a little tricky, Danny, since I must think of your pocket first and your palate second. Okay, to make things easier and cheaper for you, I suggest Mateus Rosé. This means you won't have to have red and white wine, one with meat and the other with fish. You see, I've saved you the price of one bottle of wine already!'

'Er ... just how much is this ... er ... er ... rosé?' asked Danny hesitantly. Danny was more into beers!

"Danny, we are talking about one kwacha seventy-five tambala here, my friend.'

'MWK1.75 – that isn't cheap, Davie! What if Janet is in a particularly jovial mood and wants more wine? That would be MWK3.50 ... I think.'

'I see your mental arithmetic isn't bad at all, Danny,' I quipped.

'So, I should be looking at MWK3.50 before I have tasted a piece of my Piri-piri chicken ...' To appreciate Danny's anguish, one should appreciate that, at the time, the price of a live goat was also around MWK3.50!

'Well, it's up to you, lover-man. If it is the 21 Grill you want, get your hands on at least fifteen to twenty kwacha. And if you want to go on the list of the Grill Room's most favoured diners, keep an extra two kwacha as a tip to the waiter.'

'A two-kwacha tip!' protested Danny.

'You do not have to, but it is very difficult to get a table in the Grill Room because it is often fully booked for well over a month sometimes. This is why those who want recognition and favours next time they wish to book for a table give big tips. Consequently, the next time they call for a booking, the head waiter will do everything possible to accommodate them and not just give them any odd table in the room – one in a quiet corner of the restaurant. For bad tippers or those who don't tip at all, the head waiter makes sure that next time they come in he gives them a table on the way to and from the kitchen, a very noisy part of the restaurant with waiters banging the door every other minute as they work between the kitchen and the restaurant. Tips are the key, my friend. Besides, really, must you do this, Danny?'

'Davie, there is something you need to know. Janet works with a lot of Europeans, some of whom have made the odd pass at her, and because she has turned them down, they have started to belittle and bad-mouth me. They think I am too ordinary and skint, a man who cannot afford the finer things in life …'

'Like the 21 Grill?' I interjected.

'You could say that. Daniel Chikhawo is not ordinary, and I will choose to book the day some of them have booked to dine in the Grill Room. I want to show them who I am. Before we go on this date, I would like you to show us which table implement goes with what dish. I do not want us to be mocked by these snooty Europeans because I used a dessert spoon for soup.'

'They would enjoy that, I am sure, Danny. When you are ready, my dearest friend, lover-man Danny,' I said mockingly, and I do not think that bothered him at all. He was walking on cloud nine!

Weeks came, weeks went, and slowly there was less mention of Janet until one weekend when we were having our usual breakfast, a cup of tea with buttered bread, sometimes with marmalade or jam when those indulgences were available in the house.

'Davie, I think Janet is seeing someone at her office,' Danny said with a very forlorn voice.

'Nooo! How do you know this, Danny?' I asked with a visibly shocked look on my face. 'Janet cannot do that, Danny.'

'Oh yes she can, Davie, and she is doing it!'

'You know that Kenyan friend of mine, Akida? He plays golf at the Blantyre Sports Club, and he has seen Janet having a drink with a certain young-looking Welshman called Jones. He works for Mandala. And he says that from the way they sat, any adult who understands romance could tell the two were an item, no question at all!'

'Have you asked Janet about this?' I queried.

'No. I will not ask her. I want to catch her with her Welshman lover, live!'

'As long as there is no physical violence when you find them together, Danny,' I reasoned, and he promised he would be a gentleman on the day!

A few weeks went by, and one Saturday morning, when he was working a half-day, Danny told me just before he left for work that he had heard Janet would be going to the Hong Kong Restaurant with Jones the Welshman. He then planned to call her to tell her that he had to travel to Lilongwe to sort out some family matters. That way she would not think of bumping into Danny anywhere in Blantyre that weekend.

Danny booked a table for three under a fake name. The arrival time was an hour after Jones' arrival time, which was seven thirty p.m. He knew that most Westerners are sticklers for time and that the couple would surely be arriving on time. Being a romantic evening, it would have to be a three-course meal so that by eight p.m. they could be in the middle of their main course. The restaurant served an à la carte menu.

Danny did not ask Akida what kind of car Jones drove, so the only face they were a hundred per cent sure of was that of Janet's. At precisely seven twenty-five p.m., a white Datsun 120Y Coupé entered the Hong Kong Restaurant car park and out came a white guy in a black dinner suit complete with a black bow-tie with tiny shiny-white spots on it. He dashed around the car and opened the door for a lady who was wearing a long flowing blue dress with sequins around the edges, neck, arms, and the hem, which were reflectively responding to the lights outside the restaurant. The man gave Janet a peck on the cheek before closing and locking the car doors. With a gently rising heartbeat and body temperature, Danny was watching all this from a safe distance at the top of Hannover Avenue.

'We still have almost an hour to kill, guys. Let's go into the public bar at Ryall's for a drink or two before going into Hong Kong,' I proposed. Danny was now looking deserted and down. Who wouldn't?

'Danny, do you want to proceed with this?' I asked, and Danny simply looked at me. He stayed put! The night's temperature was continuing to drop, and we remained there, counting down the minutes.

Finally, it was now eight twenty-five p.m., and quietly Danny started to walk towards the few cement steps which led into the Hong Kong Restaurant car park. Quietly, Augustin and myself also started to follow him.

'Danny, so, we go in and simply ask about our booking. We get our table, we sit down strategically, and you take the chair directly facing in the direction of Janet's table. Do not say anything yet. We order our food, and I know a moment will present itself.' Fate did play its part in this project. The table we were given was right next to Janet's! Danny was sitting almost next to Janet, albeit at a different table about a metre away!

We ordered our food, and as far as I was concerned, Danny and Jones had not met before. I could sense Janet's body language had negatively changed. I guess she did not know how Danny was going to respond to this awkward situation. And, I assume, she did not know how Jones would respond to whatever Danny was going to throw at him. Come to think of it, neither did Augustin nor myself!

Our first course came. I recall it was Devil's Soup, Bird's Nest Soup, and I had chow mein. Just as Augustin and I were about to start eating, Danny turned toward Janet.

'Janet, I am glad you have mysteriously recovered. I wonder what medication you are on, my lovely lady?' And before she could answer, Danny continued, 'By the way, who is this guy, Janet?'

'Janet, who is this guy?' retorted Mr Jones, sounding irritated, in a strong Welsh accent.

'Never mind that – I asked first! Who are you? Janet is my girlfriend, and I know she should be on bed rest, and here she is going against her doctor's advice because of you!' Danny was now standing up, attracting the attention of other diners in the restaurant. Augustin and I tried to ask him calmly to de-escalate by gently and stealthily pulling his jacket from behind, but to no avail!

'Janet, Janet, Janet, I do not want to cause a scene in here. Come on, follow me outside, now!' ordered Danny angrily and assertively. He continued, 'And you, white boy, you stay put if you know what's good for you!' Fuming, Danny racially denigrated Jones. Augustin and I were now both standing up and so was Jones, whose eyes were moving from Augustin to Danny and me, as if he were sizing us up. By the way, we were all between five feet ten inches to six feet two inches tall and butch! Jones was smaller than any one of us. It was, on paper at least, no contest!

Reluctantly and slowly, Janet stood up. She removed her serviette from her chest, picked up her handbag, which she had placed on the empty chair on her left, and walked towards the main door with Danny immediately and toweringly behind her.

Jones seemed to want to follow the two outside, but Augustin warned him against that. 'I really wouldn't do that if I were you!' Augustin whispered to him, and Jones quietly sat down. He looked agitated but helpless to act!

After what seemed forever but was probably only fifteen minutes or so, Danny came back and ordered us to let Jones know that he had to settle his bill and leave and that his woman was waiting for him in the restaurant car park outside. In response, Augustin walked around the table and took the seat opposite Mr Jones, which Janet had occupied only a few minutes earlier.

'Hello. I do not think it is in your interest to continue dining in this place. My friend here is Janet's regular boyfriend, and as you can see, he is furious. Why don't you tell the waiter to pack the rest of the food, pay your bill, and leave quickly? As he has already told you, Janet is in the car park.'

Like a jack-in-the-box, Jones did not say a word and, visibly shaken, he got up and bumping into a few chairs made his way to the till. He paid his bill and collected what had now developed into an impromptu takeaway.

I thought that having achieved his goal, Danny could now relax and have his Devil's Soup, which had now been served. Not at all! He just sat there, head bowed as if in quiet prayer. We tried to encourage him to eat but he claimed he had lost his appetite. So, like Mr Jones and Janet, we too had to carry our food home.

It took Danny a few months before he resumed dating again!

My fondest memory of Danny is that he was the man who introduced me to music by The Temptations, The Four Tops, Marvin Gaye, Gladys Knight and the Pips, and Ben E. King and B.B. King. Before this, Bula's contribution to my music preference had been music by Otis Redding, Wilson Picket, Percy Sledge, Sam and Davie, Solomon Burke, and Aretha Franklin. I have, thus, mostly listened to rhythm-and-blues for most of my life, and it is all thanks to Danny and Bula.

Chapter 17

WE WERE ONLY EXPECTING
AN ENGAGEMENT

After leaving Ryall's Hotel to join my father in running the newly opened Chester's City Motel in Lilongwe, I started to see my girlfriend, Madalo, more often. She lived less than three miles from the motel.

Being a woman of her word, she reminded me of the terms and conditions she had set for me if I ever wanted to have my card stamped, so to speak! Allow me to digress a little here. I recall a story my friend in Harare, Bisiketi, had narrated to me about the problems he had faced as he attempted and eagerly waited to get physical with his girlfriend, to whom he later got engaged and married. He was living in his family home with his mother. His father had died when he was twelve. He had two younger brothers, two younger sisters, and two elder ones, whom his mother had single-handedly raised.

We had met in London in the early eighties, and by the time Bisiketi returned to a liberated Zimbabwe, we were very close. That was when he met his sweetheart, Petronella, whom he soon introduced to his mother, and she introduced him to her parents. Petronella started spending weekends at Bisiketi' place, where she slept in the main house with his mother while poor Bisiketi spent his nights alone in an outer building ten metres from the main house. His mother was a devout Christian and traditionalist. She did not believe in sex before marriage, and she made sure her son wasn't having a nibble! She did not want to imagine that perhaps these two young people were already nibbling away in some secret locations during the day. Still, months went by, and one day, Bisiketi' mother lost her first cousin, who lived around a kilometre or so away. It was on a Friday, the day Petronella usually came for her weekend stay. Culturally, when there is a bereavement in the family or a close community, people gather and spend nights at the dead person's house. Mother Chikuni had left the house earlier, and when Petronella and Bisiketi arrived later that evening, they found the house unguarded. They chatted in the main house while dreading the possibility of Bisiketi' mother returning in the night. When the clock struck midnight, they were confident his mother would not be returning that night.

The two spent the night in the outer house, which was just a one-room space. There was a toilet between this structure and the main house, and there was a water tap in the same area. At about six a.m., they heard the sound of someone washing their clothes at the tap, where there was a functional slap for laundry. Petronella peeped, and it was Mother. She had seen Petronella's car parked in front of the house and she had found that she was not in the main house! Petronella wanted to respond to a call of nature, but she just couldn't face the mother, who thought of her as 'a good girl'. That tag had been soiled as far as Mother Chikuni was concerned. Petronella also understood the weight of what had now been exposed. They had taken some wine the night before. She had emptied her bladder a couple of times in the night, but her bladder was full again, very full.

Nature forced the poor girl to muster enough courage to open the door. She did exactly that and, in a sheepish, high-pitched voice, she greeted her mother-in-law. 'Good morning, Mother,' she mumbled, to which the mother-in-law responded without raising her head to look at her. Petronella went into the toilet and then to the main house to collect her toothbrush and other hygienic necessities.

'So, you didn't move all your stuff from the house into BISIKETI's room last night?'

Petronella's response was simply, 'Sorry, Mother!'

It was within a month after this incident when Bisiketi informed his mother that he wanted to get engaged to Petronella. He informed me that this was the first time since that fateful morning that he saw his mother smile.

Madalo was my childhood sweetheart, whom I had met through Bula, whose brother was dating Madalo's sister, Irene. She went to school at Likuni Girls' Secondary School three hundred kilometres away in Lilongwe. It was, as people call it and for practical reasons, 'a distant love'.

Apart from exchanging photographs and a lot of love letters, I had only met Madalo once when she visited her sister at Bula's brother's residence in Nkolokosa, Blantyre. She was very beautiful, as she had appeared in the photographs. Her afro hair was so dark and shiny. I thought she was very proud of it and spent time and money taking care of it. She had a beautiful, rotund face, on which her small, flat nose and well-spaced chestnut-brown eyes sat joyously in unison. She was light brown in complexion and her full medium-built body looked sexually appealing to me.

Our relationship blossomed more after we had both written our O Levels and Madalo had moved back to Blantyre, where she lived with another elder sister of hers in Kanjedza.

She surprised me one day when I asked her for a date and her response was, 'All right; come home.' I did not think our relationship had reached that stage. Still, I thought, if it was all right for her, who was I to argue? So, I accepted. Her sister worked for Hogg Robinson in town, where the knocking-off time was four thirty p.m., and I wondered why Madalo had suggested I should be at their house at three thirty p.m. I was expecting an all-day date, just the two of us, alone!

The map Madalo had given me for her address in Kanjedza was very easy to follow. It was one of those houses in Kanjedza's new lines which face north towards what was then Rainbow and Queens Cinemas in Limbe.

She opened the door and allowed me in. She was wearing a yellow dress which flowed to just below the knees – that was the legal requirement for women. It was illegal to wear anything which did not cover the body up to the knees. She shyly beckoned me to sit down, pointing at the two-seater immediately after the front door. The living room was well made up and although it was bijou, the blue-fabric-upholstered lounge suite looked nice. There was also a four-seater dining set just before a door which I later observed led to the kitchen.

'Do you want a cold or warm drink?' she asked with a smile so radiant. She couldn't have guessed what that was doing to my body. I chose tea. She quickly went into the kitchen, from where I could, in no time at all, hear the kettle whistling. She must have pre-heated the water, I thought. In no time at all, a tray of teacups and cupcakes was brought in and placed on a small stool, which she pulled next to me. 'I hope you like my cakes; I baked them this morning.' They were tasty and still warm. As we drank our tea, she rummaged through a small heap of music albums from which she pulled one by Otis Redding, *Immortal Otis*, and she set the record player to play the track 'Champaign and Wine' again and again.

We chatted about our school days and the Ordinary Level examination results we were both awaiting.

The door opened and it was Madalo's elder sister, the owner of the house. She walked in and took a seat opposite me. With a smile, she greeted me and Madalo, who introduced me as a 'friend', at which the sister gave a questioning and yet knowing smile.

'So, are you from Lilongwe? I know your father has business-es there,' Madalo's sister said.

'No, we are from Mwanza. My father came from N'nenu District. Well, it was his father who did; my father was born in Mwanza,' I explained.

'But I have also heard that you were from Zomba, or at least you have some connections in Zomba?'

'Yes, you have heard that right. My father bought a farm in Thondwe, Zomba years ago. A year before I was born. He then moved his father and sisters to this farm. It increasingly became our other home as the years passed by and later, in 1963, he opened a restaurant and nightclub at Four Miles on the Zomba–Blantyre Road,' I explained, wondering what her next question was going to be.

'So, you went to school in Zomba, Lilongwe, and Blantyre?'

'Yes,' I responded. Of course, I had gone to school in the Chiradzulu district too but I didn't want to complicate my response. At this point, I felt it was time to free myself from the ongoing inquisition.

'Madam, I was about to leave when you walked in. It has been nice meeting you.' Well, it had been. Being introduced to her by Madalo gave me confidence in her seriousness about our relationship, I thought.

Madalo escorted me toward the bus stop, and we agreed to meet again at the weekend.

When I called her on the Friday before our weekend date, she told me that I should *collect* her from her other elder sister's house in Nkolokosa. I didn't mind that. When I say collect, I do not mean by car. Oh, no! It was on foot. I was going to arrive there and greet her family for the first time. I would answer a few probing questions, if what I had experienced a few days earlier in Kanjedza was anything to go by. Besides, I was in love with the sister – Madalo.

Just over two years later, my father asked me to join him to run the family business. This was when he opened a motel in Lilongwe. He had named it Chester's City Motel, now, Lingadzi Inn.

At this point, Madalo had been transferred by her employer, Gramil, to Lilongwe. She had a one-bedroom flat in Area Eighteen, less than five kilometres from the motel.

The dying embers of our romance were rekindled, and this time Madalo seemed ready to add her voice to those of her and my sisters. She wanted and demanded we got engaged. I agreed, and arrangements were quickly made by our two families. The ceremony was to take place at Madalo's home village near the old Balaka Market, Nsiyaludzu Village.

My father was not keen on me getting engaged to get married. He thought that at just twenty-one years of age I was too young to make such a commitment, but he did not stop me.

During this same period, I received a telephone call from Madalo. We had been out of touch for quite some time. Well over three years. She told me she was now working for the Grain and Milling Company (Gramil) in Lilongwe, as a private secretary to the company chairman, John Nsonthi, the ex-minister who had saved my education a few years earlier. My relationship with Madalo started in 1973 and continued throughout my turbulent, foot-loose years. It was the kind of relationship that everybody in both our families and all our friends knew about. They also knew that I was not ready to settle down yet from observing other things I was getting up to, which was normal in Malawi among people of my age at that time. The excuse was 'Boys will be boys', whatever that meant.

So, we started dating frequently and it was then that she asked me if I was serious about our relationship. I assured her that I was. She then continued by telling me her eldest sister was inquiring about when I was going to make our relationship official. I responded by telling her that I was going to ask 'How do you think I should do that? I thought we were already official. Apart from your parents, all your seven sisters have met me.' Now, five years later, it had finally happened and, as they say, the first cut was the deepest. Madalo was pregnant. Because of the bond which existed between us, I decided to pack up my sporting gear and become an 'honest' man!

Did I love Madalo? Yes, and I trusted her very much. Madalo was beautiful, elegant, caring, and extremely romantic. Sadly, at that time in my life, that was not enough. For some reason, I also craved and hunted for more excitement. Father did not think things would work out between us because, in his opinion, it was too soon after the tragic affair that which just ended with Allena, but he still gave me his unreserved blessings.

We were both Ngonis by tribe, just like we were with Allena, and as is expected in our tradition and culture, plans were made to go to Madalo's home village, where her parents lived, for what is called 'Chinkhoswe' – an 'engagement' ceremony at Nsiyaludzu Village, close to Old Balaka Market.

From what we observed when we arrived, it seemed either we had been wrong-footed or Madalo's people had perfected their approach and the meaning to the word Chinkhoswe. The thinking on our side was that we would do away with this cultural necessity before being married at a time of our choosing some time in the future and preferably in church.

The advice and guidance I received from my elder brother, who was already married, were that I was expected to buy a complete traditional gown for Madalo, a basin, four plates, two cups, a hoe, a large knife, a sickle, and an axe. Madalo was supposed to see the colour of her gown one month before the ceremony, and all this was observed. The reason for this was that her maids should also buy, tailor, and be adorned in a similar colour on the agreed all-important day.

This was easier to handle than it had been for my friend, Bisiketi. That had been according to the Manyika culture, where an uncle, Mr Borerwe, had mustered the art and science of representing nieces and nephews in ceremonies like this one.

He used to carry money in different denominations, which he placed strategically in different pockets. During the ceremony, the side representing the bride would say something like, 'We now ask for fifty dollars, because when this girl was growing up, she went to school very far outside Harare. We want that expenditure recovered.' At this point, Borerwe would stand up, very slowly put his hand in the appropriate pocket and slowly take the right bank notes out and just as slowly place the money in a plate placed in front of him for the purpose.

'You know the bride is a graduate. You are not getting a simple wife; ours is a woman the groom will be very proud of. Besides, she will also be contributing financially to the family coffers – five hundred dollars for that.'

'You are now injuring us,' Borerwe would respond as he would stand up and this time even more slowly put his hand in the next pocket, giving the impression he didn't have adequate cash on him. You can imagine the anguish caused by the waiting each time there was a charge to be paid. Apparently, even when the charge was as low as a dollar, Borerwe would still wish to haggle.

'How much do you want us to charge, Baba Borerwe? You are having difficulties paying one dollar. Do you really want to take our daughter as your bride?' the other side would complain in a good-natured albeit frustrated way. That's how Borerwe would know his approach was working, frustrating the opposition into submission. We didn't have to go through that in Balaka.

Family members from both sides travelled from Blantyre and Zomba and the rest of us from Lilongwe to Balaka, where Madalo's parents lived. Apart from my family, I had two friends alongside me for moral support: Francis Mbilizi and Fred Chunga. I was advised by those who had been to such a ceremony that I would need them.

As soon as the car we were travelling in turned onto the dust-road approach into the village, we were welcomed by a group of singing and dancing women waving small leafy branches from the trees which lined the narrow road. It was quite overwhelming and yet exciting. I was beginning to realise the wisdom of having one's chums close by for comfort and to help take one's mind off things in situations like this one.

Outside Madalo's big rectangular brick-and-plaster light-yellow-painted house there was a large and leafy fig tree, under which a few reed mats had been spread out on the hard red earth. We were invited to sit down as the local chief was sent for.

Our local chief, Chief Kumbengule, otherwise known as CheMana, had accompanied my mother from Zomba. They were both given modern wooden dining chairs. After a while, the local chief arrived on the scene and after greeting us, Chief Kumbengule and my mother were ushered into the house.

Four girls, all dressed in similar gowns, came out of the house in single file and sat a good four metres away from where my chums and I were seated, the two chiefs together with my mother and this time followed by Madalo's elder sisters. They, the women, apart from Madalo's team, sat on a reed mat next to ours, and at that point the local chief asked me to identify my lady, the lady I had come all this way for. This I managed to do successfully, because although all the maidens had their faces and heads covered, Madalo had tipped me off earlier. She had told me to look for the one sporting a duku (headgear) with a red thread along the hem. She was the only one who had used that colour specifically for this purpose. In the olden days, failure to successfully pick your woman meant you did not know her that well and the ceremony would be cancelled, and you would be ordered to try again later!

Then the local chief stood up and gave a speech, saying, and I paraphrase, 'I'm so pleased there is a new bull in the village. Tomorrow, I'll show you where to plough. There has never been a divorce in Madalo's family, and there are five sisters before her, all happily married. Looking at the two of you, I don't think that record will be broken.' This pronouncement was followed by applause. I don't know if the chief had heard something about me!

It was now time for my chief to give his speech. It was a hot and windy day, the sort of day when one could easily see the distant mountain ranges melting into the sky with their identical shades of light blue, each shade of blue representing a different and further distance, the furthest being the palest of blues. He started, 'If you look at the distant horizon, Dave and Madalo, you'll see the smooth outline of the mountains. Try to follow them. At first, the colour looks a very pale blue, then it starts to change to a darker blue, very dark, then many miles nearer, the colour changes to a dark green. You then start to notice giant rocks and individual trees. As you climb the mountains, there are lions and leopards, not to mention snakes and caves. But you'll also enjoy the natural and sweet sounds from the different birds singing, the sounds of frogs and crickets, and the wonderful smell from the different flowers. That is marriage, Madalo and Dave. It can be fun and full of joy. Don't either one of you run away from it at the first sound of a lion's roar. Get your spears ready. You're here to stay! Here you are, two individuals brought up in different families with an emphasis on different things. Now you must grind away those scratchy edges so that you can have a smooth dovetailing leading into an enduring union for years to come. Marriage always has a give-and-take element to it.' There was applause as he concluded.

I have not forgotten that speech over the years. It is as timeless as time itself.

The last person to speak was Madalo's eldest sister, Mrs Matako. Her speech, coming after my chief's, did not register until the very end when she said, 'You can now take Madalo wherever you want – she is yours,' followed by applause, and she continued, 'Should you wish to go to church for a blessing of your union, that's all up to you. As far as we're concerned, this is it. Our Madalo is now married to you! Should you want to start having babies, it's all fine as far as we are concerned. This is it!'

It? Well, that was indeed, it! I almost shouted to my mother, 'Mother, tell them we didn't know this was *it*!' My thoughts flew momentarily to my friend, Highton Jia, who got married on a weekend somewhere in Likuni, west of Lilongwe without intending to!

Not that I minded marrying Madalo. I loved her, but I simply was not prepared to enter marriage at this point. I did not feel married, but I got used to behaving like a husband, although my family always referred to her as my girlfriend.

Madalo's flat was located about three miles from the motel. As it seemed more convenient for her to stay there, I started to spend most of my time there too. For reasons of privacy, we decided to make her flat our home and not the motel, where I had a room just like any paying guest. No privacy at all. As far as I can recall, we never exchanged any angry words during this period. The horizon was still pale blue and smooth.

Despite this tranquillity in our relationship, I still was not comfortable looking at myself as being married. Either because of a misunderstanding on a cultural point between the two sides or my feelings, I felt inadvertently *tricked*. If an engagement is a confirmation of a serious intention to marry, why complain when the other side decides you should take their daughter as your lawfully wedded wife with all the rights of a husband right away? To refuse this offer could also raise a red flag as to how serious one's intentions are.

It was during this period that Madalo became pregnant, proof that, although I was not ready to be a husband, I was more than prepared to enjoy the status of being a husband, albeit an unwilling one.

The issue of a wedding taking place in the future was discussed between us. Although I showed interest, I always made sure the date for such an event was in the hazy, distant future. I could see Madalo was beginning to doubt if I was interested in completing the marriage process by having a church wedding with her. Still, time went by, and the pregnancy she was carrying started to show, and chins were wagging! And in the meantime …

Chapter 18

ENTER SUZAN – HOW FRENCH!

Young hearts run wild.

I remember a damp January night in 1979 when I was working at Chester's City Motel in Lilongwe. I was busy printing the menu for the evening meal when a sudden burst of noise startled me. It sounded like gunshots. When I peeped through the louvres, I noticed a station wagon was just driving into the front yard. The rain had just stopped, and the air was thick with humidity. White ants swarmed around the lights in the lobby and there were even more around the car park lights. The bushes outside were alive with the croaking of frogs and the chirping of crickets. Some late-sleeping birds were still flying around, snatching the white ants in their beaks as they performed their acrobatic aerial manoeuvres, catching as many white ants as possible in their beaks with each move.

The sound of the misfiring Land Rover being revved continuously made me want to get a closer look. I walked out of the lobby and watched the driver negotiate a parking space. The vehicle was a dark Russian green in colour. From the way it looked, one could tell it had seen better days. It was not dusk yet, although the sun had just sunk over the far-away mountains to the west which were barely visible under the dispersing rain clouds after the earlier tropical rainstorm. I could easily see the driver. He was a Caucasian middle-aged man of medium height, I observed when he alighted from his vehicle. With him was a black woman. The woman was about five feet eight inches tall and slim, African-slim – curvy without being overweight. She looked rather sophisticated but at the same time, and when I greeted her, I observed she had a kind and yet melancholic look about her. There was also something familiar about her, but thus far, I could not put a finger on it, so to speak! A porter followed immediately behind them carrying their luggage. After being greeted at the reception area, the man asked if there was a double room available for a week. There was. The receptionist processed them, and I didn't see them again for the rest of the evening.

On day two and without mAllena aforethought, I invited the man and woman for dinner in the motel's Ligowe restaurant. The man, Aaron French, was an engineer, as he had explained to me earlier that morning when I had greeted the two of them over breakfast. He was relocating from Zambia and would be proceeding to Blantyre, three hundred and fifteen kilometres from Lilongwe, where he intended to set up his new company rewiring car alternators.

Over dinner that evening, the woman, Suzan, appeared in a black flowing chiffon dress with a very low neckline. She also wore a gold necklace with a dainty crucifix, which rested on her ample bosom very attractively. She looked stunning! Aaron French appeared in a T-shirt and a pair of khaki trousers. I was on duty, so I dressed up accordingly in a dark-grey suit complete with a necktie.

Dinner went down well, and there were a lot of issues to chat about, except politics, for obvious reasons. And as we wound up for the night, Suzan invited me out for dinner the next time I was in Blantyre. She called the waiter who was serving us and asked him for a pen. She quickly wrote her full name and phone number on the back of one of the bar bills littering the table. 'Please call us,' she said as she handed me the piece of paper.

As I lay in my bed, still looking at and mentally reading the information on this tiny little piece of paper, I wondered, had Suzan caught me looking at her bosom when I was admiring her necklace? Or had I made such an impression on her that she wanted me to be *their* friend? I would have travelled to all corners of the world just to see this woman again. Giving me her phone number, confusing as it was, gave me hope of seeing her again in the future ... the least of my hopes!

Three weeks later, Aaron French returned to Lilongwe on his way back to Zambia. He told me he was going to close his Zambia operations now that the Malawi project was taking root. He was back from Lusaka after a week, I think, and told me he was awaiting the arrival of the truck which was carrying his company's equipment and other personal goods.

After a few days of staying at the motel, Aaron and I became close. Eckson, a long-term resident at the motel, even made Aaron an honorary member of the motel's darts club called Nyenga – yes, Nyenga Darts Club! He fitted in perfectly. Aaron loved his drink – a model customer, I thought. During the second week of his stay, he received news from Blantyre that the lease on the workshop, which he had applied for on his first visit, had been approved. This news meant he could go and start doing up the place, although he was still waiting for a work permit.

Aaron was only away in Blantyre for less than a week when he called us to book a double room the following Tuesday.

At around one o'clock that Tuesday there was the sound of a misfiring car approaching, then stopping, followed by the sound of two doors closing, or one door closing twice. It was Mr French, and this time he had Suzan with him. As they were filling in their accommodation cards, I observed that Mr French was physically very expressive of his love for Suzan, touching her in a manner which demonstrated in no uncertain terms that he was her man. In response to the petting, she seemed a little withdrawn, even embarrassed at Mr French's public display of affection. Still, I felt a twinge of secret wild jealousy.

The weather on that day was like it was responding to the mood these two were in. There was a gentle, cool breeze, the temperature was warm without being stifling; it was a humidity-free summer's day. Their inner world might have seemed, just like the day, especially tranquil and still.

'You remember Suzan, my wonder-woman?' asked Mr French, even though I had met the two of them less than a month earlier.

He then playfully squeezed her in a 'half-nelson' hold. The discomforted look about her persisted, but Mr French seemed oblivious to it. She gently forced a smile, revealing a full set of brilliant snow-white teeth. I must admit, at this point, I envied Mr French a smidgen more than earlier. It seemed to me Suzan was the kind of girl who was certainly born on a Monday, the first day back at work for God when all the necessary parts were in stock! Suzan was given the crème de la crème of them all, from head to toe, so I felt.

During their stay, it became increasingly difficult for me not to betray my wicked thoughts in front of the couple, who were, after all, our customers, our guests. I just about managed to maintain my silence and keep my own counsel. I just had to! The possible ramifications resulting from any amorous actions towards Suzan would simply be unthinkable. What would Father say? What would other couples intending to book with us say? What a thought! The publicity would be bad, very bad for business and, besides, it is simply not encouraged in the industry, and control is the by-word, painful though this might be. All the same, when they left the following Friday, I was glad to see the back of them, particularly Suzan's, which I observed with deep concupiscence, in the same way I did her face. They did not know that they had unwittingly made my life a misery, emotionally, simply by being at the motel.

A couple of days later I had to drive Madalo's youngest elder sister to the city centre at around nine in the morning. She had come to visit from Blantyre. She pointed out to me a female figure with a young boy waiting for a bus. It was Jane, one of my former girlfriends, whom Madalo and her sister had heard about. I was not keen to offer them a lift for fear of being misunderstood by my sister-in-law, but she insisted we stop to give them a lift. Jane was a very pretty girl, tall and leggy. She was the first girl I had seriously wanted to marry, although Madalo was always in the background. She had the most beautiful voice I have ever heard and a way of mentioning my name which made my hormones go wild with desire. Our affair started in 1974 when I was about to go to Blantyre to start my job in the hotel industry. Nothing much happened then, but after the first year, I started visiting her in Lilongwe, three hundred and fifteen kilometres from Blantyre, at weekends and on holidays. Her parents knew about our relationship, but I had not gathered enough courage to tell mine. By coincidence, Jane's elder sister, who was married, lived a mere five-minute walk from my house in Kanjedza in Blantyre. She liked me a lot and told me Jane and I were *an item made to order.*

One Saturday evening I had been expecting Jane to arrive by the seven p.m. express coach from Lilongwe and had arranged with Danny and Kelly to give me a lift to the coach station to pick her up. The plan was that we would all go together to pick her up and then I would drive my friends to a disco and take the car home. They would find their way back from the disco. When we arrived at the coach station, there was no sign of Jane. Her best friend, Virginia, who had just come off the coach, told me that as far as she knew, Jane was still in Lilongwe. There was only one express coach service operating between the two cities departing at each end at seven a.m., one p.m.,, and seven thirty p.m.

'Hey?' was the only sound which came out of my mouth as Virginia hurriedly walked to the waiting taxi a few yards away.

I just could not believe Jane had decided not to come to Blantyre. How could she? I had spoken to her the day before and she had sounded so keen to travel to Blantyre. She had also added that Virginia would be her travelling companion. I turned towards Danny, full of despair. 'I have to go to Lilongwe,' I said.

'You do realise it's well over three hundred kilometres away, don't you? And I don't think you can make the disco tonight,' said Danny, tongue in cheek.

'Nkulu Chikondi Chakupha,' ('Old chap, love has killed you,') added Kelly, who I could see was finding it difficult to keep a straight face. They both then burst into fits of laughter.

'Are you all right, Dave? Maybe you should go next week. I'm not saying you shouldn't go tonight. But must you? Think about it. The coach won't arrive in Lilongwe until tomorrow morning, and you're on duty Monday morning, which means you must be back before then,' Danny tried to reason. Deep down, my mind was already made up. Nothing they could say was going to change it. As the seven thirty p.m. express coach took off, I waved goodbye to my two friends, who stood with their mouths wide open, riveted to the spot, unable to move. I was travelling on the wings of love, engulfed in the dense, soft, all-pervading fog which was Jane, and at this point, nothing else mattered.

The coach arrived in Lilongwe around four a.m. Only two taxis were at the rank at that time of the morning, and about twenty or so possible clients were alighting from the bus. Fortunately, one of the drivers recognised me and wanted to know why my father had not sent anyone to pick me up. As he started instinctively to drive me towards the airport, where the family home was, I had to redirect him to Area Eighteen, where Jane lived. Asking the driver, on arrival, not to go until I was safely inside, I knocked on the door, and a female voice answered. It was Jane's mother, and to say she was surprised to hear my voice would be something of an understatement. She told me Jane had left by private transport, which must have reached Blantyre earlier than the coach. Not even waiting for her to finish, I ran back to the taxi and asked the driver to take me to the airport. At that moment I wished I had a private jet to take me straight back to Blantyre, or at least enough money to order the taxi driver to go south, and fast.

By the time we had covered the ten kilometres to our family home, it was about five thirty. Gently knocking on Chalela's bedroom window, I saw a curtain move followed by the window itself being opened. Quickly and quietly, I jumped inside, being careful not to awaken my father, who was sleeping three rooms away. I would have had a lot of explaining to do had he known the manner of my arrival. He never encouraged us to do anything without proper planning and he was not the kind of man you could easily lie to either.

Chalela could not believe the reason for my unannounced visit.

'Young man, I have known love, but this is something else. Her name is Jane, yeah?'

'Yeah!'

'Well, whatever it is she has, it must be great,' said Chalela as he slowly and reluctantly climbed into his clothes. I needed him to take me back to the coach terminal for the seven o'clock Blantyre Express before Father got up. Chalela's Ford Cortina was parked next to the old man's car, and he suggested to me that the best approach to the problem of leaving home without arousing too much attention would be to push the car to the main road, a distance of almost twenty-five metres. As I pushed, I felt my brother was not pushing as hard as I was, and I told him so.

'Listen, young man, I've just got up. You're the one who has got the energy to burn, not me,' retorted Chalela. 'Go on, push!'

I rested my case and engaged my back and hands into top gear. The things I did for love!

As Chalela started the car, my mind wandered a little. I imagined Jane in bed, tossing and turning, unable to sleep, wondering what had happened to me. I just had to get back to Blantyre quickly. I had to see her.

I fell asleep as soon as the coach left Lilongwe Central, waking up several times on the journey, hoping we had reached Blantyre and being disappointed on each occasion. When we reached Zomba at about eleven o'clock, the coach stopped for five minutes, which seemed like hours to me. Just before setting off, I complimented the driver. 'I'm so happy with your careful driving, mister,' I said. 'I feel so safe, I even slept.'

'Don't speak too soon, my brother. There are another fifty miles we have to cover,' remarked the driver. 'Perhaps you could put your compliment in writing to my boss,' he added with a wink.

As we were driving past Kanjedza at exactly ten minutes to twelve, I knew I had to do something. The Blantyre bus terminal was another five miles off, and there was no way I would be able to go that distance and still find Jane in Kanjedza, even if I came back by taxi.

'Er … er … is there any possibility of dropping me anywhere along the road?' I asked the driver humbly. 'I live just across the stream,' I concluded, pointing towards the stream which divided Chichiri and Kanjedza.

'Only if you promise to write the letter I suggested to you earlier,' the driver joked as he slowly applied the brake pedal. 'You know I shouldn't be doing this.'

'I know, it's just that I need to be home before twelve twenty p.m.,' I urged.

'How about us?' complained one of the passengers.

'Yes, how about the rest of us?' joined in another.

'Who do you think you are?'

'Drive on, man! We also need to get to our homes early.'

The cacophony of angry voices followed me as I made my way out of the coach.

I ran across the narrow stream as fast as I could without even stopping at my own house, which was on the same route. Instead, I headed straight for Jane's sister's house, where I found the front door open. Tired, hungry, and almost foaming at the mouth, I came face-to-face with the star herself, Jane. I automatically smiled, my arms outstretched, but she kept her distance, arms folded. She did not move an inch. She did move a finger, though. 'Yes?' she asked, with a wave of her hand.

'Yes, what?' I answered.

'Is your faith in me so thin, David?' she remonstrated. 'Honestly, I told you I was coming over. Just because I did not arrive on the Express, it didn't mean–'

I interrupted. 'Jane,' I said, 'Jane, I'm sorry.'

'All right, all right. Come on, give me a big hug then.'

Lord knows how I looked forward to that moment.

'I suppose a cup of coffee at my house is out of the question, then?' I said, chancing my luck.

'You must be kidding! Do you want us to have coffee? I'll be expecting you in Lilongwe next weekend, all right?'

Just then there was the sound of a car at the front of the house.

'It must be your transport, Jane,' shouted her sister from the kitchen.

So much for our romantic weekend. Within minutes, Jane was on her way to catch her Lilongwe-bound coach at the Wenela bus terminal.

It was time for me to leave too, to go to my house for a well-deserved rest, in bed, alone. Just at that moment, Jane's sister appeared with a tray of coffee and some sandwiches.

'I wasn't listening, but I thought I heard someone say something about having coffee.' She was a good Roman Catholic and she had not decoded our private shorthand! Or had she?

After my visit to Lilongwe the following Friday, Jane told me it would suit her better if she came to see me in Blantyre the following week, because, she said, 'I just love the city.' Her visits to Blantyre increased and so did the level of my cup of lovee . A couple of months passed, then I received a telephone call at work and heard the words most single and foot-loose young men dread. 'David, I'm pregnant. You're going to become a father!' After the initial shock, I was thrilled.

Despite the fear young and single men have of making a girl pregnant without planning, there is a certain joyful feeling which such shocking news brings, the feeling of satisfaction that one's soldiers are battle-ready.

I loved Jane and was prepared to marry her. I felt ready for fatherhood, ready and prepared for the fact that we were going to become parents. I started buying cotton nappies and assorted clothes for the coming event. When Jane came over, we would go shopping in town and I would buy her a few gowns suitable for her present condition. We were happy, very, very happy.

A week before the baby was due, Jane's sister went to Lilongwe to be with her at the delivery. She promised she would telephone me as soon as there was any news. After she left Blantyre, it took two weeks for her to get in touch and when she did it was in person. She came to my house and told me Jane had given birth to a healthy boy, which made me smile from ear to ear. I waited, willing her to go on. 'It's a coloured child,' she said. 'The father is her boss, an Indian man.'

'Uh!' was all I could muster. There seemed to be a huge frog blocking my voice channel. I felt deceived, embarrassed, foolish, even. How would you feel under such circumstances?

Jane's boss was a man from Mumbai whose parents had come to Malawi a generation or so earlier to work on the country's railway project, which the colonial government had embarked upon. He decided to remain in the country afterwards. I imagined Jane calling his name like she had called mine, with the same kind of feeling. 'Mahit,' I thought. 'Mahit, darling, where are you now?' I imagined too many painful images of them, and the more I processed these thoughts, the more distressed I became. I just couldn't help it!

My friends in Blantyre were all expecting the good news, which was not to be. Still, the truth had to be told sooner than later. Jane wasn't to remain pregnant forever.

Suddenly, there was some sort of relief. Unknown to me, during her pregnancy, Jane had been living with another boyfriend called Evans in Area Fifteen, another Lilongwe suburb. Their colleagues in the city of Lilongwe and elsewhere knew them as man and wife, customarily speaking. Evans had also bought many small items as an expectant father, just as I had done. As Jane delivered the baby, he was sitting, sweating and chain-smoking next door in the hospital's waiting-room. Figuratively speaking, he was inadvertently about to witness the 'accident' live, after the baby was born and he was invited to hold it, a cruel gesture if you ask me! I was informed that he left the ward in tears and at great speed to the car park. He drove back to the office, where he ashen-facedly explained to his boss about the unfortunate event and its Hiroshima-bomb fallout for him personally. The boss, who was also a Malawian, seemed to have appreciated his subordinate's predicament and granted him his wish to be transferred to Mzuzu, a location over three hundred and fifty kilometres away. He was not seen in Lilongwe again for quite some time.

The child Evans had run away and stayed away from, the child he was certain was his, the child I had bought clothes and nappies for, the child Jane had told me I was to become a father to was now just over four years old. Seeing him for the first time I felt sad. I would have loved to have been his father, for I had truly loved his mother. How little the innocent soul knew. Maybe just as well. He didn't know what was going on in 1974 between his mom and others, me included.

***

One morning, after stocktaking in the motel kitchen as usual, I left for the market. Everything was running smoothly, although two weeks earlier Father had had an accident when his car overturned on the way to the lake in Mangochi. He was9alone and luckily he was unhurt. The accident, his first in over forty years of driving, happened during the day on a straight piece of road. He said he could not understand how the whole thing had happened, but as a result he had decided not to drive for a while. When I got back from the market around eleven thirty a.m., he called me into his office.

'Son, they've ordered us to shut all our businesses today. I was called to go to the Ministry of Trade; they sent a driver. I met the permanent secretary, who told me it was a presidential directive.' His voice was faltering. I saw, for the first time in my life, tears rolling down his sixty-seven-year-old face, a face hardened by political battles. A cold chill went through my body. I just became so weak. The immediate numbness of those words and the sight of my father at that moment paralysed both my body and my brain. The weight and implications of this news were very hard to comprehend .

My father had spent the best part of his life building up his businesses. During all that time, I never saw my father ill. He never missed a day at work. He slaved, he planned, all so his family would have something to hold onto, continuity and self-fulfilment. He did not want to want for anything. He certainly did not want his family to want for anything either. Now it was all gone. One person had decided so. For what reason? None was given. None has ever been given. I still remember us sitting in that office looking at each other with an air of total confusion and resignation. The date was the 9th March 1979 at around eleven a.m.

Father called a meeting for all members of staff to attend. When the news was broken to them in that meeting there was not a dry eye in the room. It was as if someone, a well-loved family member, had died. It was certainly the killing of the golden goose. 'Should things change, of course, all of you will be recalled,' was Father's sombre conclusion of that meeting, words uttered more in hope than expectation, I thought. I just couldn't see under what circumstances the government would reverse that decision. There was no court which would hear a case like this one, a case against Dr Hastings Kamuzu Banda's government.

Father went to the Malawi Congress Party Headquarters in town, where the regional minister, Aaron Gadama, told him there was not much he could do because he did not know anything about the case. On the same day, Father then drove to Zomba, where parliament was sitting, hoping to speak to someone nearer to the president, but all doors were closed before him. He drove back on the same day, disappointed, tired, and beaten. Mind you, the Zomba-to-Lilongwe road was a narrow, bumpy, and dusty road at the time and my father was sixty-seven years old then. I had never seen him in that state before.

Why would anyone do such a thing to an innocent man who had not broken any law of the land? Father knew nothing else but hard work all his life. His brain was, I am sure, programmed by his routine. Now all that had stopped, abruptly. My mother, who had seen worse during the political turbulence of the early sixties which Father went through, took everything in her stride. She told us to accept the situation. 'God knows best,' she advised quietly.

'Dave,' said Father, 'I've done my best. This tragedy is something I do not think I can deal with. I cannot go to any court and expect justice. I could even be jailed for suing the government.

I've told your brother, Chalela, in Zomba the same over the phone. I know it's going to be harder for him. All he knows is running this business and nothing else. Anyway, we'll see how things progress. I've got enough to live on with my wife. It's you I'm worried about.' He forced a smile. 'So, it's back on the job hunt then, Son.'

I just sat there, rigid, like a rock, head bowed, nothing to do, nowhere to go, certainly, nothing to say.

For the coming days and weeks, I had no reason to leave my bed in the morning. What a ghoulish prospect. What sin had a man committed that all that his sweat had given him had been taken away? There were no answers, not even muffled echoes from the past – only silence.

The reasons for our family's tragedy were not explained. Let us assume it happened because Allena's mother, (Lady Bhekimuzi Mukarakate), who was Malawi's 'First Lady', felt that I had not shown respect in the way I had handled her daughter. As soon as there was a rejection of my proposal I was on my way with another girl. Who did I think I was? The president might have given her a free hand, Judas Iscariot-style, hence the reluctance by the police to guard the properties and the lack of any explanation as to why it happened.

Assuming the reason lies somewhere in between, my guilt will always be there. Father, although he kept quiet on that possibility, might have had similar thoughts. His behaviour towards me did not change though. If anything, it got better, a lot better. On the day he died, I promised my mother that I would be her provider. She must want for nothing. I told her this because I was closer to her than I had been to my father but also because I felt I might have possibly contributed in no small part to the family tragedy, although my father had rubbished that thought.

I spent a month not knowing what to do, and potential employers were not keen to employ me or anyone called Katsonga. The refusal by the government to allow my father to dispose of stock like drinks and various foods, some of which were bought on credit, simply added to my father and the family's stress.

Luckily, the bank manager at the National Bank of Malawi, one, Mr 'Alcock'[sp], was kind enough to cancel the loan my father had with the bank.

We were also not allowed to dispose of stock like furniture, beds, bedding, etcetera. When Father asked for permission from the Ministry of trade, the response he got was that he did not have a trading licence and thus he could not legally exchange any of his goods for cash, which is trading. Despite our predicament, there seemed to be no one willing to deal with us in any practical and helpful way. We had become 'hot' – too hot to touch. Even the suppliers of most of the drinks turned us down when my father offered to return the drinks to them free of charge. We ended up giving all the meats and fish away to members of staff and people in the nearby village at the now old airport. An entire cold-room full of these foods! The same was done with most of the beers and lagers.

In the meantime, on the job front it was becoming very difficult and frustrating to make progress. There seemed not to be any brave, perhaps even suicidal, potential employers willing to take the chance of offering me or any of my siblings a job. The fear was that something nasty could befall them through being guilty by association – old Roman-style political punishment! It was in the public domain that Dr Kamuzu Banda was an avid admirer of everything Julius Caesar!

I had spent six weeks without a job when Mr Nicholson called me with a job offer. "You have to obtain a police clearance certificate. It will be telling the hotel that there is nothing wrong with anyone employing you in the country.

One evening, as I stood outside the hotel's main entrance, I noticed an old Land Rover parked down Hannover Avenue. I was sure it belonged to Aaron French, unless, of course, he had sold it. It did not take long for my question to be answered. I saw Mr French coming out of the main bar, which was down in the basement at the front of the hotel. Our eyes met.

'Sorry about the bad news, Davie. Suzan told me about it and that you were now working here. She swore she saw somebody like you when she was here for lunch last week,' Aaron said as we shook hands. He went on to tell me how his business was now on the rails and that things were not looking at all good on the home front either. To complicate matters, he said, his Chinese wife, who had hitherto still been in Zambia, had now joined him in Malawi. 'I'm confused now, Davie. I suppose you might be hearing of a divorce sometime soon.'

'Why, Aaron?' I prodded.

'You know, Davie; I just can't leave Suzan. Life can be cruel at times. How I wish I had met Suzan three years ago,' he lamented, and I could tell from his sharp blue eyes that he was really troubled, and intoxicated.

Changing his mind about leaving, he invited me for a drink and continued his narrative, telling me, among other things, about a fight he had almost had with a priest whom he strongly suspected of having an affair with his beloved Suzan. I found it all rather improbable. 'Priests do not do that sort of thing,' I argued.

'Yes, they do,' contended Aaron .

I met Suzan and Aaron around the hotel on several occasions after that. They seemed very happy and in love. During this period and after what he had told me, Aaron was nearly always under the influence of the bottle, and his girlfriend was acting like a pillar of strength, quite literally, on the occasions when Aaron could not walk straight. Privately, he continued telling me about his tortured soul, Suzan and the priest, about him and his wife and the inevitable turmoil. I still challenged him in defence of the priest, telling him his suspicions were unjustified and perhaps unfounded. After parting company with Aaron at around nine thirty p.m., I moved to the bar counter, where a few regulars were chatting while nursing their favourites. At this point, I had been working at Ryall's for around three months.

As the duty manager on a quiet night in the hotel activity-wise, I continued chatting with customers. I moved to the area around the counter where some regulars were nursing their last orders. The Dugout Bar closed at ten p.m.

I found the regulars engrossed in an argument about wives' responses to situations with their husbands. Although I was the youngest in this group, they considered me old enough to contribute to such matters despite being handicapped by being a bachelor. Perhaps there was something here to prepare me for the future. They usually sought out my company every time they met at the hotel, which was very frequent. One of them, whose name was George, was of mixed race and came from Trinidad. He worked for the Bell Telephone Company, was of medium height, stubby and kept an afro with thick sideburns, which were developing shades of an invading grey colour, which he appeared to sport with a degree of pride.

Perched on the next barstool was a tan-skinned six-footer with a long face and going respectably thin on top, who worked for Agency Maritime International. The other two used to call him Gentleman Bill. The third was a manager for Hogg Robinson Travel. Sadly, I was told he drowned in Lake Malawi a few years later, may his soul rest in peace. He was the shortest of the group and the most talkative. His leisurely rolling gait indicated to most people the size of the man's bank bAaron ce, and those who saw him walking had no doubt he was well-heeled. Not that the other two were not. I also knew this because they talked about it and the fact that they were all married with children in secondary schools.

In Malawi, I did not know anyone, apart from the politicians themselves, who talked about politics in public, so when people drank together, they tended to speak about their personal experiences. So long as affairs of government were not mentioned, even obliquely, they had nothing much to fear from the Secret Police. They used to say it was treason even to dream you were the president of Malawi.

It was George's turn to buy a round. 'No, I think it's time I left. I have to go,' said Bill, draining his whisky glass. 'I don't want to find my wife asleep when I get home. She hates it.'

'Barman, a double JW Black Label for this man here before he disappears, please!' commanded George firmly.

'No, really, I must go!' insisted Bill agitatedly. At this point, the alert and businesswise barman had already served the ordered drink to the reluctant Bill.

'Listen, man, wives do not go to sleep when their husbands are late in coming home at night,' interrupted the Trinidadian. 'Barman, hurry up with a drink for him and one for me before you cost your hotel some money here!'

Bill reluctantly gave in by conduct. He took a sip from his glass, saying, 'Look, my wife does. I know her. When I get there, she'll be gone – fast asleep.'

'I think George has a point, though,' chipped in the Hogg Robinson man.

'Of course I have a point. Let me tell you this. Last month, I went to a party in Limbe given by Mr Sacranie, the attorney. My wife refused to go because she wanted to get up early to go to church early Sunday morning. I promised her I would be home no later than midnight, so we could go to church together. Well, the party went on forever, and I could only leave around three in the morning. I knew I was in trouble, and I made sure I did not make any noise from the moment I approached and entered the gate to the moment I entered the house. I just didn't want to disturb her sleep and didn't want to answer any questions at that time of the morning, you know what I mean?

'There is a gentle slope from my gate to the house about thirty metres away. I had the headlights and car engine switched off, and the car rolled in silence to a stop in front of my garage. I stealthily opened and closed the car door and sneaked behind the house. I thought I would have fewer doors to open if I used the kitchen entrance. So, there I was, about to insert the key into the padlock when the door opened, so gently, from the inside. My wife was standing right there in front of me in her nightdress. "Come in, darling," she softly whispered. "This is your home. Why do you bother yourself with all this?" Guys, I felt like a teenage boy. How would you feel?'

After hearing this, Bill rushed to the payphone at one corner of the bar, and to his surprise, it rang only once before his wife answered. As predicted, she had not been asleep, but then you can never tell with wives, I was later to discover!

***

Meanwhile, Madalo's pregnancy was in its final stages. One afternoon, at around two o'clock, the phone rang at the cottage. It was a call from Madalo's brother-in-law in Lilongwe to say he was calling me from the hospital where they had taken Madalo. She was now due for delivery. 'I'll be here until she has delivered, so you just wait there by the phone and I'll call you as soon as there is some news,' he said with a degree of excitement. Luckily for me, I was off-duty that afternoon, and waiting by the phone is exactly what I did. Each time the telephone rang before the crucial call came through, whoever it was on the other end must have thought I was either drunk or had some serious mental problem. 'Will you please call me tomorrow!' That was all I could blurt out before I hung up. When the all-important call finally came through, I recognised the voice at once. 'You're the father of a bouncing baby boy. Mother and child are both all right.' I was so excited. My heart was filled with a kind of joy I had never experienced. For the first time in my tender life, I had shared the pregnancy and the expectation of the birth of a child wanted and cared for, and whose mother I loved. That night, when Madalo telephoned me, I almost ordered her to come home as soon as she was able.

We were both happy, and so were our immediate parents and extended families, who kept calling to check on the health of the child and his mother.

It was pleasant being a father when Madalo finally joined me. I felt so different and somehow more grown up coming home from work every day to be with a wife and a baby, my son!

Madalo's and my happiness was complete when the company she was working for in Lilongwe (Gramil) gave her a transfer to move to their Blantyre branch and be with the father of her newly born child. I knew the news was of great significance to her, because apart from being ambitious and hard-working, she also enjoyed working for this parastatal, and I respected her even more for that.

Now that Madalo would be returning to work soon, one of her elder sisters recommended to us a nanny who had worked for her earlier. In the interim, Madalo felt lonely at the house because of my shift work at the hotel, particularly the night shifts, so she started spending more time with my sister, who also lived in Blantyre. I had no objections. I thought it was a good idea, and why not?

One Saturday afternoon, I had my afternoon break at two p.m. Normally I would have had a siesta, but on this day, I decided to go to the matinée showing of a Bruce Lee movie, *The Way of the Dragon*, at the Apollo Cinema. Judging from the queues, it had to be a popular movie – I had no idea! As the queue edged forward slowly like an over-fed Boa constrictor, I thought that at any moment the management would announce, 'No more – house full.' With about four people in front of me, I suddenly felt someone by my side. It was Suzan. She was wearing a multi-coloured flowing cheese-cloth dress and she had her hair in a short ponytail.

'Would you please buy me a ticket, Davie? The queue is just too long. I don't think I have a chance of making it if I join the queue at the back,' she said as she handed me the ticket money. I was happy to oblige, and rather than buying two tickets for different seats in different parts of the cinema, I bought her one next to me. Despite my feelings towards her, I was simply not in the mood for anything other than to watch the film, which we both enjoyed rather a lot. Before leaving the cinema at about four o'clock we stopped for a soft drink. Suzan offered to drive me back to work in her brand-new navy-blue Peugeot 104, but although I was not due to start work for another two hours, I declined her offer. Suzan maintained, 'Jump in anyway. We could have a drive, if you don't mind.' I did not mind.

Suzan sped her car along the road to Blantyre Southwest, along Chikwawa Road. The area had a sea of green grass, dotted with occasional shrubs like islands. It seemed like a huge emerald carpet. The soft wind brushed by, making the plants dance in the cool evening air. With the windows down and the car crawling on a rough and narrow path, I could smell her expensive perfume mixed with the wildflowers which filled the air with their late winter scent. She turned right into a dead end and switched off the engine.

I asked Suzan to turn the car so that it faced the direction of our departure. She wondered why.

'It is easier to get away, just in case we need to make a hasty retreat!' She quietly responded to my request. We then got out of the car and leaned on the car bonnet as we continued with our chat. Now, it was no longer a commentary of the movie we had just watched.

'Now, I want to know exactly what happened to Chester's City Motel and your father's other businesses.' I did not know Suzan's background at this point and wondered how I should answer her question. Should it be honestly and factually, or should I go deeper into other issues I thought could have been linked to the family tragedy she was inquiring about?

'What have you heard so far, Suzan?' I responded, forcing a less-than-genuine smile.

'I know you are wary after all that you have been through, Davie. I will start by opening up to you.' Suzan narrated a story so tragic that my hatred for the regime in my country increased more than twofold, if it was at all measurable.

Suzan confessed to me how she had gone out with one of the most powerful politicians in the country, Mr. Chikhakhalala. That was years earlier while studying at the University of Malawi's Chancellor College. Before getting her first degree she was offered a scholarship to continue her studies in California, United States of America. When she came back home on holiday a year or so later, she had developed enough self-confidence to end the illicit affair with the feared politician. In response, Suzan was thrown in jail without trial. She was accused of being the daughter of a rebel, Henry Chipembere, and that while in America, the two of them were spending a lot of time together. That was a very serious offence at the time – a relic from Cicero's Rome, one might add.

During her time in jail and solitary confinement, Suzan was visited by people representing various human rights organisations, one of whom was a representative of the Roman Catholic Church through French priest, who took her case up with Amnesty International and the U.N.H.C.R.

Suzan informed me that Mr. Chikhakhalala had helped her get the scholarship, which might go some way towards understanding, not condoning, his anger when Suzan ended the affair later, some time in 1974.

It is possible that the pressure from these international organisations resulted in her eventual release, although it was not complete freedom. She was now banished from all major cities and towns in Malawi. She had to stay in her home village of Malembo, in Monkey Bay, Mangochi District. Others have not been so lucky. At the time I first met her at Chester's City Motel, the ban had only been lifted for around two months, and after all this, Mr. Chikhakhalala still demanded an apology from Suzan, which was not forthcoming!

In a response to a letter from him for disappointing him, Mr. Chikhakhalala had allegedly told Suzan she was the first woman in his life to end an affair with him. It had been a shock to his system, a blow to his pride. Considering the number of women Mr. Chikhakhalala is *allegedly* said to have had amorous affairs with, that is in response to Suzan's note ending the affair with, Mr. Chikhakhalala, the latter allegedly expressed to Susan that she was the first woman to end an affair with him. This revelation was a shock to his system and a blow to his pride. Given the number of women, Tembo is rumored to have had relationships with. This was quite a significant admission.

After listening attentively and sympathetically, it seemed that the courage and resolve which Suzan showed against the system and her dislike of Dr Kamuzu Banda's government dovetailed with my own very smoothly. I thought, here I had found a partner in arms!

She was now shunned by employers, on Mr. Chikhakhalala's orders, she said. No one was allowed to employ her because, they were told, *she was a rebel*. Here was a man so powerful, so rich, a man who could decide anyone's fate, intent on ruining a young woman's life all because of a lust-driven personal ego.

'How do you survive then, Suzan?'

'Oh! I was going to tell you. Do you know the priest who first discovered me in jail? It is his family who sends me money every month for my upkeep. After my release, they bought me a house in Chigumula, and I had another house around Chigumula, which my auntie, who died a month ago, also left me, as she had no child.' I wondered where Aaron French was getting the relationship between Suzan and the priest wrong!

I was now a little more relaxed and narrated my own story to her. She interrupted here and there to seek clarity, and when I looked at my watch, I noticed we had been at this secluded place for well over an hour and a half! I now had only twenty minutes to be back on duty.

As we drove back to the hotel, we discussed our star signs and, coincidentally, my birthday was coming up in a week or so – a Leo, the 6th of August – and hers was the 21st December. She was a Sagittarius.

Suzan invited me to her house, promising that she would start preparing a special meal that very same day. Suzan was a pretty girl. She had, among other things, very expressive eyes and a very expressive bum. How could I say no to a woman like that? On the other end of the spectrum, we saw each other as victims of a system which had wreaked havoc in our young lives. This strengthened the magnetism between us.

The following day, Suzan phoned me at work, asking me not to let her down, because she had started organising the birthday dinner. Let her down? If only she knew. I would have cancelled a heart-by-pass operation just to die on her dining room table on that day, my birthday. What excuse did I give Madalo? I wangled myself out by saying that I had to see my mother in Zomba. Did I love Madalo? Certainly! Nevertheless, it was a sign of red-bloodedness in men – cheating by men was normal. Other men would question your manhood if you did not cheat on your girlfriend or wife. And it was a no-no, for a man to tell on another man. There was the unwritten rule of a defence pact against probing, suspicious women. An attack on one was an attack on all of us, so we believed.

Suzan lived in a three-bedroomed country house off the Blantyre–Thyolo Road. As I entered the house, the first thing I noticed was the way she had smartly arranged her furniture. She had both western and local chairs and stools, which were punctuated by different plants, giving the room the appearance of the airy outdoors.

As Suzan gesticulated to me to take a seat, my ears pricked at the sound of music softly playing in the background. Judging by her next utterance, she knew I was already impressed. 'That's Shirley Bassey,' she told me, and I nodded, trying to hide my ignorance. And at this point, the track playing on the album was 'Bring In The Clowns'. Unintentional? Probably not. Only time would tell.

Suzan rhetorically asked me if I was comfortable, and I responded in the affirmative. She then disappeared into what I later observed was the kitchen and wheeled in a trolley of drinks, which she parked very close to me. It was as if she had in mind the fact that she was not just entertaining a date but also a hotelier, I pig-headedly assumed.

Among a variety of spirits and liqueurs on the trolley, there was an ice bucket cradling a very cold-looking bottle of Moët et Chandon. Was she showing off? Or was this how she saw me or how she thought I saw her? Whatever the reason, it did not matter. We were alone in front of a bottle of one of the best champagnes around!

Did I have an idea where all this was leading? Did I consider my feelings for Madalo at all at this point? How about Aaron French? Mind you, I was still a very impressionable twenty-four-year-old young man at the time, holding down what I thought and still think was a plum job: company car, company house, a cook and garden boy paid for by the company. I just felt I had now entered the premier league, selfishly and certainly blindly, perhaps! At the time, I was playing the kind of game boys of my age in Malawi played. If anything, I was a victim of my society. Remorse? Unquestionably! Given a chance to re-live my life again, I would conduct my life very differently and with virtue.

I remember the first course was a prawn cocktail, which was followed by fillets of chambo (lake perch) as an entree. The girl had class! No wonder Aaron French was becoming more suicidal, murderous even, by the day, if the chance permitted itself.

The main course was a straightforward grilled Piri-piri chicken, which was not quite ready. I was helping Suzan clear the table after the first course when something funny happened on the way to the kitchen. Walking behind her, my eyes could not help but steal a look at her progressively expressive rear. I pinched it gently; I just couldn't resist the temptation. Isn't it amazing how much courage there is in a few glasses of bubbly? Like a provoked feline she turned, looking me in the eye, both eyes in fact, and put the plates she was carrying on the kitchen sink. I felt hypnotised as she took from my hands the plates I was carrying, her eyes still focused on mine. Placing them on the sink, without looking at them, we started to kiss passionately. The only sound from that precious moment came from the grill a couple of metres away and the distant sound of Shirley Bassey from the livingroom.

Suzan took a step back, shyly avoiding my eyes as she quickly turned to open the oven to see how far the chicken still had to go. 'It's coming together nicely. Twenty minutes or so and it will be on the table.'

Quietly, she led the way past the dining area and to her boudoir. Well, the next thing I remember was being choked by a dark, acrid smoke which had engulfed the bedroom and the entire house. The Piri-piri powder which had been applied to the chicken made the smoke a lot worse. The chicken had been completely burnt to charcoal. We had dozed off! We must have been very tired after what must have been a very long day!

In the kitchen, the white-painted walls had taken on a yellowy look and had a sticky feel to them, and almost all the rooms next to the kitchen had had a similar treatment!

After this experience, we saw each other almost daily. I started sleeping out while poor Madalo was alone with the baby at the cottage. Slowly, a dark cloud, pregnant with a possible storm, formed itself over our home as the horizon changed from light blue to steely grey. Madalo and I did not talk about what was going on, but the tension was there for both of us to see. At the same time, Madalo also made sure my sister stayed well informed about the state of our relationship.

Suzan knew how much I loved my son, for I never stopped talking about him. From the way she responded I had no doubt she was happy for me, so when one day she asked if it were at all possible for her to see him, I promised I would think of a way of making that possible. A day or so later, I asked the nanny if I could take the boy into town for a while. I had arranged to rendezvous with Suzan in the hotel car park only about a hundred metres away from the house. As I expected, she was happy to see my son, and rather than just sit in the car park, she suggested we drive into town. Suzan held the baby while I drove, and we were back within twenty minutes, no more. With hindsight, I shouldn't have allowed this at all!

That evening I had a 'rocket' from a very incensed Madalo, because someone had spotted Suzan and me with the baby in the car somewhere in town. She was absolutely furious. I had never seen her quite like that before, and because I had no real defence, my responses showed it. After that, it was about time to return to work for my evening shift, and I did not return home that Tuesday night, Wednesday or Thursday.

As Suzan and I slept on Thursday night, everything seemed heavenly. We felt we did not have a care in the world. She was everything I had ever wanted in a woman: beautiful, better educated, conversational and politically informed. I am sure, in her own way, Suzan was at this point also very fond of me.

The time had just gone past midnight when we heard a car hooting at the gate, and when Suzan peeped out of the window, she saw two cars. When I looked, I recognised the front one as belonging to my brother, Mark. What had happened at this unholy hour, I wondered. Suzan went to the gate and was confronted by the 'hunting' party, which consisted of my two brothers, my sister, and Madalo's sister. They seemed very agitated and undoubtedly angry. In the confusion, with every one of them talking at the same time, the story unfolded that the baby had been taken to hospital and was dying of food poisoning, and the suspects were *Suzan and Davie*.

'The police have been alerted already,' added Mark. 'Both of you, jump in. We're going to the hospital,' he wrathfully ordered us.

'You, Suzan, come with us in this car,' suggested my sister.

'No. I don't want that,' I interrupted. 'We will follow you in her car.'

'Do you think this is some kind of game?' threatened my visibly angry sister.

I simply did not trust that Suzan would be safe in the company of *those* people under the circumstances. No chance!

A very depressing sight greeted us at the hospital. My little boy was connected to all sorts of tubes and wires. He looked to be sleeping, but the top of his tender skull was pumping away as if his head were going to burst open. As I stood at the bottom of the bed with Madalo on one side and Suzan on the other, I was now extremely afraid, wondering what might have happened and why Suzan and I were suspects. I tried to touch the baby but was stopped and told off by Madalo. 'Are those hands clean?' she cynically queried as she slapped my arm away from our very sick son.

'Well, Davie, we won't part peacefully, my dear,' said Madalo, 'after what the two of you have done to my son, whatever it is. I knew there was something strange going on when you took the child away with your bitch there.' She tearfully pointed at Suzan. 'We don't know whether he's going to make it or not, so you had better start talking with your woman about what you have done to my son,' Madalo said between sobs, tears rolling down her cheeks. My legs felt so heavy as I stood there like a statue, unable to respond, because I just did not know what had caused our son's illness. My mind was numb, congested, and utterly confused. How could Suzan do it? Did she do it? No, she couldn't have. But still, there we were, accused of the attempted murder of my son, which might turn into an actual murder should my son not make it! My tongue was lead-filled too. I could not speak, and we stood around that hospital bed with the young boy fighting for his life for over an hour, in silence. When I eventually asked Suzan to go, she refused at first, but after a little persuasion she agreed to leave the ward saying she would sleep in the car outside the hospital.

I was later to be dropped home by Suzan as Madalo spent the night by our son's hospital bed. When I visited the hospital the following morning, the doctor told me there had been a steady improvement throughout the night and that there was room for hope. I went to work to explain to Mr Nicholson what had happed and to ask for a couple of days off duty. The request was granted, and I returned to the hospital, where I spent the rest of the day in a very tense atmosphere. In the meantime, Suzan had telephoned her guardian, the priest, about what had happened, and he was on the scene in no time. He asked to know what the problem was and my son's prognosis. He was informed that there were many causes for such an illness.

Suzan had seen the child on Tuesday, but it was Thursday before he became ill, and the priest said he thought that food poisoning would have struck earlier than that. Madalo responded by saying that the child had been poorly right from Tuesday evening, but since I was never home, I could not collaborate her story. Looking back, I had not left Suzan alone with the baby while we were driving around town on that Tuesday. How could she have poisoned him? The mind boggled!

I had been going out with Suzan for just two months. Things had progressed from the day of *The Way of the Dragon* at the cinema, my birthday and the burnt chicken, to an attempted murder charge by Madalo. Was the Good Lord trying to tell me something? If so, I was too stubborn to listen. Madalo and the baby were back home within three days, but the situation between us was still tense, perhaps worse!

By now, it was generally accepted that I did not know what motives, if any, Suzan had had towards the innocent baby, and the doctors said the baby hadn't been poisoned at all. He had had what they called gastritis. I refused to accept the suspicions of both my brothers that perhaps Suzan might have slipped my son something while I was not looking.

For my part, I told Madalo in no uncertain terms that as far as I was concerned, there was no future for us. I just did not think that a woman who seriously considered I was responsible for my child's illness and possibly his demise could be relied upon as a long-term partner. Yes, she was responding to my unacceptable conduct but not to a level of wishing to do away with me in this way! Naturally, I continued my affair with Suzan – not that I needed much inspiration.

Working one evening a few weeks later, I was approached by the night security man. He told me there was a van at the cottage removing stuff from the property. I got there just as Madalo, and the baby were about to leave. I felt very distraught but did not wish to stop her, because I knew there was no future in our relationship anyway. I also knew I was to blame. I had, perhaps foolishly, caused the split! Madalo swept everything from the cottage, everything! I even had to borrow teaspoons from the hotel for a while as I restocked. The only items she did not take with her were those large ones needing to be dismantled to fit through the door. This was one reason I still had a bed to sleep in, albeit with bedding from the hotel.

Looking back after some months, although I was happy with Suzan, I still felt seriously unhappy about Madalo's departure. I had treated her very shabbily. Madalo was a virgin when we met, and she held on for over five years before finally surrendering to me. I thought she was faithful to me, she was loving, she was beautiful and smart, but she was not *dangerous*. There was no excitement. Why I should crave such a thing I do not know. In Suzan and at twenty-one years plus of age, I had everything I wanted, including *danger and excitement*.

My family were up in arms as news of our split spread. Mother and Father were not as vocal as the rest, who were saying all sorts of disparaging remarks against Suzan. They swore never to set foot in my house if Suzan was staying with me. It was then I started to understand what might have gone through the troubled mind of Edward, Duke of Windsor before he left for France with the American divorcee, the love of his life. There was no way I was going to succumb to their demands. Although in hindsight it is difficult to be objective, I think that had they been supportive or indifferent I might not have continued my affair with Suzan. It's just possible. Every word they uttered against, or simply about, her, could have been factual, but at the time I just thought they were being predisposed. Why should I have listened? I was completely besotted, smitten! The priest and I had become good friends by then. I believed I knew and understood the situation better than anybody else who questioned it.

When Aaron French heard about the latest situation he could, obviously, not accept it. He wanted to know why I would do such a thing. Why? Well, you may as well ask, 'Why do birds sing?' Because that is how nature planned it. But no, for Aaron there had to be more, so he decided to complain officially to my boss, Mr Nicholson, who presented me with the matter one morning, telling me that Mr French had complained that because of my ungentlemanly behaviour by snatching his girlfriend, the hotel's reputation as a safe and peaceful place for couples to come to was in serious jeopardy.

'Your assistant had stolen my woman, and you know very well I am one of your regulars, Mr Nicholson,' Aaron had said. Mr Nicholson was so nice about the whole situation, telling

Mr French that there were no rules against me asking out any woman I fancied, if there was no conflict of interest, workwise. '

'Has Suzan complained?' Mr French saw no need to answer this question. Thus, it was a private matter between the three of us. Discussion closed.

Did I not feel sorry for Mr Aaron French? Difficult question, but let me say the following: I believe in fate. The path an individual's life takes is pre-destined by a power greater than any living being. There is very little, if anything at all, that one can do to reprogramme that.

Aaron French was a married man, whereas I was *sinfully* co-habiting. In other words, he and I were playing an illicit and unfair game against our partners. I cannot defend that. Suffice to say, my competitor for Suzan's affection was, I believe, in his early forties and presumably with settled faculties. I, on the other hand, was barely twenty-two years of age, foot-loose and fancy-free like most boys of my age and class were at that time. It is only later in life and with the advantage of hindsight that the folly of what I did to a man I had hitherto sympathised with comes to the fore with much regret.

Suzan had now moved in with me at the official residence I had shared with Madalo only about a month earlier.

We didn't have many friends visiting, let alone relatives. It was mostly just the two of us alone at the cottage, surrounded by what felt like shark-infested stormy seas. Madalo had more friends and relatives in town, most of whom didn't have to cross-check the narrative they had heard from her side. Come to think of it, the narrative from my side, I am sure, supported Madalo's story. Suzan and I were literally on our own!

The priest, Suzan's guardian, was a regular visitor, and so was my old friend, Kelly. The priest's seminary, where he was the bursar, was only two miles from my parents' home in Zomba, and so he took the liberty of introducing himself to my family. He was concerned, he told them, about the rumours flying around about himself and Suzan, which he said were through sheer ignorance on the part of those responsible.

Speaking as one Catholic to another, he did not have to travel too far to win my father's confidence and trust. It was a move I found very comforting. Whatever was happening elsewhere, I did not want to upset my parents. From then on, Suzan and I used to drive to Zomba whenever I was off duty, sometimes picking up the priest before driving to Ku Chawe Inn, a hotel on top of Zomba Plateau. The scenery was simply breathtaking from up there. The manager was a good friend, so we always enjoyed special treatment. Trips to the lake, a journey of roughly one hundred and fifty miles from Blantyre, were also becoming frequent. Our destination was a small town on the southern tip of Lake Malawi, Mangochi. In the olden days, it used to be a slave post for Arabs until a British man called Johnston came along and built a fort there. Most of the hotels on the lake were in that area, and Suzan and I found the lake and swimming particularly soothing.

When I think of those days, one trip stands out. Suzan's birthday fell on a date in December, and I decided to take her to the lake whenever I was going to have a day off before the month was over. A month earlier, the priest had helped me buy a brand-new Mazda 323, apparently to partly restore the dignity I had had working at Chester's City Motel, and also for what he saw as standing up against injustice perpetrated by the Dr Kamuzu Banda regime. I suppose he saw my relationship with Suzan through political eyes as well.

My life was going through a lot of changes and at such great speed that I do not recall ever stopping for a while to check exactly what was happening to me and where my life was headed. I never stopped to smell the coffee, as they say!

During the week of Christmas, a young couple checked into the hotel, and I overheard them lamenting the fact that they couldn't get a room at any of the major lakeshore hotels until after the second week of January. Ryall's Hotel couldn't extend their stay after the twenty-eighth day of December because the hotel was going to be fully booked.

The man, who I was later to learn was a Jamaican working for Tate & Lyle in Zambia, told me his girlfriend was Zambian. I had seen them earlier around the hotel and felt sorry for them, so I offered them accommodation at my residence. Suzan did not mind. So, for two days we stayed together, and on the 30th December, Suzan's birthday, we set off for the lake. During the journey, our guest confessed that he was suspicious of my motives when I offered to give them accommodation. He thought I was after his girlfriend. He said, 'I told myself, any sign of funny behaviour and boom!' We all had a good laugh. Just as well I wasn't.

On the 31st December 1979, I was working up to eight o'clock in the evening, and soon after knocking off, our two guests, Suzan and I set off on a two hundred and sixty-five kilometre drive to the coastal resort of Nkopola Lodge on Lake Malawi. We stopped by Limbe to pick up my buddy, Kelly, whom we had invited to accompany us.

When, the day earlier, I had telephoned the manageress, an old friend of mine whom Suzan knew too, she had told us there was no room available and that we should check before setting off. A phone call that morning had confirmed the situation was still too tight, but she added, 'Come anyway; no one is sleeping tonight.' We arrived at about eleven fifty p.m. on New Year's Eve, just ten odd minutes before 1980! The place was buzzing with music and laughter, people making merry, celebrating all their achievements in the year just ending, reflecting and planning for the year ahead, giving thanks to the Lord for good health, success, and everything!

We did not waste time looking for the manageress on arrival. We simply joined the other revellers who were at one of the bars on the beach and were already away in Never-never Land. By the time the manageress saw us it was 1980.

We had been kindly given accommodation in the manager's office, into which two mattresses and bedding had been brought. Still, it could have been worse. Kelly, who had previously met the manageress, was offered accommodation at her flat that night – certainly not for sleeping, because by the time we were retiring to go to sleep, it was sunrise, and breakfast was being served. Before our heads could hit the pillow the manageress had invited us to join Kelly for a shower at her flat within the hotel compound before assembling, red-eyed, for breakfast in the lodge's spacious dining room.

We spent the first day of the year mostly in the water and swigging endless glasses of Premier Brandy and Coke. The Nkopola Lodge manageress had the evening off, so she had decided to join Kelly for dinner at the nearby Makokola Lodge. We spent most of our time that evening listening to the Jamaican's stories from and about Kingston and the surrounding areas. Some of them were scary, particularly those about organised crime (the Jamaican underworld), burglaries, muggers etcetera. He found life in Zambia and certainly in Malawi positively boring. Despite this, he told us he was considering applying for Zambian citizenship at the time.

During all this conversation, although Suzan would comment occasionally, she seemed a little far away from what was being discussed. On several occasions, I caught her eyes firmly fixed on me with a look of melancholy. I decided to engage her the first time I got a chance. I suspected perhaps she was not feeling too well because of a pregnancy – possibly?

We left Nkopola Lodge to go back to Blantyre on the 3rd January 1980. We stopped at Mangochi Boma to buy some fresh fish to take home. The Jamaican insisted on paying for the fish, perhaps his way of saying thank you.

It would take a period of well over twenty years before I could set foot on the beach of Nkopola Lodge again – not that I was aware of this at the time!

Two days later, we were, once again, alone at home, and I thought I should ask Suzan if something was bothering her deep in her heart. She was forthright in her response. She poured out her worries about my safety. She was convinced my life was in danger, if not because of her then certainly because of my name and what Authorities saw as defiance in the way I was carrying myself. She told me there was something about the way I carried myself which made people think I was rudely confident and brash! It was a perception, but others tend to make unfair conclusions about you from that. 'I know you better.'

'How do I change it, Suzan?'

'Do you think you can? Ha! It's an integral part of your persona, Davie. You were born like that! The sooner we can leave this madness the better, I think! I fear it might be today or tomorrow or shortly, at some point, they will pick us, and for me, again! You do not have to commit an offence; we will be jailed simply for being who we are. I do not think we should hang about, Davie,' she concluded with the same determined look I had observed about her when she was ditching Aaron French.

'I hear you, darling. I suppose it's time we began to plan. Let's discuss the matter with Father Fiderle when he is next in Blantyre.' The priest had now also become my confidant and advisor on most of the challenges we faced at this time.

Chapter 19

RETURN TO RYALL'S

Madalo was very supportive in my hour of need. She decided to leave her flat and join me at my half-brother Mark's house. The arrangement was acceptable to Mark, since both my brothers liked her and had known her for a long time. It was very strange getting up in the morning with nothing to do and nowhere to go. Every time I drove into town, I felt uncomfortable, because it seemed to me that everyone was talking about me or the family. It was hard to summon up the courage to face people. A few friends came by to show their solidarity, albeit quietly. Chisa was among them.

I began looking for a job, and sending CVs became a full-time occupation. The responses which came were all negative. It was now getting very depressing indeed. Then one day I recalled the final words spoken to me by my ex-boss, Mr Nicholson, and I decided I would telephone him. He recognised my voice immediately and said he had heard the sad news and that he had been trying to get in touch with me.

'I've just had to sack my assistant this morning. It's your job, Davie. All you have to do is get police clearance showing that we can "safely" employ you.'

I could hardly believe my ears. But there was a catch. How did I go about getting a police clearance letter? There was one person who would know the answer, so I drove to the airport to ask Father.

An appointment was made with the police commissioner, for it was he and he alone who gave such clearances. I still remember waiting in his office for that all-important piece of paper. 'I don't know why they say you should get this clearance,' said the man who oversaw the whole police force in Malawi as he signed the letter. 'You don't need it; you've done nothing wrong as far as we're concerned.' From the police headquarters, my first stop was by a photocopier. I dared not trust such an important document to memory alone should the original be misplaced.

Father was pleased this obstacle had been removed, and when we spoke to Mr Nicholson on the phone, Father thanked him sincerely for giving me the job. I asked when I should go to Ryall's. 'Tomorrow,' was the reply. 'You don't start work for another ten days but come anyway. You're welcome to come as soon as you can make it.'

It was roughly five in the morning as I peeped through the window to the eastern horizon, which was bathed in the light greyness of dawn, not yet completely lit by the faint dark-orange streak threatening yet another hot summer's day. It was time to get out of bed if I was to catch the early morning express bus to Blantyre, the same service I had used a few years back when I was running after Jane. Mother was already up and in the kitchen. As soon as I finished having a quick bath, breakfast was already on the table: fried green beans rolled in a flat omelette and some diced game, steamed, washed down with a cup of lemon tea. No one makes tea as well as my mother, not even the experts at Ryall's.

Mother said, 'Your father and I wish you well. He says, and I agree with him, don't comment to anyone about what we've experienced. You never know who such people possibly are. Apart from that, your father says you know what is expected of you.'

The door opened and in came Father, still wearing his dressing gown. 'You don't have to finish your breakfast, you know. There isn't much time,' he said. 'The Express leaves bang on time; hurry up, now. Namu, bring me the car keys. They're on the side table in the bedroom.' Turning back to me, he continued, 'I'm sure your mother has told you everything already. Don't trust anybody. You don't know who you are dealing with any more these days. A wrong word to the wrong person and you'll find yourself in jail, so just be careful and bury all the bitterness inside your heart. If I can manage that, so can you, Son.'

'Are you going like that, Phiri?' my mother asked Father.

'Just bring my coat. I won't be leaving the car, I promise.'

So it was that I found myself being driven to the coach terminal by my half-dressed father. Throughout the seven-mile drive we hardly spoke. Father may even have suspected that his car had been bugged.

I arrived at Ryall's around two in the afternoon, just before Mr Nicholson left for his afternoon break. After the usual 'hallos' and a few comments about the Big Story, he asked for the clearance, which I gave him.

'You're now the senior assistant manager for the hotel,' he announced. 'The company bought me another house a mile from here, which means you'll be taking over the cottage, my beloved cottage.'

I could not help but smile at this arrangement. 'There are also extra perks,' he added. It became clear that he had fought the board over my appointment and that if I messed up, I would be putting his neck, as well as my own, on the block.

'I've got a lot of confidence in you, Davie, otherwise I couldn't have done it,' Mr Nicholson said as he handed me the keys to the cottage. Shaking my hand, he wished me a good rest. I had eight days. Among my perks, I was to have two servants – a qualified cook, and a garden boy. I was entitled to hotel food, this time even when off-duty. I had not expected anything close to this. I was simply overwhelmed. It felt like the long-lost son's return home.

The cottage was as old as the hotel, built in the late 1920s. It had a raised foundation, about a metre high, so that one had this air of majesty standing on the porch when welcoming guests as they walked up the steps. There were two bedrooms, both ensuite. The living room was as big as an airfield with a front porch to match. The kitchen was just as grand. It was simply a dream. It did not replace what we had lost, but it did help cushion the weight and the force of the blow for me and, in a small way, for the family.

As I prepared to start work on the first Monday, several things were troubling me. Would I be able to do as well as (or better than) I had the last time? Would the same forces which had ruined my father follow me here? As it happened, the first question was easier to answer. Members of staff responded to me as though I had never been away. They realised I had more authority than before and responded positively. Both my servants were delighted to work at the cottage. I was truly happy – we all were. To enhance our working relationship, I made sure I knew their wives and children, so when they told me one of them was ill, I knew exactly who they were talking about. I also wanted the wives to feel free to approach me should they have any social problem they felt I should know about, problems such as a husband nursing a hangover or being beaten up by an angry husband for 'no reason at all' – things like that. It all helped to strengthen the bond between us.

Mr Thawale, who was still at the hotel, was the only person not happy with my return, and he showed it in subtle ways. His little house was near the hotel, only about five minutes' walk away. He was allowed to use my front garden as a shortcut, which meant asking my garden boy to open two gates for him, one leading to and from the hotel and the other to the outside road. The garden boy reported to me that Mr Thawale was demanding spare keys to the gates so that he could pass at any time. When the boy refused, Mr Thawale had reportedly said to him, 'Don't push your luck, son. Your boss might not last here and you'll need me then, remember that.' Although the cook bore witness to this incident, I decided not to confront Mr Thawale with the matter for the time being.

That night, when I went to bed around midnight, I was very sleepy that night. Sleeping hadn't been easy since that call from Mr Nicholson., and as soon as my head hit the pillow, I was in La-la-land. Sometime later, something woke me. I do not know what. The outside security lights were sending artificial dawn rays into the bedroom as I lay face up, now fully awake. I became aware of a figure at the bottom of my bed and as I watched, it moved slowly towards me and then gently and quietly sat on the bed, almost on my feet. I was now in a cold sweat, for I could not tell what this man-like figure was. I recalled, years back, my mother telling me how to deal with such things, and as bravely as I could, I managed to say, 'Look, as far as I know, there is nothing I've done against you. If I have, please forgive me; it wasn't intended. Please leave me alone. I'm only a kid when it comes to acts like this.' Slowly and soundlessly, the figure stood up and simply vanished towards the bathroom door.

I had never been so scared in my life. Further sleep was impossible. First thing in the morning I telephoned my father for advice, and he suggested I contact my sister, who lived in Nyambadwe, west of Blantyre. He said she knew a man who could help me with my problem and sure enough, when I spoke to her, she said she would come to the cottage the following day around two p.m., and we could go to visit him together.

During the day, Mr Thawale, who was my prime suspect, avoided me whenever he could, and when he could not, he did not respond when I greeted him. That night, I experienced the same visitation, forcing me to sit up until dawn. True to her word, Naphiri arrived at the cottage a few moments after two o'clock, and we set out to see the 'man'.

He lived in Blantyre East, in an area called Chigumula. His grass-thatch house was in the middle of a small nesting on a hillside overlooking the shire valley below. It looked isolated and was surrounded by a vast pine forest. I can recall not seeing any human settlement for well over eleven kilometres after leaving the Thyolo–Limbe road.

We were received by a middle-aged lady who quickly brought out two chairs before greeting us properly. She, without being prompted, brought us two cups of water. This was a traditional greeting. 'Madala is seeing some people, but I do not think he will be long,' she said almost apologetically as she stood up from the reed mat which was a couple of feet away from where our chairs were to go into the kitchen hut, which was to our right.

In less than ten minutes, we saw coming out of the house a squat and balding gentleman in his late forties. We both stood up as a mark of respect to Madala. He greeted us, and I could tell from the exchanges that he knew my sister well. He invited us into the house, where there were two similar chairs to those we had outside. He started by saying to me that he was sure I was the main reason we were visiting him that day. 'Problems at work, isn't it?' Well, there were no handphones at the time and there he was, telling me why I was there. He then asked my sister to give us some privacy. He then produced a gourd from a sack. He started to rub it as he spoke to me as if in a trance. 'I see a man, an older man, who is unhappy with your current position at the office. Is that correct?' He raised his head and looked at me searchingly. It was scary. I had been told that such people existed, but until now I had experienced nothing like it. 'You've made a brave decision, coming to see me,' Madala said. 'You're dealing with (I was not dealing with) a very bad and powerful man. At this very moment, he is aware that you're here. He feels that since you came in, his influence on members of staff has gone down. Don't worry. I will do something for you.'

I waited in silence while the man left the room. He must have been gone for about thirty minutes, and when he came back, he was holding a little cushion-shaped object wrapped in a grey piece of cloth, about one and a half inches square. 'Put this in your pocket and keep it with you at all times, and as soon as it goes, as soon as you lose it, hurry back to me.' He refused any payment.

The following day, I had my little 'cushion' in my pocket. I was aware of its presence as it brushed against my outer thigh as I walked. I certainly did not want to lose it. Mr Thawale's attitude was becoming quietly more hostile by the minute. Just before lunch, around eleven o'clock, it was time for what we used to call the menu check. All three menus we had in the hotel were taken to the respective chefs in the kitchen to check (taste) what they had prepared against the menus. I decided to visit the cloakroom before this activity and privately locked myself in one of the cubicles to check in my pocket for the cushion. To my amazement, it was not there. It had simply disappeared. I had lost it. How could I have done? I had not sat down since the last time I looked, and there was no hole in my pocket. There was only one thing for it – another trip to see Madala. I was now becoming even more scared of Mr Thawale. Outwardly, we were two senior members of staff working closely, albeit silently, together. Deep down, there was dangerous skulduggery going on.

By two o'clock, as soon as I finished work, I was on my way. Madala told me what had happened before I could even open my mouth. 'You're dealing with a professional here,' he added. 'I'll handle him; don't worry. What do you want to happen to him? Because we can either give him blindness or paralysis, or we could just do away with him.'

Do away with him? I felt a sense of guilt. That's a bit drastic, isn't it, I wondered to myself.

As if he had read my thoughts, Madala said coldly, 'That's what he wants to do to you. He wants to kill you.'

'Does he?' I asked miserably.

'What do you think? Do you think he will simply toy with you and let you be? He's not a fool!'

I was becoming increasingly afraid, and in a shaky voice I asked, 'Can you stop him? Do something that will show him he can't do anything to me? But do not physically harm him, please?' I suggested with a plea.

'All right, I can do that. Tomorrow, at around five in the evening, I'll come to your house with some medicine which will end it all. After that, he will have no illusions at all as to who he's dealing with. I will introduce myself as your uncle when I arrive at the hotel.'

That day, I arrived back at the cottage around five thirty p.m., in good time to be back at work by six p.m. The garden boy had gone for the day and the outside gate was locked as usual. I stopped in front of the gate, opened it and drove in. After parking the car, I went back to lock the gate, which was roughly thirty metres from where the car was parked. As I shut it, a big green mamba appeared from the direction of Mr Thawale's house, heading towards me. Instinctively, I jumped up and away and it missed me, only touching my ankle with its tail as it disappeared into the hedge, not that I went looking for it. I cannot abide snakes, and the green mamba is one of the most dangerous of all. I went to work that night feeling rather shaky. Petrified! Fortunately, I was duty manager for the evening, which meant I was free to be anywhere in the hotel, which made it easier to avoid my adversary.

Back at the cottage that night, I was awakened by the sound of footsteps on the front porch, which sounded like one person pacing up and down non-stop. These noises continued until the early morning hours. I did not look. I had heard some very disturbing stories about such phenomena, how if you peep you go blind, or even receive a big slap on the side of the face, leaving you paralysed on one side. Lots of stories. I suffered quietly.

At five o'clock in the evening on the following day, Reception called me in the kitchen to inform me I had a visitor. 'He says he is your uncle,' the receptionist said. I was in the kitchen at the time and due to finish work at half past five. When I went to Reception, my 'uncle' was sitting down in one of the chairs with his back to me, facing the main entrance. He was dressed in old colonial-style khaki trousers, with a beige shirt and a tatty checked jacket, which made him look like a character from the *Zulu Dawn*. Mr Thawale was looking at him with questioning and sceptical eyes. It was as if he knew there was more to him than met the eye. He was probably aware that there was. My 'uncle' noticed my arrival before I reached where he was sitting. I greeted him and invited him home, which was when he pointed at his bike parked across Hannover Avenue. On the carrier there was a large sack, and I asked one of the front-office staff to push the bike to the cottage.

'I wanted to look as authentic as possible,' Madala told me. 'It would have looked rather suspect if I had come with nothing from the village – uncles do not behave like that!' He laughed. I responded likewise. 'So, I brought you some uncleaned rice from my little field. We've had a bumper harvest this year.' I thanked him. After a cup of tea, I released my cook so that I could be alone with my 'uncle'.

'Something tells me I've already seen the man today. My heart skipped a little when I was sitting down in Reception. I knew the man was there; I could feel his presence.' He was right, and I told him so.

'What I've brought you is some herbs to protect you at home and at work. Should anyone try to harm you in any way, they'll only end up harming themselves. Where is the bag of rice?'

When I brought it round, Madala opened it and took out two big bottles containing light-brown liquid, with a few roots floating in both.

'This one you add to your bath water just before you start having a bath. Do it for the whole week, and I think you should start now, while I do my part to protect the house.'

As directed, I had a bath, and as I came back into the living room Madala was also coming back into the house from the garden. It was very dark outside. He had, so he told me, treated all the four corners of the house, and he had done the same to the four corners of the fence. You ask, what had he done? 'Treated them' – that's all I know.

'One more thing now,' he said, producing a little sachet from his shirt pocket. 'I'll have to make a couple of cuts on your body, one on the skull and the other on the chest.' I had not expected this turn of events, but having had medicinal cuts for lesser needs on my body before, I did not resist the idea. Madala asked for a razor blade, which I provided, and when the small incisions were made, he applied a little black powder to the bleeding cuts. As he rubbed it in strongly with his rough thumbs, he whispered some words which I did not quite catch. I suppose I was not intended to hear them. He stayed the night at the house, and there were no unexplained strange disturbances.

The following day, I was not working until six in the evening, so I offered to drive Madala home. He refused, saying there were several things he had to do in town. That was when I handed him an envelope in which I had put the equivalent of fifteen pounds, but when he opened it, he said, 'No, I won't accept this, my nephew. The medicine hasn't worked yet. If you want to thank me, come and see me in a month.' It was a little after nine o'clock that morning when I saw him off at the gate.

When I saw Mr Thawale later that evening, his dislike for me was written all over his face. He used to pretend to smile and greet me every time we were in the same area, but not so now. He tried not to find himself alone with me. This was hard, because with the never-ending string of party bookings in the hotel we had to work closely in the kitchen to make sure all was being done properly. With what my 'uncle' had done for me, all the happenings at the cottage had ceased. I was now more relaxed and began to conduct myself like one who had just signed a contract with immortality.

Years before I joined the company, a man was rising rapidly through the ranks with the strong possibility of overtaking Mr Thawale, who had started to show him the same kind of hostility he was now showing towards me, and it did not take long. The 'pretender' was found dead in his sleep one morning and, perhaps unfairly, all fingers pointed at Mr Thawale. Members of staff who had noticed the way he was behaving towards me never stopped warning me about him. With my newly found confidence, I began to throw veiled challenges at him. I would joke with any one of the chefs, knowing Mr Thawale was within earshot, saying, 'Look here, old man, I hope you've checked the menu. I know some of you are trying to intimidate me with your magic. You can't win against me, you know. I've gone deeper than you can ever imagine.' I would confidently challenge them, believing the herbs the traditional healer had given me would protect me against any witchcraft. 'So, you just do your job and I'll do mine, okay?' or something to that effect. It used to cause a lot of laughter among the staff, for they knew who I was referring to. Whenever I said anything like this, Mr Thawale used to look down or leave the kitchen altogether, leaving the staff tittering. He eventually gave up. As the old saying goes, 'When you can do no more, sit down on your front porch, watch the river, and wait for the day when the corpse of your enemy floats by.' I suppose this is what he decided to do, and I was determined not to give him the pleasure.

Chapter 20

WALKING THE PLANK

Growing up in a dictatorship, in a country where everything readable or watchable is censored, does not prepare one for the open and competitive world outside. Kissing (mere kissing) scenes in movies ended up on the cutting-room floor, and even simple tourism brochures showing women in bikinis were blacked out. Books such as *Animal Farm*, to name but one, were banned.

During my latter years at Ryall's, I remember getting excited when we became the only importers of a fruity, dry, strong red wine from the Rioja province of Spain, called Banda Azul. After the first consignment arrived, duty paid, we were in the process of cutting a stencil showing the new wine for the hotel's wine list when my boss was called into the office to take a phone call. He told me it was from the security branch, instructing him to return the wine because it bore the words 'Dr Kamuzu Banda'. There was only one Dr Kamuzu Banda in Malawi, who may have been dry but not fruity! We were, therefore, well and truly lumbered with the offending wine in our cellar, for we had no market for it. Eventually, a compromise was negotiated with the appropriate officials allowing us to export the bottles to Zimbabwe, where the local populace did not mind 'drinking' our great leader. The financial loss was immense. Did we claim? Not in Malawi. We considered ourselves lucky the matter was not taken further, for, say, anything less than treason – the president's name was one of the protected emblems of State in those days.

When a reporter, or a tourist, visited Malawi, one of the first things they noticed was the marked reluctance of the locals to answer any questions they thought were political, no matter how obscure they might be. I grew up in a society where you always mistrusted the next person until they proved themselves, which was almost impossible to do. Despite all this, life carried on normally, well, as normally as possible.

My boss, Mr Nicholson, was always nervous when we had a booking from the Malawi Congress Party HQ, the Ministry of Youth and Culture, or, above all, the Reserve Bank. The first two organisations were led by very ambitious and utterly ruthless individuals who were, like the third, a law unto themselves. The man at the MCP head office was the then regional minister and secretary general to the party, Albert Muwalo Nqumayo, a man who was linked with all the punitive actions the Malawi Congress Party was meting out to all those they suspected of being anti-MCP or anti-Kamuzu Dr Kamuzu Banda. Sometimes the two were one and the same. He was deeply feared by most people in the country. Anyone suspected of not towing the party line – it was Albert Muwalo Nqumayo they faced. He was responsible for the implementation of the Forfeiture Act, and all ministers and MPs were petrified of his name, not to mention his person. He came from my tribe. Alas! Another man, from the Ministry of Youth and Culture, called Gwanda Chakuamba Phiri, had the advantage of having a degree of control of the Malawi Young Pioneers, Dr Kamuzu Banda's utterly merciless private army. Malawi's equivalent of MI5 was, at the time, recruited from their ranks.

Mr Nicholson had the misfortune of being summoned to appear before Albert Muwalo Nqumayo on two occasions. First, because his wife was seen by MYP boys sunbathing 'naked' in her fenced cottage garden. There were laws against such things in Malawi. I do not recall if they applied to people in the privacy of their home. He was warned that he was held responsible for his wife's (un)dress sense, and they could both face deportation should this be repeated. The second time was when we had a booking from the regional minister's office. A table for ten was booked in the 21 Grill for the Honourable Chidzanja Nkhoma himself and a group from the Women's League. Most people who used the Grill Room at lunchtime were those working in town who had to hurry back, thus they did not order heavy meals. Not so for the honourable minister and his (alleged) 'harem'. They were in no hurry, so they ordered 'the works', including the famous 'Plank Steak'.

Because of the British love for tradition, the steak, a T-bone, was served on a wooden plank. There were over ten such wooden planks in the kitchen, and they all looked worn after being repeatedly in use since 1921 when the hotel opened its restaurant services. Marks made by steak knives and forks over the years were all visible, and the centres too had become concave as a result. Most people enjoyed this because it represented years of the restaurant's experience in top cuisine. However, on this occasion, when the waiters brought the main course, big sizzling T-bone steaks, possibly from a huge Nguni-breed beast, served on old pieces of wood, the minister hit the roof. 'Where is the manager?' he demanded angrily. In no time at all, poor wee Mr Nicholson in his navy-blue double-breasted jacket and grey slacks was standing before the Great One.

'Look here, you so-called manager, we know you people think you're still ruling this country. Those days are gone forever.' I am sure Mr Nicholson was wondering what all the fuss was about. 'Look around you,' continued the minister. 'You won't see anyone else eating their food off a plank. Why? Is it because they are white, like you? So, because we're black, you order your chef to serve us using these old pieces of wood? That's it, isn't it? Don't you know who we are? I can make sure you're deported by tonight if you're not careful!'

'I'm sorry, Sir,' breathed Nicholson.

'Yes, and so you will be if you don't mend your ways. Food off a plank! Indeed!'

By now, the whole restaurant was quiet. The solemn faces of the whites on the other tables grew even whiter with fear and wonderment, and on the faces of the handful of Malawians was engraved deep shame and embarrassment at the minister's unfamiliarity with what to expect at such top restaurants. It was not the time to explain anything to the livid man, so Nicholson ordered the steak to be served again, this time on china. There was a message on the following morning for my boss to go and see the general secretary of the party. We all knew why, so Nicholson took the precaution of taking the menu with him. Fortunately, the secretary-general was quite au fait with the hotel's way of doing things and he had a good laugh about the complaint. He apparently turned to Mr Malawi, the other assistant manager who had accompanied him, saying, 'Komanso nduna zinazi ndi Mabulutu eti?' (This translates as, 'Some of these ministers are brutes, aren't they?') Mr Nicholson had survived yet again. This informational malnourishment has continued to afflict the country to this day, although the restrictions have been gone since 1994. Very low education standards have largely contributed to this situation.

The palace became concerned about the rising powers of Albert Muwalo Nqumayo and Gwanda Chakuamba. It is hard to say who at the palace was concerned. My view is that Hastings Kamuzu Dr Kamuzu Banda had a lot of trust in these two individuals to a level where others feared they were losing out in the pecking order.

To support the above point, a couple of years earlier, in 1974, when I had just finished writing my O Levels, I went to the Trade Fair grounds on the 4th July in mid-afternoon. I had walked from Kanjedza, a mid-density suburb of Blantyre, and as I approached this location I could hear police sirens blaring from the Blantyre end on the Kamuzu Highway. At the time, this kind of siren sound was only used for Hastings Kamuzu Dr Kamuzu Banda of Malawi. It was also customary that when one heard that sound, one had to stand erect, facing the road, clapping hands until the motorcade passed. I joined in doing all this until the convoy came to a stop just at the gates into the Trade Fair grounds, and who came out of the main Mercedes Benz S-Class? The Honourable Albert Muwalo Nqumayo. I could not interpret the reaction of those who witnessed this incident clearly. Was it that of shock or admiration that this man had now climbed to this level, where he could legally and officially mimic the

President of Malawi, Ngwazi Dr Kamuzu Banda? Or was it that people thought the secretary-general was beginning to overreach himself by usurping some of the president's trimmings of power? What did I think? I was too numb to think. The thought of this man taking over from Kamuzu Dr Kamuzu Banda was no less scary than the thought of allowing the despotic self-serving Kamuzu Dr Kamuzu Banda himself to continue to trample upon citizens' basic human rights.

Nevertheless, a plan was devised to limit the influence of Albert Muwalo Nqumayo and Gwanda Chakuamba, who were perceived by some top politicians as growing too powerful, even with Dr. Kamuzu Banda's approval. Subsequently, Nqumayo was charged and found guilty of treason based on questionable evidence that would likely not hold up in an impartial court. He was executed shortly thereafter. Chakuamba was also charged with treason, found guilty, and sentenced to over twenty years in prison.

Does this version meet your expectations?

And then there was Aleke Dr Kamuzu Banda, who stayed in jail for twelve years at the pleasure of the president. For all the years he was in jail there was no charge against him. The intervention by Amnesty International may have saved his life and given him back his liberty. Whispers making rounds in the country at the time Aleke Dr Kamuzu Banda was arrested were that when he had visited Zambia a week or so earlier, a journalist had asked him who he thought would replace the ageing president of Malawi and he, apparently, answered that he was 'Number Two'; in other words, he was positioned to take over power from Ngwazi Doctor Kamuzu Dr Kamuzu Banda when he died. But he was president for life! Aleke Dr Kamuzu Banda paid with a twelve-year loss of liberty at one of the most secure jailhouses in the country for those words, if indeed he had uttered them. So, one by one, the top potential successors were being eliminated. Now the crowded top echelons of the MCP were looking less crowded. The only one who survived the purge into the top four at that point was Mr. Chikhakhalala, the Reserve Bank governor, who also held a very long list of parastatal chairmanships, including that of the National Celebrations Council.

Nevertheless, in the mid-eighties, Mr. Chikhakhalala was forced out of his position as governor of the Reserve Bank of Malawi, when the World Bank refused to give Malawi new loans so long as Mr. Chikhakhalala was governor, because they suspected at the very least that Mr. Chikhakhalala was incompetent, or at worst, corrupt, so it was reported. It was said that the president of Malawi was powerless to act against him because of Lady Bhekimuzi Mukarakate's influence over him, so it finally became necessary for the World Bank itself to replace Mr. Chikhakhalala. They recommended a Malawian who was already working with the World Bank in America; his name was Madinga. Although I do not know what was agreed, it is likely that when the matter was discussed at the palace, they gave the World Bank positive signs that there was no problem with Madinga's appointment. In due course, Mr Madinga returned to Malawi and was seconded to a parastatal organisation, the Malawi Development Corporation (MDC), while negotiations over the main appointment were continuing between the World Bank and the Malawi government. Within a month of his return, Madinga was dead. Allegedly, his car collided with a police lorry on the Blantyre–Limbe road near Maselema.

By morning, the only sign of the accident was Madinga's car, which had been shunted to the road by *some people*. There was not a mark on the road showing the exact spot of the accident and no screeching tyre marks to reflect the drivers of both vehicles having tried to avoid the collision. There was no cordoning off of the area where the late Madinga's badly damaged vehicle was to show that the police had been to the spot and that they were investigating the 'accident'. Most of the people who saw the police lorry were those coming from the nearby Chisakalime Nightclub after closure in the small hours of the morning. This was probably another successful job by the Malawi Mafia. There were whispers that Madinga's family tried to find out how the accident occurred, but to no avail. As far as I am aware, no one has been brought before a court of law on that issue.

At this point, it was now left up to the palace to pick the name of a suitable candidate, so they picked Mr Chakakala Chaziya (in power 1984–1986), who, apparently, turned out to be even less competent than Mr. Chikhakhalala himself, and he did not last. The next choice the World Bank accepted for the position of governor of the Reserve Bank of Malawi was Mr Chimwemwe Hara, (in power 1986–1988), a Malawian who, like Madinga, was working for them in America at that time.

Mr. Chikhakhalala was appointed as Minister of Finance as early as 1966 when Malawi became a republic after attaining independence in 1964. In 1971, an MCP Convention was held in Dowa, and Mr. Chikhakhalala was the 'primary' sponsor (while another two seconded) for Dr Kamuzu Banda to become the 'Life President' of Malawi. To show appreciation for what Mr. Chikhakhalala had done, Dr Kamuzu Banda gave him a scholarship to go into postgraduate studies in central banking in Britain and France. This study put him in good stead when he was later appointed as governor of the Reserve Bank of Malawi, a post he held for more that twelve years.

Mr. Chikhakhalala's appointment as Minister of Finance, and even his previous post, was the first sign of nepotism and the grip Lady Bhekimuzi Mukarakate had on the president (then prime minister). Mr. Chikhakhalala was a simple secondary-school-teacher without the necessary qualifications to move up the ranks as fast as he did. There were better qualified individuals to hold that position and the president knew it, of that I have no doubt. Of the crop of politicians around at the time of the Cabinet Crisis, only Mr. Chikhakhalala survived and was still active in 2009, having seen off a good number of potential opponents should a vacancy in the top job avail itself in the future.

According to Wikipedia, Mr. Chikhakhalala and Lady Bhekimuzi Mukarakate slowly but surely started to build a fence around the president, a fence with only one gate, which was guarded by

Lady Cecilia herself. To see the president, one needed her permission. She and Mr. Chikhakhalala were deeply suspicious of anyone they thought might pose a political threat in the future. There was no way the populace could find out any truth from the president, because his truth was Lady Bhekimuzi Mukarakate's truth or Mr. Chikhakhalala's truth. Thus, the president had lost his sight and was using Lady Bhekimuzi Mukarakate as his guide dog. If the dog jumped, so did the president, without asking whether the jump was over a thorn a stone or just a joyful jump for all the power the dog had amassed. Nevertheless, it is also probable that Lady 's position was as difficult as those who worked directly under the Ngwazi. One could assume she had her limitations as to how far she could go in opposing some decisions the Ngwazi was making. At the same time, she couldn't completely ignore alleged requests for support from her uncle, the Honourable Mr. Chikhakhalala. She was perhaps just like others in her position walking a very tight rope and who lived to tell the tale.

One morning, I received a call from the Reserve Bank to book a private party for twenty-five people over the coming weekend. The governor, Mr. Chikhakhalala, was to be the host. That weekend, Mr. Nicholson was going to the lake, and I was to be in overall charge, supported, albeit unwillingly, by the ungodly Mr. Thawale. I chose a good team to deal with the function, and everything was well prepared. It was customary for the hotel manager to welcome large parties, and on that day I was turned out in my best bib and tucker. So was Mr. Chikhakhalala. He arrived wearing a cream designer suit, crocodile-skin shoes, and a gold wristwatch, all signs of the good life. I bowed and stretched out my hand to shake his. He looked up and made sure I knew he had noticed me and my gesture and then withdrew his hand and shook the hand of the person next in line. It was Mr Thawale's. I had been publicly shunned by the second most powerful person in Malawi and the most ruthless. What next?

When Mr Nicholson returned, Thawale was the first with the story and all its possible ramifications. Two days later, Thawale received a visit from an official from the Reserve Bank, a chap called Magareta, who was known as Mr. Chikhakhalala's right-hand man. He was someone, so rumour had it, who did all manner of unsavory chores for his boss, including scouting for girls. He asked Thawale how it was that I had been given a job at Ryall's a second time around and what my position was. My boss felt safe in the knowledge that I had produced a valid police clearance, signed in person by the chief of police, Mr Kamwana.

A week later, I saw Magareta in the Dugout restaurant. He called me over and offered me a drink. I refused the offer but still had a few minutes to spend with a customer.

'I see you're doing very well here, Mr Katsonga,' Magareta started with mock courtesy.

'I didn't know you'd been observing me, Sir,' I countered, my short-fuse temper already rising to the bait and registering inside.

'People are talking. They say you're too self-centred, pompous, and getting too big for your boots. That's not very nice, is it?' There was a thinly veiled threat in his voice, and I had great difficulty modulating mine in reply.

'Mr Magareta, people will always talk. If minding my own business is seen as such, what do you expect me to do? I'm not bothered by these things, if I've not knowingly done anything to annoy such people.'

'Incidentally,' he said and paused, 'how is Suzan?'

'Who wants to know?' I answered impertinently.

He forced a laugh. 'You'll find out, you'll find out,' he repeated and went on, 'Mr Katsonga!'

I got up from the chair and walked away. I had had enough. I was now more than aware that I was in trouble, big trouble. Allegedly, several young men had had their careers curtailed just because they crossed Mr. Chikhakhalala's path over women. I remember one chap living in Kanjedza, who was having an affair with a stewardess from Air Zimbabwe rumoured to be Mr. Chikhakhalala's girlfriend and who had just arrived the previous night and was booked to stay in the hotel. I do not know if the young man spent the night with her, but on the following day, I met him on the veranda nursing a glass of beer. He had some mutual friends with him. They were talking about going to the Mount Soche disco that evening and he excused himself by telling the others that he wanted to go home and change his clothes. Less than thirty minutes later, news got to us that he had died. His car had been involved in a collision with a police truck soon after crossing the Mudi Bridge on Victoria Avenue. A baker who witnessed the 'accident' and was prepared to give evidence mysteriously vanished. I was now living in fear!

I grew up believing in fair play. If you did something wrong and were caught, you deserved to be punished, but not if you were innocent. It did not matter who was the accuser or the accused; wrong was wrong and right was right. I was prepared to face the music for that belief and for the woman I loved. The fact that individuals were lurking in the bushes ready to harm anyone they didn't like didn't seem to slow me down. Looking back now, how stupid! As they say, there is little difference between insanity and love!

The following day, I had a visit from my brother-in-law, Augustine. His friend in the Special Branch had whispered to him to warn me that a file had been opened at their headquarters on my 'activities'. Mark, my stepbrother, approached me with a similar message a few days later. When the priest came home that same week, he was arrested, taken to MCP Headquarters and questioned about his activities. They suspected him of being a spy and warned him that his movements were being monitored.

At this juncture, I felt so hopelessly helpless and afraid. It looked like the end of the road. There was nothing but darkness around me. The island on which Suzan and I had taken refuge was slowly sinking. The hurricane was gathering strength, and the weather reports were forecasting worse to come. It is easy to understand how helpless Robert Maxwell might have felt during his last hours on that boat when you find yourself in a situation where there is only one outcome – a brutal defeat. I had to do something, but I did not know what. What had I done to deserve this kind of attention? I was lost. My soul was seriously troubled. It was not a problem my family could help me sort it out. I was on my own with Suzan, who was now pregnant.

Chapter 21

LEAVING WAS NOT WITHOUT STRESS

When the weather was favourable, to escape the grave which my gluttony had dug, I needed to shed some pounds. Suzan concurred. So we would drive past her rented house in Chigumula, a suburb on the Blantyre–Thyolo road. The road took us to the green rolling hills of this district where tea bushes grow. There, I would run in the crisp and fresh air, sheltered by the windbreaks from the howling winds. Suzan would slowly drive behind and within sight of me. And on the horizon, the majestic Mount Mulanje rose above the clouds, a sight which made my efforts more bearable.

We were laughing and joking on our way back home to Blantyre when a lorry seemed to prevent us from overtaking it. Finally, it gave way by indicating, and just as we were about to add speed and begin to overtake, the driver quickly blocked us. A crash was unavoidable at this point. I tried to brake, but it was too late. I put my foot down on the brakes, but it was like there was no brake pedal. The car now seemed to have a mind of its own, uncontrollable. I pressed even harder, but nothing changed. The road was too narrow to swerve, and the truck was too close to avoid hitting. Suzan screamed and I panicked as we crashed into the lorry's rear. The car was smashed, but we were spared. The lorry drove on, oblivious to the sound of metal meeting metal. The driver didn't hear the crash, or the scream, or the screech. He just kept going, perhaps unaware of the damage he had helped cause.

We drove home slowly since the radiator had been punctured and the vehicle needed water at short intervals. Luckily, there was a gallon of water, which Suzan travelled with in case of emergency. As for stopping, we used the handbrake. We never spoke a word to each other about the *accident* until we got home, shaken by our narrow escape.

When the car was checked at a garage the following day, the mechanics discovered that the tubes which carried brake fluid to the brakes had been tampered with, severed by a sharp instrument. This was too close for comfort. At this point, we knew we were living on borrowed time, but we had not envisaged events taking such a nasty and dangerous turn at this rate.

Did we go to the police? Which police? In Malawi, there was no dividing line between the various sections of Dr Kamuzu Banda's government. The presidency, judiciary, press, security, and the ruling party were all one. Reporting such an incident was one sure way of getting oneself picked up by the secret police. Apart from the priest and my boss, Mr. Nicholson, we told no one else about it. These were difficult and dangerous times for us and many Malawians.

During that same period, Suzan was building a house for her mother in her village near Monkey Bay on Lake Malawi. Three weeks or so had elapsed since our accident when Suzan was able to gather enough courage to drive there on her own, but as a precaution, we sent the car to the garage for a general service the day before. Suzan left early for her mother's village before I went to work, telling me to expect her back before seven that evening. Working a straight shift that day meant I was home at six, and because I wanted to prepare a special meal for two that night, I asked the cook to knock off earlier that evening. The Indian fellow from Kanabar House, who supplied the hotel with seafood, had given me two lobsters that afternoon, and I planned to surprise Suzan with lobster thermidor when she returned that evening.

Having finished my preparation, I mixed myself a drink, South African Oude Meester, brandy, and Coke, then under the security lights, I picked up my darts and began throwing them at the dartboard hanging on the other end of the veranda wall.

Eight o'clock came and went, then nine o'clock, and there was still no sign of Suzan. I was getting extremely anxious when she eventually arrived by taxi, telling me the car had lost one of its front wheels and overturned. Fortunately, she was not badly hurt, suffering nothing more than a few bruises, but the car needed a lot of work done on it.

I was alerted by Thomas that Mr. Thawale was now spreading the news about my difficulties with the political classes to the hotel staff. I knew the noose was getting tighter – I could feel it. Thomas wanted to know the true story of what was happening in my life. I obliged him partially! It was hard to trust anyone in those days.

I then got a call from my brother, Mark, who asked to see me somewhere in Soche, insisting I had to be alone and that I should go by taxi. Mark was at the time living in Lilongwe, where he worked for Lever Brothers as a regional marketing manager. I wondered what had brought him to Blantyre!

An old friend in the Special Branch, whom Mark had known since his years in the Special Services during the Rhodesian War, had advised him that he had eavesdropped on a conversation his colleagues were having at the office in which my name had overtly and prominently featured. The story was that they were under orders to make sure that I *disappeared*, or that some grave misfortune should befall me – the emphasis here being on grave! The order had come from 'above'. The friend had told Mark to warn me in no uncertain terms that the woman I was going out with was a *treacherous woman*, that I was playing with fire, and that the sooner I stopped dating her, the better.

'Things have reached such a stage that if we're sent to go and pick your young brother up, that's what we will do. The chief is resisting the whole idea, but as you know, he can't hold out forever,' the informant had added and continued, and I paraphrase, 'It looks as though Gold Finger's feathers have been well and truly ruffled.' Gold Finger was one of the nicknames Mr. Chikhakhalala had been given by the middle-class public. There was no question he was a very well-heeled man. He oozed worth and lots of it and he flaunted it!

'Davie, you left a decent girl, Madalo, and opted for a very dangerous woman like Suzan, who will certainly get you hurt;

how clever is that, my young brother?' Mark rhetorically asked, looking at my face as if searching for some written response on it. I think he got none because this is what he said next. 'Whatever she has done to you must be irreversible. Well, do not say there was no one to warn you. I will be driving to Zomba tomorrow on my way back to Lilongwe, and Father will be informed.' I simply nodded to indicate I had heard and understood what he had said, and our conversation shifted to other less controversial topics. I then thanked Mark for the message he had brought me and bid him farewell.

I did spend several hours thinking over the warning Mark had brought to my attention. Was my beautiful Suzan Poison Ivy? Should I leave the country? Where was I to go? Having talked the matter over with Suzan, we decided on Zambia, but the priest, on being told of our plan, suggested I go to London. His thinking was that Zambia was too close to Malawi, but I wanted to be closer to my elderly parents, I protested. Nevertheless, the priest was against the Zambia destination, because, he had said, 'Malawi has more spies and assassins based in Zambia, Zimbabwe, and Mozambique than in any other region of the world. They can organise a hit within days. History has shown that they do, and they can,' he had warned.

We approached our friend in the Zambia High Commission, who had some knowledge about our situation, to check whether he would assist us to escape into his country as a stepping stone to our destination of choice. Malawi shares her western border with Zambia.

The Zambian was kind and helpful, but he had to check with his superiors first. That took time. Then, our plans hit a snag. The immigration guy who was handling Suzan's passport got scared when he discovered that her file was locked in his boss's office. It was in the cabinet reserved for files for enemies of the state. This was when we decided I should leave the country first and find a way of bringing Suzan out of the country later. This approach might give the plan a decent chance of success. We had to get legally married first and fast. The understanding was that without a marriage certificate, it would be difficult to make a case for Suzan to leave the country, considering the issues she had with Gold Finger. It was our only option. I loved Suzan and wanted to marry her anyway, so we booked the registrar. I asked my uncle, Mr. Sanderson Chole, the one in whose home I had stayed when I was looking for a job, to be my Nkhoswe (representative) at the registry. He agreed.

The reason for the secrecy surrounding the registration of the marriage was that Suzan was pregnant and there was the possibility of the Church not being keen to assist her with her case for freedom if they found out that she had *sinned*. The priest, who was helping us, had to keep his own counsel for the same reason. He wasn't the Church! The degree of negative commentary about our union among family members, mostly on my side, simply added to the impetus for the cloak-and-dagger approach. 'We do not mind people knowing after the event but surely not before!' We had informed my uncle, but he was not informed of our planned escape soon after we got the marriage registered. We felt it would be safer that way.

An arrangement to meet with the Zambia high commissioner to Malawi was made by Father Fiderle. Suzan and I had to travel to Lilongwe for this within a day or two of getting this information. Everything went well, and the arrangement was that we would be driven in separate vehicles at night to go to Kachebele Major Seminary, which is located on the border between Malawi and Zambia, and that we would be picked up by the Zambian authorities soon after crossing the border. We were informed by Father Fiderle that it was very easy to cross into Zambia from the seminary without being detected by the authorities.

Understandably, the high commissioner could not simply proceed with this request without consulting his superiors in Lusaka, and this seemed to be dragging a bit! We were now concerned, because we did not know how many people at the Ministry of Foreign Affairs in Lusaka would be privy to the documentation and whether some of them might not be as discreet as they were required to be. We had to look for another option.

A secret meeting was arranged between the priest, Suzan, my boss, Mr Nicholson, and me. For my trip to go smoothly, my boss had to be involved. He had to know what the end game was. It was a huge risk but one worth taking. Luckily, he understood my predicament. The plan we hatched was that I was being sent on a working holiday for two months. We believed that with an official letter from Ryall's Hotel, I could then apply for an international passport from the Ministry of Home Affairs. Once I had left, the priest would do the rest, that is, he would bribe someone within the system. Yes, it was the only way! I suspect that in the sacrament priests are anointed with, it is acceptable to protect innocent life by any means necessary – just a thought! I will ask Monsignor Tamani[5] for confirmation. He could not do so immediately because Suzan was slightly over six months pregnant at this point, and if I was merely on a working holiday, it would look suspicious to be seen leaving on such a trip with a very pregnant wife at home.

Mr Nicholson understood the danger I was in and was thus willing to assist. The Priest e emphasised the need for total secrecy, needlessly but understandably. Suzan was in complete agreement. Out of necessity, all these plans were hidden from my family. They would certainly have resisted the whole idea or made a fuss, with the possibility of inadvertently endangering the whole plan. It had to be done that way. The author John Gwengwe[6] described Malawi in one of his books some years earlier as, 'Dziko losawuka ndi Mantha (A country with fear-induced poverty). To survive during those days most Malawians had to appear pathologically modest!

---

5 Was in the early nineties the spokesperson for the Roman Catholic church in Malawi. Respected nationally for having a quick brain.
6 John Gwengwe served as a minister in the Kamuzu Banda government and was also a businessman and author of several Chichewa books. His career in government came to an abrupt end, and he faced personal repercussions including imprisonment due to a phrase in one of his books that was interpreted as critical of the Kamuzu Banda's regime.

The Zambian high commissioner was officially made aware of our second and latest plan and so was the Blantyre-based Zambia Airways representative in Malawi, a very tall chap, about six foot six, handsome, with a long narrow face. He always had a Petronella smile. I only remember his first name as James. His six-foot frame seemed short by comparison when he was accompanied by his Ugandan Watusi wife. She was close to seven feet tall and had a body and face which even Hitler would have capitulated to, thus changing the course of world history! She was certainly a wife to look up to!

The high commissioner in Lilongwe delegated the chore to the Zambia consular general called Francis Chalabesa stationed in Blantyre. Both men were regulars at Ryall's Dugout Restaurant – particularly the bar. It was thus not unusual for me to join them for a drink now and again. The difference this time was that there was something very serious cooking, and it was not in the hotel's kitchen. This was a matter of life and death for Suzan and me!

Zambia Airways had to be included in the escape plan because we reasoned there was a distinct possibility that I would be stopped from boarding the plane by Special Branch officers stationed at the airport if the rumours we were hearing about plans to polish me off were anything to be believed. Such actions were not unknown in Dr Kamuzu Banda's Malawi, and on advice from James, it was arranged that my name should not appear on the passenger manifest until the plane had taken off. Apparently, all manifests were checked by intelligence officials long before boarding. They did that to collar those they wanted to have a word with and who were trying to do a runner. The diplomat promised he would be at the airport on the day to make sure our plan worked smoothly, and if it did, to take the matter up to higher authorities outside Malawi.

We picked the 17th May 1980 as the day to secretly register our marriage at the district commissioner's offices in Blantyre and the 31st May as the day of my escape through Chileka Airport. The two weeks in between felt like perpetuity itself to me, not knowing what might have leaked to the intelligence department now that the circle had widened quite a bit. Zambia Airways, the Zambia consular general in Blantyre, The Zambia high commissioner in Lilongwe and their Ministry of Foreign Affairs in Lusaka, the Roman Catholic Church, and the Malawi government had spies swarming everywhere. It was almost impossible to remain calm and comfortable under such circumstances.

I acted normal at work for a week, giving the impression that there was nothing afoot. It was hard. Suzan and I agreed to avoid talking in the main rooms of the house for fear of electronic bugs. The bathroom was our haven. We filled the tub and kept the taps on, letting the water drain now and then. Mark had taught me this trick some years earlier. He had said to run a bath if one wanted to muffle any conversation. We were desperate!

With a week to go, I asked Suzan if I could go away for two days. I wanted to be alone, to take stock, to reflect on the road which had taken me this far. At first, she opposed the idea, but when I persisted, she eventually relented with the words, 'Just you be careful, now.' I thought, because I did not want to make my movements too obvious, it would be safer to hire a car. My destination was Lilongwe.

I arrived in town at around one o'clock in the afternoon and headed towards the airport. Halfway there was the last primary school I had attended before going to Blantyre for my secondary-school education at Soche Hill Secondary School. I turned into the narrow, dusty road full of potholes which led to the school and stopped at the local shop, where we used to buy pencils and biscuits, among other things. Nothing had changed. Same old buildings, same old oxcart carrying wood or sugar cane entering the village down the road. Looking up the sloping playing fields, I could recall my early days doing physical education and playing football with friends like Philip, Willard, and Garnett, whose father's two front teeth were, allegedly, knocked out by our servant, Mr Shoti, over a bar hostess. Please do not ask why he was called Mr Shoti!

Garnett himself was the chap who had confounded the medical profession for a week in 1970. He had become disillusioned with his mother's cooking and decided to leave home, quite understandably, some might say. His desired destination was the Lilongwe General Hospital, but the trouble was that he lacked the necessary qualifications to be admitted there, so what did Dozy Garnett do? He stole from the kitchen a bottle of red food colouring and, after passing water, he added a few drops into the toilet bowl and started to scream. His doting mother rushed in. 'Blood! You're passing blood, my son!' she might have cried before whisking him off to the local doctor immediately. The first thing the doctor asked for after taking Garnett's particulars was a sample of his urine. Garnett obliged. He performed his trick in the nearby bathroom and brought the sample back to the doctor.

The doctor was most perplexed by what he saw under his microscope, declaring, 'I do not know what to say, Madam. I think we shall need to do more tests. We are going to keep the young man here overnight, Madam.' So, Garnett was given a bed in one of the wards in the hospital.

A week went by without finding anything with this patient, and after four days his mother brought him clean clothes and took what he had been wearing hitherto. Because of the various tests he had undergone, Garnett was exhausted and sleepy when they arrived, and when they left, his doting parents took his dirty clothes with them, where they discovered the 'blood' bottle in one of his pockets. They made a U-turn back to the hospital, which was around ten kilometres away.

Garnett's mother managed to disguise her fury for a while and taking her seat next to Garnett's bed she said, 'Garnett, the doctor wants a urine sample. Please oblige him?' Garnet quickly got up and rummaged through the bedsheets for his stuff but to no avail. 'Garnet, hurry up; the doctor is waiting for the sample.'

Garnett's mother got up and gave him a few slaps before producing from her handbag the offending bottle. 'Are you looking for this? Yes, are you? Yes?' The racket brought in some nurses and security to see what was going on. The duty doctor, who was in the next ward, was also on the scene. It was he who, with tongue-in-cheek, suggested Garnett should remain in the hospital for another day to recover from the beating. Come to think of it now, I never asked him if the hospital food was to his liking!

We all used to walk home together after school with Eleanor, Maria, and all the others. As I drove from the school it seemed like only yesterday when I was part and parcel of this landscape.

At our old home at the airport, although the nightclub was not exactly falling apart, there was a ghostly look about it, probably from disuse. It's corrugated-the iron-sheet roof was now rusty brown with dust, and the windowpanes, chameleon-like, were catching the same colour. The old car park, which used to be alive with customers' vehicles every night, was now overgrown with weeds, apart from a little patch nearest the main building, where car tyre marks could still be seen. Probably they were made by those old customers who had not heard of the nightclub's fate.

I decided to drive down the narrow, winding road into the nearby village of Mafosha to see our old houseboy, Elia. He was the kind of boy who always looked undernourished but sinewy. At almost six feet tall and extremely reedy, his deep, dark-brown eyes seemed to carry some sadness about them, until, that is, he opened his mouth and then you had with you a very funny and sensitive friend. He taught me a lot about hunting, more than Uncle Willard ever did, and about the local customs.

Elia's mother and my mother were very close, and every Boxing Day my mother would make a point of giving Elia's mother a food hamper. She was a very nice lady, who never let her poverty affect the way she responded to people more fortunate than herself.

She was the one who informed my mother about local politics, for example, what the local chief's opinion was about us settling there. We were, after all, 'foreigners in Lilongwe. My parents would then plan what their next move might be when they saw the chief. When I arrived in the village, I was disappointed to find Elia and his mother were away for the day, so I simply left a message and a parcel of dried fish I had remembered to buy for them.

I did not stop at Chester's City Motel. The name had now been changed to Lingadzi Inn and was being run by Hotels and Tourism. Despite not stopping there, I still felt a deep resentment and, I think, some degree of bitterness, but where could one turn to justice in this land so impoverished with fear and prejudice?

I did not want to visit any crowded areas where somebody might recognise me, so I spent the rest of the afternoon driving around the outskirts of the city among the large and small maize and groundnut fields where people were harvesting their crops. Most of the men had their shirts off, their bodies looking lean and sweaty. They were at the end of the agricultural cycle. During that year the rains had been good. The government would be able to earn the nation some foreign exchange through agro-produce exports, I thought. As I drove past, some of them turned to look at me with sullen, troubled interest, to which I found it difficult to respond in any noticeable way. I drove on. My thoughts were in turmoil, and I was too confused to speak rationally with anyone.

I eventually arrived at the Capital Hotel at around nine in the evening, and luckily for me, there was a room available. Only a few years old, the hotel was the largest in Lilongwe at the time. I paid cash and gave my name as Phiri, which is my totem and a very common name in Malawi, then quickly disappeared into my room, where I spent the rest of the evening in contemplation. I knew Special Branch officers visited all hotels at around seven a.m. to check the hotel registers, and from the lists they either picked a few names at random to follow during their visit or they already knew their quarry. As the chances of them recognising me were about six to four, I had to leave early. Having already paid for supper, which I had served in my room, before retiring for the night, I was able to slip away slightly after six in the morning. I did not want to give the police any reason to suspect I was up to anything.

By seven o'clock I was over sixty miles away, somewhere in Dedza District, on my way down south. The terrain in this area is so mountainous. Like a serpent swimming in dark green waters, the long and meandering road, which acts as the border between Malawi and Mozambique, wound its way southwards, relentlessly eating into the miles as it did so. Now and then I would pass several women selling their agricultural produce, mostly tomatoes, onions, cabbages, potatoes, and a variety of tropical fruits. Whenever a car approached, they would lift a few items, hoping to attract the attention of the occupants, just in case they were not conspicuous enough.

I remembered a few trips I had made as a passenger in my parent's car when my mother had habitually insisted on stopping at a particular place along the way. She was impressed by the quality of the product and the humour of one of the traders, so she always bought from her. My next stop being my parents' home, I decided to buy them something as a surprise, something to lift their dampened spirits, if only for a few hours, perhaps a day.

There were more traders than usual when I arrived at that place, about seven of them, and their produce looked pretty much the same, so I decided to buy at least something from everyone, not forgetting to buy the bulk from my mother's favourite. I had only bought some fruits and a few cobs of fresh maize when one of the women, who I later identified as my mother's friend, said, 'Si inu mwana wa a Chesitala?' ('Aren't you Mr Chester's child?') She asked this rhetorically as she walked toward me. 'I never forget a face. Your mother always bought from me – don't disappoint me now, son,' she continued, this time holding me by the hand, pulling me towards her display. I asked her to prepare a big parcel for Mother. 'What of?' she asked with a grin, revealing a huge gap between her front upper jaw and a doorway to heaven for the country's dentists.

'You know what my mother bought from you, Grand Mom!' I replied.

'Okay. Just leave it to me then. You do look like your father.' She turned to a younger trader next to her. 'Nakhoni, remember a Chesitala? Doesn't he look like his father?'

'Mother why is everybody asking me the same question?' I said gently, embracing her.

'These days you never know,' she replied softly, releasing herself from my arms and looking enquiringly into my face.

'I simply came by to give you some products from your favourite lady from Mozambique. Coming from Lilongwe, I stopped at Lizulu for some vegetables.' I moved to get the packages from the car.

'Don't bother yourself,' said my father. 'Amini! Amini!' he called to the servant. 'Will you get some things from the car?' I explained to the servant which packages he should bring out.

Mother was quite delighted. 'Is she still there? I have not seen her for some time.'

'She said the same about you, Mother,' I told her.

I explained to them about my trip abroad. I did not tell them the whole truth, because I was convinced they would not approve, so I stuck to the 'official' version of going away on business for two months. They wanted to come to the airport to see me off, but I discouraged them. I told them I did not want any emotional farewells and that I preferred to keep everything quiet. They somehow accepted my wishes. My father was then sixty-seven years old, and I thought he looked a little thin, and so did my mother. I understood, and for a moment my inner anger and bitterness silently surfaced, but I had to quickly suppress them.

Mother brought me my favourite supper of nsima with mpiru, plus grilled beef. As we ate, I knew that this could be my last meal with my parents. The thought hurt.

'You look absent-minded,' commented Mother.

'It's the trip. You know I'm scared of flying.' We all laughed. 'Just pray for me and all will be fine.'

As I left my parents, my mind was racing with a lot of 'What ifs'. In my country, you cannot afford to be too sure of anything. Too much had happened to too many people over the years for me to think otherwise. What would my parents say? So many questions which I could not answer. What I did know for certain was that if I stayed, my freedom would be curtailed. I was afraid to think of anything beyond that probability. There were any number of possibilities.

Joining the main Blantyre-to-Zomba road, I turned right and looked at the old rusty car bodies to my left. This used to be Silombera's garage, the man who had fought on behalf of Henry Chipembere. It was now a grave for old disused cars, and its ex-owner himself was in a special government graveyard four or five miles away. Cause of death? I supposed a broken neck suffered when he was hanged in 1965.

A few metres ahead were the big, old, leafy mango trees, where a party activist called Mteketa had hidden when the other side was after his blood. The man owed his life to those lovely mango trees. He was as fat as a well-fed maggot, and the very idea of him climbing into a tree was enough to make those who knew the man break into laughter. Those were dangerous times, and nothing seemed to have changed over the years.

The drive back into Blantyre was quick, less than an hour, and I decided to return the car to the owners before I went home. When the transaction was completed and after I had paid the bAaron ce due, the owner was kind enough to drop me back at the cottage.

After failing to unseat me with his supernatural powers, Thawale started, among other tricks, to work with Mr. Chikhakhalala's people. As soon as I arrived at the hotel the following day, he approached me with a message that two Special Branch people had been asking for me. 'Whatever it is they want to see you about, they looked very serious,' he said. 'There was also a man from the Reserve Bank, who has just left. He wanted to know your whereabouts,' he concluded with a grin. He gave me the impression of someone who was enjoying all the intrigue. Having done his worst and failed, he was now working on Plan B – 'The enemy of my enemy is my friend'.

I told Mr. Nicholson I might not see him again before my departure and thanked him for everything he had done for me. For once, I noticed, he was emotional. Biting his lower lip he said, 'I don't want to repeat what I said to you when you were going to join your father, but if things don't work out for you this time, I will visit you wherever they put you. Good luck and God bless,' he concluded in verbal shorthand as we were interrupted by a knock on the door. It had already been agreed that Suzan could stay at the cottage for up to six months after my departure.

My air ticket was to be issued at the airport, and as I did not want to be seen in town, Suzan had done all the shopping I needed. That evening we had a delicious meal of grilled chambo (freshwater perch) on the bone, prepared by Suzan and washed down with a bottle of South African sparkling wine from KWV Wineries. We were alone for the last supper – possibly the Last Supper. As we finalised our plans, we discussed the possibility of my being stopped at the airport by the Special Branch. We thought there was a good chance I would be stopped, but I had little choice. What else could I do? The net was closing in. I had to leave, to give it a try, otherwise there would be no room for me. Suzan was both encouraging and very supportive of my plans.

Suzan and I drove to the airport alone to catch my flight on Zambia Airways at one p.m. on that warm and slightly windy Saturday afternoon, the 31st May 1980. The sky looked bluer than usual, and my mind was unsettled. We had been advised to arrive late and to leave my suitcase in the car until the last minute. Our Zambia friend, the diplomat, was there to bid me farewell. With a few minutes to go before departure time, we went to the airline desk and when my ticket was issued, he advised me to check in and proceed through the departure gate without delay. I rushed out to the car to pick up my suitcase, which was handed in, and I was given my boarding card. Everything was done so quickly. I kissed Suzan goodbye and left her standing there, rigid and motionless. Before disappearing behind the gates, I turned and looked back and she was still there, waving, the tension and sadness showing on her face, fear and sadness etched on mine. Passing through Customs, I was pulled aside by an unsavoury-looking character in civilian attire, and I thought, that was it!

'How much foreign currency have you got on you?' he harshly queried. I told him how much.

'How long are you going out for?' I told him how long.

'Is this the only luggage you have?'

'Yes,' I confirmed.

'Go behind that cubicle for a body search,' he said, pointing to my right. In the cubicle, I was stripped to the bare necessities, but they did not find anything suspicious. What next, I wondered? Was I carrying extra undeclared foreign exchange on my person? Yes, I was. I had folded the bank notes in a small pouch, which I had nicely and tightly folded between my scrotum and my back passage. I had been guided by the priest that this was a safe area to hide a small package. 'Most regular body searches don't go beyond the underwear,' he had said. It looked like the conclusion as to what to do with me had already been reached, and it was now a case of trying to find legitimate evidence, any evidence, and on this occasion, they almost got it.

The immigration people were, thankfully, quiescent, and I was soon on my way to the aircraft. Once seated, a Special Branch officer, whom I knew as Robert, left the people he was talking to and came over to speak to me. He casually asked where I was off to and when I was coming back. He was interrupted by the diplomat, who had also come on board. Pretending to be surprised at seeing me, he asked where I was going and joked about getting lost in London. We all laughed. He also asked me if I was spending any time in Zambia and when I said I was, he gave me his brother's name at Lusaka's Intercontinental Hotel and recommended that I stay there. As we had already finalised arrangements for my stay in Zambia, his real aim was to misinform the Special Branch man.

We said our goodbyes and the aircraft doors closed on them. The aircraft's engines began to ratchet up the decibels, and I could see through the windows that the plane was now in motion as its engines continued to roar even louder. I was still apprehensive. Anything could still go wrong. At this point, I still feared the plane could be turned back by Security. Then it reached the final stop on the runway just before take-off, at first slowly, then it gathered speed for what felt like an eternity, and agonisingly I finally felt the aircraft's undercarriage leave the runway. We were airborne. As it cleared the clouds, I could now see the small villages get smaller and smaller as the aeroplane increased its attitude. With each foot it rose there was a decrease of tension and stress in my heart, but there was still a mixture of the conflicting emotions of relief and trepidation.

From geography, I had a rough idea about what route the journey would take, and sitting next to the window on the left-hand side, I could see a large river. It had to be the Zambezi. It was the only west–east flowing river of that size in the area. All the others were north to south, so I knew at this point that I was closer to Lusaka than I was to Blantyre. What if I am refused entry into Zambia, I worried to myself. Thank God it was not to be. The image of Suzan, seven months pregnant, waving goodbye, and that my parents doing the same when I had gone to bid them farewell all weighed heavily on my mind. I was out of the Motherland, a land of poisoned spears and arrows, of shadowy figures in the night. I had left my home, my heavily pregnant wife, and my friends. My joy at having eluded possible untold horrors was tinged with deep sadness. Little did I know of the trials which lay ahead and that this was just the beginning.

Chapter 22

TWO ALIENS IN MUTARE AND
THE GREAT CHICKEN MASSACRE

In 1988, my good friend, Bisiketi Chikuni, had asked me to join him in Mutare, where his family had been invited by his brother-in-marriage, Dan Mobane, for the Christmas festivities.

By now, oodles of water had passed under the bridge, and I can't say it was clean water either. Suzan had been and gone in a messy divorce in 1982. At this point we had been blessed with a son and a daughter. If you may indulge me at this point, this story will be in my next offering entitled *The Sound of Keys*, available towards the end of 2024.

Bisiketi knew I was going to be in Harare from London during that period because my company, dck Images, was sponsoring, for the second year running, an invitation squash tournament from the 27to the 31st December at the Medical School Squash Courts, University of Zimbabwe.

The case for custody of my children from Suzan was still ongoing in the United Kingdom's Family Courts, and a representative for Essex Social Welfare, whom I am going to refer to as 'my companion' in this chapter and elsewhere, had been officially informed of my intended absence from the jurisdiction for three weeks. On learning about this break, she had then asked me for more information about Zimbabwe, and she later told me that she liked what I had told her about the country, I am sure, she must have spent some time reading and asking others about it. She decided to visit the country during the time I would be there to make her tour a little easier travelling with someone she knew well, so to put it!

We arranged to travel together. At this point, we had become intimate. It all happened by accident, in my view. On my second supervised visit to see my children, the children, having been collected from their foster home by my companion, refused to come out of the car when they arrived at the pre-arranged meeting venue. They, particularly the boy, were very hysterical. I found the reaction rather confusing since the first supervised visit had gone particularly smoothly. The visit was thus cancelled. My companion told me to wait in the nearby Thurrock McDonald's restaurant while she dropped the children home.

I was feeling very low emotionally, even tearful! My own children had screamingly refused to see me. I felt worthless, small, and alone! I was depressed. How would you feel!

My companion returned in less than thirty minutes and joined me by ordering a cup of coffee for herself. I was already having one. She explained to me why there was such a response from the children on the second visit, the first one having gone so successfully. Apparently, the children had innocently informed the foster parents that the visit had been very nice and that they were looking forward to the next one. They then added that the social worker had dropped them just outside the house with me in the car, meaning that I had now known where the children lived. This was a breach of the arrangement the Family Court had put together. This made them feel unsafe that this perilous black man had this information. Perhaps that's the image of me they had been provided with by my ex-wife – I do not know!

So, when my companion went to collect the children for the second supervised visit, the foster parents would not have it. They accused her of breaking one of the rules of these supervised visits, that the children should be held at a neutral venue until the court had received a positive report of the supervised visits. Although she had the legal powers to force the issue, the children knew that by seeing me again they were making their 'parents unhappy, even furious! I became increasingly tearful as my companion explained all this. She defended her position by saying that since the first supervised visit had been a huge success, she didn't see any reason why I should not see where my children lived. Just the location. She then clasped my hand with both her hands in an attempt to console me. The restaurant was filling up, and she asked me if we could go somewhere more private to continue the talk and what we should do next in response to what the foster parents had done. They had poisoned the children's minds against me.

My friends in Zimbabwe knew my girlfriend, who was also Zimbabwean and living in London. I felt awkward arriving in Harare with a woman they did not know and one who was legally handling my custody case, even-handedly, so I believed. We thus had to put together devious modus operandi which would help mitigate the situation.

I was going to arrive in Harare two days earlier and would stay with my friend, BISIKETI, in Emerald Hill, a suburb of Harare. My companion was to be accommodated five kilometres away in Sundridge. This was our tournament chairman's residence.

My companion was to be introduced as the marketing manager of dck Images, hence her presence in Harare during the tournament. We agreed that there would be no sign of any closeness between us which would belie the narrative.

My companion arrived on the 22nd December, and she was welcomed by the team in a very grand fashion. After a shower and a late breakfast at the chairman's residence, she said she needed to sleep, since the flight had been very bumpy and she did not sleep at all on the flight. There was to be a brae (barbeque) hosted by Bisiketi and his wife at their residence to welcome her into Harare, Zimbabwe. That went down very nicely. My companion and I kept to our script throughout dinner, after which she was driven back to her temporary residence at the tournament chairman's house. On the 23rd December, the chairman's wife offered to take my companion on a tour of Harare. They took their lunch somewhere in town. In the meantime, Bisiketi and I met the chairman and others to update each other about the tournament's arrangements.

The chairman's wife and my companion found us at the house just before we were about to part company for the night. No, the chairman and his wife wouldn't have it. They decided to detain us for yet another impromptu brae. Bisiketi called his wife on the ground phone to join us. Once again, there was no sign that there were suspicions that there was something untoward going on between the two of us. Very encouraging, I thought.

On the morning of the 24th December, we started off for Mutare at around eleven. Bisiketi, his wife, their two children, and the two of us packed the Mazda 323, which Bisiketi had been allocated for use as he did his PhD research on the effects of the pesticide DDT on human health – mostly on suckling babies.

The two-hundred-and-fifty-five-kilometre drive was to take us just over three and a half hours. My companion kept commenting on how lushly green the country was. She also informed us that until she had landed at Harare International Airport, her image of Zimbabwe, and of Africa in general, had been that of a desert, all brown with a few green patches spaced here and there.

Bisiketi took advantage of my companion's Essex links and proudly told her of his Alma Mater, The University of Northeast London, where he did his first degree. The rest of the drive was spent discussing inconsequential everyday matters. We stopped at Rusape to stretch our limbs and to respond to biological stresses.

We were now climbing the last mountains before descending into Mutare when Bisiketi announced that we were now almost at our destination. I saw the indicators flashing left, and in the near distance I could see the buildings, which to me looked institutional. One was the forestry college where Dan was the principal. On the final turn into the college's campus, I noticed the architectural similarities between these college buildings and those in similar institutions in Malawi. They were all built during the federation period, before 1963.

I had met Dan and his wife a year or so earlier in Harare at one of Bisiketi's family gatherings. He was small in stature, dark brown in complexion and stood at about five feet four inches. He was very talkative and even more so after taking a beer or two.

After welcoming us at his official residence, which was within the college's campus, BISIKETI's wife, the children, and my companion were taken into the house by Dan's wife while Dan took us to a spot under a big flame tree, where he had a huge cast-iron camp pot with three legs on the fire. He proudly told us he was cooking mazondo, to you, Davie, cattle-scratchings, as a part of our Christmas lunch the next day.

'After cooking them, they taste better when kept overnight,' he smugly added.

'Is there anything we could be doing right now then, Dan?' asked Bisiketi.

'Oh! I have a few bottles of Viceroy brandy in the house. Perhaps you want a beer?' he asked, with his eyes questioningly shifting between Bisiketi's and my face like a searchlight.

'Well, I think some Viceroy wouldn't be a bad idea,' Bisiketi replied as I nodded, eager to agree. Dan called out to some young man in his early twenties who I assumed was his home help. Dan spoke to him in a low voice, and after a few minutes the young man returned carrying a full tray of glasses, three cans of Coca-Cola, a silver bucket of ice, and a full bottle of Viceroy brandy.

Dan wanted to serve us but was stopped by Bisiketi. 'You are my Baba Mukuru; you cannot serve me.' Dan was married to the elder sister of Bisiketi' wife, Petronella.

'Yes, you are right, but since you are my guest, that rule will temporarily be shelved.'

'And that makes me Baba Mudiki? You mean distance and ownership of residence affect these cultural titles and etiquette, Dan?' asked Bisiketi as he gently grabbed and opened the Viceroy bottle with deep intent and longing engraved on his face. He loved Viceroy brandy and after all, it was Christmas Eve!

'Now, since I am not Baba anything here, what else is there to be done by a title-less visitor like me?' I jokingly asked Dan.

'Now you have reminded me, we must slaughter some chickens – five of them.' Once again, he called the young man to show me where the chickens were and said that he should allow me to do the slaughtering. 'It's an honour in our culture to allow your distinguished visitor to slaughter an animal, in this case chickens, for his meal so that as you are chatting, he would be salivating, for he knows what his dinner will consist of.'

I did not look at this task as having any difficulties. In Malawi, most young men begin to kill a chicken for the family mat (table) from the tender age of ten, some even younger. It is normal, as it is expected that it is a part of growing up, an integral part of becoming a man. So, with my Viceroy brandy mixed with icy-cold Coke in hand, I followed the young man behind the house, where the chickens had been kept in what looked like a one-and-a-half-metre-square chicken mobile-house.

I did the needful, and the young man helped me with feather-plucking and gutting. Dan, with Bisiketi in tow, appeared to appreciate progress and I was then told that two of the chickens were for charcoal roasting; the other three were to be split in half. One was to be fried, and the other half was to be stewed by the wife. I offered to do the frying and roasting if the wife would allow me. She did.

We did not go to bed that night until late, very late! The two sisters had a lot to share, and they probably wanted to show my companion that they were happy to have her in their midst. The other younger members of the gathering could also be heard chatting away throughout the night. As for Dan, Bisiketi and me, we were on our second bottle of Viceroy – remember, it was Christmas Eve!

Before retiring to bed that night, the family informed us that their father and mother-in-law would be joining us for Christmas lunch the next day.

The senior in-laws arrived at about eleven on Christmas day. It was not the first time for me to see them. The father-in-law had just retired from the Zimbabwean civil service as an administrator. He was a district commissioner for Chitungwiza Township, thirty-five kilometres southwest of Harare. I couldn't describe him as slim, although it was his height which made him look slightly plump. He had a dark mahogany skin, and he did not have much hair to talk about on his head. A dream client for a barber! The mother-in-law was of medium build, light brown in complexion, lighter than her husband. She must have stood at five feet three inches. He sounded and looked jovial, but I was later told by Bisiketi that she was the powerful one in the family. She was the one who carried the cane!

The moment they took their seats on the veranda, the Christmas dinner began. Samosas, sausage rolls, and more magical dishes were coming out of the kitchen, some with decorations one wouldn't wish to eat without being viewed as a philistine. Soon after twelve, three other brothers and sisters to the hostess and Bisiketi's wife arrived from Harare. The dinner table had fourteen covers. It was a long table, with the father-in-law and his wife at the top table and everyone else sitting in descending order up to the end. Your guess is as good as mine as to where I sat. You got it right – I was number fourteen and right at the end of the dinner table. How did I feel? Not too good, but as an outsider, I think this was one of their practical solutions. I might have done it differently, but I did not allow the seating arrangement to ruin my appetite. No, seriously, there was nothing wrong with the seating arrangement.

The whole table was littered with all manner of dishes served by three young ladies in uniform. I thought they had been hired specially for this ceremony.

After the father-in-law said grace and we started to eat, the table was quiet apart from the clatter of silverware against or hitting the wedgwood plates.

It was at this point I thought I should break the silence. 'Dan,' I called, lifting my upper body and looking in his direction, 'the mazondo is very delicious, and as a matter of fact, the food is really tasty. My thanks to the chefs!'

'Thanks to you too for killing, cleaning, and roasting the chicken you prepared; it is very nice,' came the response from Dan's wife.

'Oh! It's you who killed the chicken, Davie?' queried my companion in a sharp and cutting voice.

'Yes,' I proudly responded, not knowing or trying to understand why she had asked the question in the tone she had employed. I could not see anything anti-social in slaughtering a chicken for consumption.

'Mmmmm, I didn't know you could do that,' was all she could say, but looking at her demeanour, she looked rather unimpressed and not at all happy.

'I didn't know you could cook, Davie?' bellowed the voice of the father-in-law.

'I try; my first career was in hotels, Sir,' I answered in a low and timid voice.

'In Malawi, what do you call mazondo?' he continued.

'*Dziboda*.' At this point, there was no sound of cutlery to be heard at the table. It was like a bad ghost was passing by – dead silence!

'Do you know why the table has hushed?' asked the father-in-law.

'No, Sir,' I replied, wondering what I had done wrong.

'It's because, in Shona, dziboda is a woman's inner thighs, with sexual connotations.' I felt like hiding under the table now. It was extremely embarrassing, and the father-in-law must have recognised this, as he immediately changed the subject to other general issues.

It is disenchanting and discouraging for a Nyanja- or Chewa-speaking person to learn Shona in a hurry without once or twice embarrassing themself. For example, the word 'bvudzi' means 'hair' in Shona, whereas the same word means 'pubic hairs' in Nyanja and Chewa. The word 'zimatha' (spelt differently) in Nyanja or Chewa means 'thank you', whereas in Shona it means 'buttocks', etcetera.

The next day, we bid farewell to the other guests, who were staying longer, and after thanking our hosts, we were on our way back to Harare in the same car we had come in. The atmosphere between my friend from London and me was visibly and audibly frosty. Bisiketi and Petronella tried to de-ice the situation by introducing various issues for discourse but to no avail.

We had a prior arrangement to tour the Nyanga Highlands at Trout Beck Inn. Despite the not-so-conducive atmosphere between us, I decided to keep the arrangement, and we travelled there in Bisiketi' car. It was a good four-hour drive of listening to a music cassette, which kept repeating, and none of us felt like changing it. It was perhaps a foil to the conversation, which was absent. The drive was, thus, obviously uneventful. I tried very hard not to make any reference to the chicken massacre, which I thought had annoyed my companion so much and completely changed her perception of me – a man capable of killing a chicken can kill anything! Although we were booked into a double room, it would have been just as good, better even, to have booked ourselves into two single rooms.

Now that we were in a different environment, I decided to introduce the chicken issue on the 24th December 1988. As soon the word 'chicken' came out of my mouth, my companion intervened and said, and I paraphrase, 'I did not know you were capable of spilling the blood of another living thing. You must be heartless, cruel even. You could kill a human being!' All this because I had killed chickens for the Christmas lunch. I tried to explain the issue away by looking at it from an African cultural angle, something her British middle-class upbringing probably hadn't taught her, so I suspected. Alas! Just as well she had not seen or heard of me killing goats, and sheep, and helping in putting down bulls at traditional functions in the old country. That would have made her flip her lid!

Back in Harare, I heard from Bisiketi that she had spent three days touring other places of interest with the tournament chairman's wife.

On the 31st December 1988, the tournament proceeded smoothly, and prizes were to be awarded at the chairman's house, followed by a massive New Year's Eve party. Looking around me that night, no one was sober, and we were leaving the venue around four p.m on the 1st January 1989. In my condition and that of my hosts, it was difficult to imagine we were to be hosting another barbeque that day at one p.m.

Guests started to arrive around twelve p.m., claiming they thought we might need help considering the exertions of the night before, and they were right. By one thirty p.m. the fire was ready and so were all the extras in the garden. My companion arrived around two p.m., and I with the hosts greeted them with joyful smiles, well, as joyful as I could manage to appear. Then, I saw my companion talking with Bisiketi's wife and pointing at me or in my direction. Then I saw Bisiketi's wife beckoning her husband and talking to him with a very serious look on her face. I wondered what was going on, but I didn't have long to wonder because Bisiketi came to me and whispered, 'The cat is out of the bag!' My companion had apparently complained to her hosts that I had ignored her the entire evening and that I hadn't danced with her enough, preferring to dance with one girl she suspected I was probably dating. Yes, I knew the girl in question. She was a very good dancer and I enjoyed dancing with her. She then revealed to them the whole unholy plan we had concocted. Was I ashamed? Entirely. I felt I had disrespected my friends' families and the participants in the squash invitation tournament. I was very upset with her, given that there was nothing ethical or holy about our scheme. She was a married woman on separation, so she had told me, and I had a steady girlfriend at the time.

The remaining days of my stay in Harare were like an exercise in watching paint dry. I couldn't leave Harare for London fast enough. I heard my companion had rescheduled her itinerary with the help of her hosts, who might have viewed her as the victim in this escapade. The original departure date remained unchanged; we were to leave on the same flight.

From that afternoon to the day we left Harare, we did not speak to each other. I recall that when checking in my companion shouted out to the tournament chairman, 'Make sure my seat is not close to his.' I couldn't see her on the flight. The chairman had obliged her request, I thought, not that I was looking for her. My hopes of an attempt to clear the air dissipated when I heard her give that instruction at the check-in desk. I now feared that she may cause a scene if I spoke to her solely for the element of rapprochement. I decided to stay put and awake for the entire nine-hour flight – I just couldn't sleep.

The last time I saw her was as we both walked *very* separately towards the car park at Heathrow Airport. She walked together with a gentleman I assumed was her estranged husband, who was pulling her wheeled luggage. I had also been welcomed by my girlfriend.

A year passed before I heard from her again. I received a call in which she said she wanted to talk to me about a case she was facing at work. Her employers, Essex County Council, had information that she had breached their disciplinary code on ethics by having an intimate relationship with a client. She wanted us to meet, and I obliged her. I didn't realise that this would be the beginning of a nightmare I am still struggling to wake up from, and in the words of Aristotle, I should have known better!

Our behaviour as we grow up mirrors the society in which we are born and raised. I feel very remorseful for all the deliberate and forced errors I made against all the young hearts I met on my journey from adolescence to becoming a man. Everything I did seemed normal since there was no one I knew, growing up at the time, who didn't behave as I did. I hope these women have it in them to show some compassion and forgive me. To those who broke my heart, I say, all is forgiven. It's much easier to understand the errors of my ways looking in the rear-view mirror than it was all those years ago. I should have known better.

Episode II, *The Sound Of Keys*, to follow.

EIN HERZ FÜR AUTOREN A HEART FOR AUTHORS À L'ÉCOUTE DES AUTEURS MIA ΚΑΡΔΙΑ ΓΙΑ ΣΥΓΓ
HJÄRTA FÖR FÖRFATTARE UN CORAZÓN POR LOS AUTORES YAZARLARIMIZA GÖNÜL VERELIM SZ
CUORE PER AUTORI ET HJERTE FOR FORFATTERE EEN HART VOOR SCHRIJVERS TEMOS OS AUT
SZÍVÜNKÉRT SERCE DLA AUTORÓW EIN HERZ FÜR AUTOREN A HEART FOR AUTHORS À L'ÉCOU
 DORAÇÃO BCEЙ ДУШОЙ К АВТОРАМ ETT HJÄRTA FÖR FÖRFATTARE Á LA ESCUCHA DE LOS AUTC
AUTEURS MIA ΚΑΡΔΙΑ ΓΙΑ ΣΥΓΓΡΑΦΕΙΣ UN CUORE PER AUTORI ET HJERTE FOR FORFATTERE EEN
YAZARLARIMIZA GÖNÜL VERELIM SZÍVÜNKÉRT SERCE DLA AUTORÓW EIN HERZ FÜ
OS SCHRIJVERS TEMOS OS AUT ... RAÇÃO BCEЙ ДУШОЙ К АВТОРАМ ETT HJÄRTA FÖ

The author

D. C. Katsonga is a Malawian politician with a bachelor's degree in business administration and a postgraduate diploma with the Chartered Institute of Marketing. He also obtained a master's degree at the Southbank University in London, United Kingdom.

The author is a former hotelier, who spent much of his working life as a politician in Malawi, serving his country as a cabinet minister in six different portfolios and as the Speaker of the National Assembly.

Reluctantly Surrounded by Politics portrays different stages of D. C. Katsonga's life and is the first of several books intended to lay bare all aspects of his interesting and colourful life.